China's Hydro-politics in the Mekong

China's Hydro-politics in the Mekong explores the intricate processes of conflict and cooperation over the use of water resources in the Mekong river basin between upstream China and the downstream countries of Laos, Thailand, Cambodia, and Vietnam. The book tackles two gaps in the empirical literature: first, the neglect of international hydro-politics as one specific and increasingly important issue area of China's foreign policy behavior, especially its neighborhood diplomacy; and second, the disregard of China's role in Mekong River politics.

In particular, this book scrutinizes the 'spring 2010 Mekong crisis' and the events surrounding it which led to a series of complex multi-level, security-related interactions among various state and non-state actors in the region, with China at the center. Analyzing this crisis, the book not only employs securitization theory as its theoretical framework and adds a couple of innovations to this theory, but also gives a detailed account of China's hydro-political behavior in one specific and particularly revealing case study. Moreover, the book embeds China's Mekong hydro-politics in the bigger picture of its (sub-)regional international affairs, as the former does not take place in a vacuum, but rather is a part of China's overall foreign relations with its neighbors. The book acknowledges this link and provides new insights into the role of hydro-politics and its relationship vis-à-vis other issue areas of China's foreign policy.

Sebastian Biba is Lecturer at the Institute of Political Science at Goethe University Frankfurt, Germany.

Routledge Contemporary China Series

For our full list of available titles: https://www.routledge.com/Routledge-Contemporary-China-Series/book-series/SE0768

Corporate Social Responsibility Reporting in China
Evolution, Drivers and Prospects
Jieqi Guan and Carlos Noronha

China's Generation Gap
Jiaming Sun and Dongmei Cheng

China Reclaims World Power Status
Putting an end to the world America made
Paolo Urio

The Economic Roots of the Umbrella Movement in Hong Kong
Globalization and the Rise of China
Louis Augustin-Jean and Anthea H.Y. Cheung

Economic Policy Making in China (1949–2016)
The Role of Economists
Pieter Bottelier

The Power of Relationalism in China
Leah Zhu

China's Financial Opening: Coalition Politics and Policy Changes
Yu-Wai Vic Li

China's Hydro-politics in the Mekong
Conflict and Cooperation in Light of Securitization Theory

Sebastian Biba

LONDON AND NEW YORK

First published 2018
by Routledge
2 Park Square, Milton Park, Abingdon, Oxon OX14 4RN

and by Routledge
711 Third Avenue, New York, NY 10017

Routledge is an imprint of the Taylor & Francis Group, an informa business

© 2018 Sebastian Biba

The right of Sebastian Biba to be identified as author of this work has been asserted by him in accordance with sections 77 and 78 of the Copyright, Designs and Patents Act 1988.

All rights reserved. No part of this book may be reprinted or reproduced or utilised in any form or by any electronic, mechanical, or other means, now known or hereafter invented, including photocopying and recording, or in any information storage or retrieval system, without permission in writing from the publishers.

Trademark notice: Product or corporate names may be trademarks or registered trademarks, and are used only for identification and explanation without intent to infringe.

British Library Cataloguing in Publication Data
A catalogue record for this book is available from the British Library

Library of Congress Cataloging in Publication Data
Names: Biba, Sebastian, author.
Title: China's hydro-politics in the Mekong : conflict and cooperation in light of securitization theory / Sebastian Biba.
Description: New York : Routledge, 2018. | Series: Routledge contemporary China series ; 186 | Includes bibliographical references and index.
Identifiers: LCCN 2017050153| ISBN 9781138553606 (hardback) | ISBN 9781315148663 (pbk.)
Subjects: LCSH: Water resources development–Political aspects–China. | Water resources development–Political aspects–Mekong River Region. | Water security–China. | Water security–Mekong River Region. | China–Foreign relations–Southeast Asia. | Southeast Asia–Foreign relations–China.
Classification: LCC HD1698.C5 B53 2018 | DDC 333.91/620959–dc23
LC record available at https://lccn.loc.gov/2017050153

ISBN: 978-1-138-55360-6 (hbk)
ISBN: 978-1-315-14866-3 (ebk)

Typeset in Times New Roman
by Taylor & Francis Books

To my grandfather Alois

Contents

List of illustrations viii
Acknowledgements ix

1 Introduction: China and water 1
2 Securitization theory and China's international hydro-politics 25
3 China and Southeast Asia 42
4 China and the Mekong 69
5 The spring 2010 Mekong crisis, part one: China faces criticism 96
6 The spring 2010 Mekong crisis, part two: China responds 129
7 Conclusion: Making sense of China's (Mekong) hydro-politics 162

Index 185

List of Illustrations

Figure

3.1 China's overall foreign policy goals   44

Maps

1.1 China's shared river basins   11
4.1 The Mekong River and its riparian countries   70
4.2 The Mekong mainstream dams   77

Tables

1.1 Selected countries' total renewable water resources (m^3/inhabitant/yr)   6
1.2 Different continents' estimated water availability (m^3/per capita/yr)   6
1.3 Water dependency ratio of China and its riparian neighbors (2014) (%)   12
3.1 China's trade with the MDRCs (various years in US $ million)   50
3.2 China's position in the MDRC's world trade in 2009   51
3.3 China's outbound FDI flows to the MDRCs (2004–2009 in US $ mil.)   51
4.1 The Mekong River Basin and its riparian countries   70
4.2 China's dam cascade on the Mekong River   78

Acknowledgements

The origins of this book go back to my PhD studies, which I started at National Chengchi University in Taipei, Taiwan, in September 2009 and finished at Goethe University Frankfurt, Germany, in October 2014. During this intense educational journey of mine and until the completion of this manuscript, I have received the help and support of a great number of individuals and institutions. I should like to take this opportunity to express my gratitude to a few in particular.

I would first of all like to extend my heartfelt thanks to Heike Holbig who kindly agreed to assume the role of supervising me at Goethe University when my PhD project was already well beyond its initial stages. Had she said no, this book would probably never have come about. Ever since her yes, she has always had a sympathetic ear for my questions and concerns around and beyond this manuscript, providing me with invaluable academic advice on numerous occasions. Also, she was patient with me when I preferred pursuing other projects first to turning my PhD thesis into a book. I am moreover grateful for Gunther Hellmann's offer to function as my PhD co-supervisor without even knowing me at the time. Since then, he has challenged me on this project several times, but this has only meant that my thoughts became clearer after his constructive criticism. Further thanks go the other members of my committee, Jens Borchert, Claudius Wagemann, and Phil Langer. Apart from those with official function, several more colleagues in Frankfurt were supportive in various ways: I thank Christian Rosen (for being a very pleasant office neighbor), Johannes Lejeune, Christina Maags, Marion Reiser, Philipp Erbentraut, Claudia Hülsken, Martina Neunecker, Iris Wurm, and Markus Liegl. In addition, I would like to say thank you to Janet Lin, Miriam Nikitka, Leonie Hasselberg, and Mei Chen for providing useful research assistance.

The birthplace of this book, however, in many ways is Taiwan, not Frankfurt. I spent three years at the International Doctoral Program in Asia-Pacific Studies (IDAS) at National Chengchi University. This time was essential for arousing my interest in and laying the conceptual groundwork for this project. Several professors provided valuable support. I would especially like to thank Lee Chyungly for having me as her research assistant and familiarizing me with the field of non-traditional security. Besides, I have to extend my gratitude to Liu Fu-kuo, Chang Chung-young, Raviprasad Narayanan, and William Su for sacrificing their precious time to go through my various research proposals and give feedback, thus helping me set this project in the right direction from early on. Besides, only through their cordial assistance could I transfer to Frankfurt with a research project elaborate enough for Heike Holbig to agree to take over. Further, I would like to express my appreciation to all IDAS staff from 2009 to 2012 for their administrative support as well as to National Chengchi University, the Taiwan National Science Council, and the Taiwan Ministry of Education for various scholarships and travel grants that facilitated my life and my research abroad a lot.

A few more scholars gave important advice during various stages and on various aspects of this project. Among them, special mention goes to Richard Hu who functioned as my advisor during an exchange semester at Hong Kong University in fall 2010 when I was about to fix important theory questions related to this book as well as Rita Floyd who was kind enough to provide excellent comments on an early draft of my thoughts on developing securitization theory. Moreover, I would like to say thanks to all the participants of numerous panels on several international conferences where I presented different parts of this research over the years and where I usually received knowledgeable comments that were helpful for continuing this work. Receiving great and very positive feedback was certainly true for three anonymous reviewers of my 2016 article in *Security Dialogue*, 47(5), 420–439, which also uses material presented in this book, as well as for the two anonymous reviewers of this manuscript. I am thankful to all of them, as the remarks made helped improve this work markedly. I also extend thanks to Stephanie Rogers and Georgina Bishop at Routledge for their professional support during the review and production processes of this book.

Special thanks, moreover, have to go to all my interview partners in China, Thailand, Laos, Cambodia, and Vietnam with whom I had very interesting discussions and who provided great insights – even though this sometimes meant that they had to share sensitive information. While they must remain unnamed here, I am deeply grateful that they were ready to share their knowledge with me and thus contributed enormously to my research. What is more, while I met all of them for the first time in summer and fall 2012, many of them I have since met, or at least corresponded with, again and again. Our conversations have grown much deeper and much more trustful over time, and I nowadays even have a few academic friends among them that enrich my research considerably.

Finally, I would like to express my heartfelt thankfulness to my family and closest friends who have always given me unconditional support and have always been there for me. They encouraged me to go on when I got stuck and they distracted me when I was too focused to see the forest for the trees. Sabrina Habich-Sobiegalla offered important guidance and encouragement during the early stages of this work. Markus Rohé and Simon Dankert could always be counted on for good rounds of skat that have been extremely unwinding. Simone Kamps, through her unswervingly positive and ever cheerful character, has pulled me up whenever I could use a little solace. My parents, Rosemarie and Walter Biba, along with my sister, Katharina Biba, have been my biggest supporters, not only during the time of this project but throughout my life and academic career. They have never doubted that I would cut my own path and to know this has given me great strength and confidence. My grandparents, Elisabeth Bilz and Elfriede and Alois Biba, have provided significant additional support whenever needed.

Despite the enormous number of persons who have contributed to this manuscript, I am solely responsible for any errors in the work.

1 Introduction
China and water

China's rise ...

China's foreign policy has been one of the most widely and most controversially debated topics in International Relations (IR) and Area Studies literature for many years. One of the prime reasons why the spotlight has been more and more thrown on China is the country's phenomenal rise. Ever since Deng Xiaoping in 1978 launched his "reform and opening up policy" (*gaige kaifang zhengce*), China has been on a path of tremendous economic growth and modernization. As a matter of fact, decades of continuous near-double-digit annual growth rates in its gross domestic product (GDP) have turned China into the world's second-biggest economy, only trailing the United States (US).[1] When measured in real purchasing-power terms, China even overtook the US as the world's leading economy in late 2014 (Arends 2014). What is more, China in 2009 replaced Germany as the global "export champion" (Atkins 2009) and has accumulated the by far greatest amount of foreign exchange reserves, at one point in 2014 nearing incredible US $4 trillion (Noble 2014). China's economic success has even produced sustained discussions about a generic "China model" of development – combining a free market and an authoritarian state – and its chances to supersede the prevailing "Western model," based on capitalism in democratic settings (e.g., Zhao 2010). Militarily, China has also caught up enormously and meanwhile ranks second after the US in terms of worldwide military expenditure. In the period between 2006 and 2015 alone, China's spending grew by 132 percent (SIPRI 2016: 3). China has furthermore articulated its intentions to build a blue water navy and in 2012 commissioned its first aircraft carrier. Besides, China has been able to initiate an ambitious space program, becoming the third country to launch a human being into space in 2003 and the first nation to launch a "hack-proof" quantum-communications satellite in 2016.

On the political front, China has steadily extended its influence through evolving into one of the key players in most areas of global governance. China is not only a permanent member of the United Nations Security Council and a driver behind the G-20, China has likewise increasingly become a heavyweight in the World Trade Organization, International Monetary Fund, and World Bank. Moreover, China has joined, or at least affiliated itself with, the most important regional organizations in East Asia, including the Association of Southeast Asian Nations (ASEAN), the Asia-Pacific Economic Cooperation, and the East Asia Summit. More recently, China has even proceeded to (co-)establish its own regional and transregional institutions, such as the Shanghai Cooperation Organization, BRICS (consisting of Brazil, Russia, India, China, and South Africa) and its New Development Bank, as well as the Asian Infrastructure Investment Bank (AIIB). The newest and grandest expression of China's increasing ambitions is certainly its Belt and Road Initiative (BRI) officially launched in the fall of 2013.[2] Consisting of the Silk Road Economic Belt and a New Maritime Silk Road, the BRI envisions the creation of a highly integrated, cooperative, and mutually beneficial set of maritime and land-based economic corridors linking China to Asian and European markets. The initiative is said to include more than 60 countries with a total population of over 4 billion. Often framed as a purely economic enterprise, BRI also carries geo-economic and geo-political agendas (Swaine 2015). Last but not least, on the cultural level, the proliferation of Confucius Institutes around the globe since the new millennium is indicative of China's increased resources also in the soft power area. All in all, it is in particular the speed and comprehensiveness with which China has catapulted itself in its current position as the world's potential "challenger number one" of US predominance that must be seen as unprecedented.

At the same time, it is exactly China's unique trajectory that has stirred very ambivalent reactions. While for the Chinese, their ongoing rise constitutes nothing else but a "national rejuvenation" "granted by nature" (Yan 2001: 33–34) – after all, in the last 2000 years, China has enjoyed the status of what would nowadays be called a "superpower" several times – for the rest of the world, feelings about China's rise have varied widely, from outright "China threat" to enthusiastic "panda hugging." The single key question related to China's rise certainly is whether this process will (continue to) be peaceful, as proclaimed by China, or whether it will ultimately lead to war, possibly even great power war, thereby following the historic precedents of the rise of Prussia and Wilhelmine Germany in the run-up to World War I as well as the ascent of Nazi Germany and Imperial Japan during the inter-war period.

Those who have studied China's rise and its potential consequences using IR theory have reached very different conclusions. For example, for offensive realists, China's rise is bound to lead to war with the US, as China will try to dominate Asia and maximize the power gap between itself and its neighbors, whereas the US does not tolerate peer competitors and will go to great lengths to contain and weaken China (e.g., Mearsheimer 2006, 2014). China's "new assertiveness" (Yahuda 2013) primarily witnessed in the East and South China Seas since around 2009 seems to be grist to many realists' mill. However, an opposing view is held by neoliberal institutionalists. Probably most prominently, Ikenberry (2008) has argued that the post-World

War II US-led international order has created unusually "accessible, legitimate, and durable" institutions that will be able to accommodate China's rise in a way beneficial to both the US and China. The global order is also an issue increasingly in the focus of power transition theorists. Seeking to examine in how far a rising China is (dis-)satisfied with the existing international system, those theorists have, among other things, pointed to China's accelerated building of pillars of a parallel structure (including, for instance, the China model as well as organizations such as BRICS and the AIIB) in order to demonstrate China's growing dissatisfaction with the US-led order (e.g., Lim 2015 and Biba 2016a). Others, however, have maintained that China is by no means a revisionist power aspiring to overthrow the existing order. Rather, so it has been posited, China is a "reform-minded status quo power" that finds the US-led international system flawed and works to rectify this system from within (e.g., Li 2011 and Ren 2015). In contrast to these various arguments, yet another very different assessment comes from scholars who do not black-box the Chinese state, but in fact put a lot of emphasis on China's domestic situation in order to explain possible foreign policy outcomes. Those scholars have oftentimes questioned the sustainability of China's rise and with it the ability to wage a major war in the first place, referring to China's huge arsenal of grave domestic problems such as rampant corruption, widening social disparities and severe environmental degradation, potentially even precipitating regime collapse (e.g., Chang 2001 and Gurtov 2013). Meanwhile, however, it has also been acknowledged that internal dynamics, above all China's sometimes virulent nationalism, could likewise give rise to a much more aggressive Chinese foreign policy (e.g., Hughes 2011 and Zhao 2013).

Against this twofold backdrop that, first, the evolution of China's rise is of critical importance for peace in Asia and the world, as well as that, second, China's foreign policy is a key perspective through which to examine China's rise, one thing is striking. That is, one of the foreign policy fields that bears potential to influence the future nature of China's rise to an enormous extent has so far been largely neglected from analysis, at least in this particular context. This field is China's international hydro-politics. Hydro-politics, or water politics, at its simplest, can be defined as "politics affected by the availability of freshwater" (Biba 2012: 603). As Elhance (1999: 3) expresses it, "[h]ydropolitics is the systematic study of conflict and co-operation between states over water resources that transcend international borders." This book intends to provide much-needed insight into this significant and, in fact, increasingly relevant aspect of China's foreign policy.

... and its neglected links to fresh water

The links between freshwater resources and China's rise, or the potential impacts on this rise, are more diverse than one might think. On the one hand, there is the sometimes loosely recognized link between China's domestic water woes (see details below) and the country's rise (e.g., Economy 2004 and Hofstedt 2010). The logic, in somewhat simplified terms, goes that China's grave domestic water problems could set in motion a causal chain reaction from water shortages to economic downturn to social instability and, eventually, to regime collapse. Such a chain reaction could, at any point, interfere, in one way or another, with China's current rise trajectory. Yet, this domestic side of China's water equation will – while not fully ignored – not be in the focus of this book.

On the other hand, there is also a link between China's rise and the country's *shared* water resources, that is, in particular, its many international rivers (see details below). For as its domestic water resources have increasingly come under enormous pressure – and this is where the domestic water situation impacts on international hydro-politics – China feels the need to more and more utilize water running down its shared rivers in an effort to guarantee sufficient supply for the various water-related needs of its huge population. Quite possibly, this will not be without serious consequences for China's many downstream riparian neighbors. In fact, the building of Chinese upstream dams (sometimes coupled with the alleged planning of water diversion schemes), the various potential impacts on downstream countries, and reactions from the latter represent one issue-complex that has already been discussed extensively for rivers such as the Mekong (e.g., Menniken 2007; Li et al. 2011; Magee 2012; Pearse-Smith 2012; Räsänen et al. 2012; Kuenzer et al. 2013; Yeophantong 2014; and Fan et al. 2015) and, to a somewhat lesser extent, the Brahmaputra (e.g., Holslag 2011; Sinha 2012; and Zhang 2016). Apart from a few exceptions (see Liebman 2005; Biba 2012; and Ho 2014, 2017), though, the existing literature has largely missed out on comprehensively dealing with at least two significant and inter-related aspects. First, that China's politics of its international rivers is intertwined with other areas of China's foreign relations as well as the country's overarching foreign policy objectives and that this bigger picture has to be kept in mind has seldom been acknowledged. Second, that China's international hydro-politics as a *de facto* more and more important field of China's foreign policy bears potential, and increasingly so, to both constrain China's rise and derail its peacefulness has not commonly been recognized. Therefore, this book will shed light on the characteristics of China's international hydro-politics, how this hydro-politics is linked to China's overall foreign policy and its goals and what China's behavior in this field can tell us, at least implicitly, with regards to China's rise.

Per se, China's international rivers have not, until recently, even ranked particularly high on the agenda of China's foreign policy makers. In fact, many in China have long held the belief that every drop of water flowing through Chinese territory is a domestic matter and thus could be used absolutely freely and without taking the interests and concerns of riparian neighbors into account. Yet, this approach has in recent years already caused simmering friction between China and several of its riparian neighbors. Meanwhile, China's foreign policy has also put a premium on its so-called "good-neighborly policy" (*mulin zhengce*) as a part of the country's peaceful rise (*heping jueqi*), later renamed peaceful development (*heping fazhan*), strategy that has itself been further supplemented by lofty slogans such building a "harmonious world" (*hexie shijie*) and a "community of common destiny" (*mingyun gongtongti*). Sharing borders with 14 sovereign states, China has attached great importance to its adjoining regions already since the late 1980s. The key principle of China's neighborhood diplomacy is "becoming friends and partners with your neighbors" (*yulin weishan, yilin weiban*), which is itself aimed at "building an amicable, tranquil and prosperous neighborhood" (*mulin, anlin, fulin*) (Zhao 2011: 54, 57). The idea behind this approach has been to have stability and peace all around China's vast periphery so as to create conditions favorable for concentrating on the promotion of its own domestic development and, at the same time, also to foster a positive image of itself abroad. The problem for China now is that conflicts over shared water resources could completely derail this neighborhood diplomacy. In the meantime, Chinese scholars have begun to recognize the potential for water conflicts between China and its neighbors (e.g., He et al. 2014).

The rationale behind potential water conflicts between China and its neighbors is rather obvious. In most regions of the world, water availability levels have been falling tremendously over the last decades. Asia indeed stands out in several respects of an impending global water crisis. As a whole, Asia has undergone the world's fastest growth in freshwater withdrawals from rivers, lakes, and underground aquifers during the 20th century (Chellaney 2011: 8). Recent data on Asian countries sharing water with China reveal that in the time period from 1962 to 2014 (that is, from the earliest to the most recent data available) all (except Russia, but including China itself) have suffered from steep declines in water availability per capita, ranging between 50 and up to 75 percent (FAO 2016; also see Table 1.1). Nowadays, Asia – after all, the most populous and most rapidly developing continent on the planet – is the region with the lowest fresh water per person ratio in the world (Chellaney 2011: 26; also see Table 1.2). Meanwhile, water demand in large parts of Asia has risen enormously. Reasons for the diverging trend of sinking water availability and increasing demand are manifold. They include high population growth, coupled with increasing rates of urbanization, spiraling household consumption, and changing diets. They also comprise rapid economic growth and the concomitant degradation of existing reserves of fresh water and the destruction of water tables through deforestation, overexploitation, and pollution. Weak governance and mismanagement have frequently aggravated this process (Dupont 1998: 62; Chellaney 2011: chapter 1). In the future, climate change already felt today will likewise loom large as yet another serious problem impacting on water resources.

The problem that could cause conflicts is that the twin trend of declining water availabilities coupled with rising demand of water carries huge potential for severe adverse impacts. Fresh water is essential to human existence and has no substitute. More precisely, water is at the center of various complex, but vital nexuses, most significant of which are probably the water-food nexus

Table 1.1 Selected countries' total renewable water resources (m³/inhabitant/yr)

Country	1962	1982	2002	2014	Decline(%)
Afghanistan	6,992	5,157	3,040	2,008	71.28
Bangladesh	24,044	14,289	9,007	7,621	68.30
Bhutan	404,772	218,692	135,361	100,671	75.13
Cambodia	78,995	68,553	37,541	30,562	61.31
China	4,175	2,759	2,161	2,018	51.66
India	4,083	2,617	1,753	1,458	64.29
Kazakhstan			7,221	6,150	
Kyrgyzstan			4,698	3,976	
Laos	150,225	98,233	60,614	49,030	67.36
Mongolia	34,421	19,573	14,239	11,761	65.83
Myanmar	52,034	32,355	23,988	21,671	58.35
Nepal	20,256	13,478	8,574	7,372	63.61
North Korea	6,498	4,310	3,319	3,067	52.80
Pakistan	5,237	2,958	1,711	1,306	75.06
Russia			31,165	31,543	
Thailand	15,082	8,903	6,838	6,454	57.21
Vietnam	25,490	15,529	10,793	9,461	62.88

Source: FAO (2016), Aquastat Main Country Database.

Note: Kazakhstan and Kyrgyzstan belonged to the USSR until 1992. Therefore, separate figures for these two countries, as well as Russia, only exist since then.

Table 1.2 Different continents' estimated water availability (m³/per capita/yr)

Continent	Water availability
Asia	3,037
Africa	4,008
Europe	8,941
America (North & South)	20,928
Oceania	32,366

Source: adapted from Chellaney (2011: 26).

and the water-energy nexus (e.g., SEI 2011). On the one hand, to grow food, water is indispensable. Generally speaking, the social and political stability in many Asian nations has hinged upon governments providing their people with sufficient and affordable rice or wheat. However, as Asia's population keeps growing and simultaneously changes its dietary patterns, more water for even more food will be needed. For example, it takes ten times more water to raise a kilogram of beef than to grow a kilogram of rice or wheat. Meanwhile, water shortages across Asia jeopardize growth in agriculture and thus also put enormous pressure on the very sector that holds the key to poverty alleviation in the region, given the considerable number of people working in agriculture. Huge waves of migration, rural-to-urban as well as across national borders, could be one result, together with all the social and political instabilities likely attached (Chellaney 2011: 14, 35).

On the other hand, generating energy likewise requires water for the extraction, mining, processing, refining, and residue disposal of fossil fuels, as well as for producing biofuels and for generating electricity. In fact, the prioritization of water usage for energy generation over water usage for agricultural purposes is increasingly common in Asian countries, as the former usually yields a much higher economic output, however also causing inter-sectoral controversies. Energy generation constitutes the backbone of economic growth in many Asian countries. In order to maintain economic growth, energy demand has been soaring in most places. Higher energy demand, however, usually also implies more stress on water resources. One example is the generation of hydroelectricity through often large-scale dam building that has increasingly come into the focus of many countries in the region. Governments often see it as an "ecologically friendly" way for energy production and more and more believe that hydropower is without any alternative. At the same time, however, dam building, especially in transboundary river basins, brings along its own set of complicated political, social, economic, and environmental challenges (also see Biba 2016b).

In sum, both China and its neighbors are in dire need of more water in the future, while already today they all have increasingly less water at their disposal. As a general result of this major trend and given the character of water as a life-giving resource, water issues are already tied to matters of national security across Asia (Chellaney 2011: 12). At the same time, much of the water available for China and its neighbors is shared between them (see below). While earlier predictions that future wars will be fought over water (e.g., Starr 1991 and Gleick 1993) have – fortunately – not become reality yet, shared water resources certainly have here and there turned into a dividing factor between riparian neighbors across Asia. De Stefano et al. (2010), for example, have detected a recent trend towards less cooperative interaction between countries in several Asian river basins and have additionally found that the two most controversial issues in transboundary relations are infrastructure development and water quantity issues. As a look at this larger context already indicates, China's shared rivers play an increasingly important role for the country's entire foreign policy, especially its neighborhood diplomacy. Hence, whether China continues to rise and whether this rise continues to be peaceful will also be decided by China's international hydro-politics.

China's domestic water situation

As briefly mentioned above, China's international hydro-politics is to some extent driven by China's domestic water situation. This is why an initial look at this situation is useful and, in fact, necessary. In many ways, China represents the epitome of Asia's water woes, for the country has been faced with incredible domestic water problems. In qualitative terms, more than 75 percent of the river water running through China's urban areas is regarded as inappropriate for drinking or fishing, and around 30 percent of the river water throughout the country is deemed to be unfit for use in agriculture or industry, as an estimated 20,000 chemical factories are dumping at best marginally controlled pollutants into China's rivers. Similarly, 50 percent of the groundwater in urban cities is "too polluted for drinking." In 2006, almost half of China's major cities did not meet state drinking-water quality standards, and a third of surface-water samples taken were deemed severely polluted. In 2014, the water quality of 68 percent of Chinese domestic lakes was considered either "bad" or "very bad" by official standards, and nearly 300 million rural residents in China did not have access to safe drinking water (Economy 2007: 43; Gleick 2009: 81; and Li and Wu 2017: 60).

Quantitatively speaking, while China is the fifth-richest country on the planet in terms of water resources, its annual water availability on a per capita basis has been reduced to only one-third of the world's average (Li and Wu 2017: 60). In other words, while the population in China accounts for more than 20 percent of the world, it has less than 7 percent of the global freshwater resources at its disposal. Of the country's more than 650 largest cities, the Chinese government has classified almost half of them as short of water, with 108 identified as "serious" and 60 as "critical." The annual urban freshwater shortage is estimated at 5–6 billion m^3, while irrigated areas experience shortages of 30–35 billion m^3 per year. Groundwater tables around Beijing, for instance, have already dropped 100–300 meters. On top of that, water use in China has been surging, with urban and industrial demand growing at 10.1 and 5.4 percent respectively per year (Hofstedt 2010: 72–73). After China's first national water census conducted in 2013, about 28,000 Chinese rivers – more than half of the rivers previously expected to exist in China – appear now to be missing and have been removed from state maps (Ford 2013).

Meanwhile, the overall distribution of water in China varies widely in both time and space. For instance, while the south is more or less abundant with water, the north, which possesses 40 percent of the country's total population, half its agricultural land, and more than 50 percent of its GDP, receives only 12 percent of China's total precipitation (Economy 2013: 1–2). Put differently, while China's average renewable water resources amount to roughly 2,000 m^3 per person and year (see Table 1.1), this figure is only 700 m^3 in the country's north (Chellaney 2011: 52). With 1,000 m^3 of total renewable freshwater resources per person annually marking the officially recognized line for water scarcity, China's northern parts thus face critical conditions. To relieve the enormous pressure on water resources in many places of China's north, the leadership has heavily relied upon a large number of water transfer schemes. The by far biggest and most prestigious is the South-to-North Water Transfer Project. The goal is to eventually divert 44.8 billion m^3 of water annually from southern rivers over different routes to supply the population centers of China's north. Construction began in December 2002 and completion is planned for 2050. The cost is expected to be around US $62 billion, more than double the sum for building the Three Gorges Dam (Water Technology 2016).

Until now, China's water challenges have already incurred immense health and economic costs. The Organization for Economic Co-operation and Development (OECD 2007: 95) has estimated that hundreds of millions of Chinese are drinking water contaminated with inorganic pollutants as well as toxins from untreated factory wastewater, but also inorganic agricultural chemicals. As a consequence, major outbreaks of illness, including cancer, have been reported in heavily polluted regions, raising health care costs and public concern (Gleick 2009: 79, 81). In fact, more than 450 "cancer villages" with cancer rates considerably higher than normal have been identified in China, most of them clustered around rivers with high pollution (Economy 2013: 3–4). At the same time, the World Bank has estimated that China's water crisis is equivalent to a GDP reduction of 2.3 percent, with 1.3 percent caused by water scarcity and 1 percent by pollution (Economy 2013: 4). The Chinese Academy of Sciences assesses economic losses due to water shortages in the urban areas of northern China alone as equivalent to 3 percent of the total Chinese GDP (Hofstedt 2010: 72–73).

However, while China's domestic freshwater resources have been dwindling down to a dangerous degree, thereby precipitating grave national consequences, the country still boasts the world's greatest potential for producing electricity from flowing water (Smil 1998: 937). Unsurprisingly, as China's economic growth has long resulted in an extremely high energy demand, China's leaders have increasingly sought to utilize this asset. In 2016, China by far ranked number one in its share of worldwide hydroelectricity use, consuming approximately 29 percent of the global total and up from 15 percent in 2007 (BP 2008: 38; BP 2017: 42). China furthermore pursues the goal to generate at least 15 percent of its total energy output by 2020 using renewable energy sources, mostly through water (EIA 2015). With more than 87,000 dams, some 25,000 of which are large dams (with a dam height of at least 15 meters), China nowadays is the country with the most dams by far in the world (International Rivers 2016).

In sum, the above facts paint a rather grim – albeit complex – picture regarding China's domestic water situation. What is more, however, are the

10 *Introduction*

linkages of domestic actions to the international theater. Three examples may elucidate these connections. First, not only Chinese citizens are affected by the country's extremely poor water quality, China's river pollution has also been a serious matter for some of its riparian neighbors. One of the most well-known examples is the infamous 2005 Songhua River incident that temporarily cut off the water supply for nearly four million people – including those living in Russian cities along the Amur – after a chemical plant explosion in the city of Jilin had contaminated the river, which is the largest Chinese tributary to the Amur, with 100 tons of benzene-related pollutants (Gleick 2009: 83). Second, the amount of water flowing out of China and into its riparian neighbors is already decreasing due to increasing demand and consumption of water within China (Feng et al. 2015: 329). Third, as China has already fully developed most of its major domestic rivers, the country has increasingly shifted its hydropower focus towards shared watercourses. As a matter of fact, 70 percent of the total potential hydropower within China is located on its international rivers in the country's south (Feng et al. 2015: 329). It is this complicated background against which China's international hydro-politics is set.

China's international rivers

Regardless of its domestic water problems, China's geographical position makes it play the role of an unrivalled "multidirectional, transboundary water provider" (Chellaney 2011: 2) around its entire periphery. The country is home to the Qinghai-Tibet Plateau, where the largest freshwater reserves outside the polar ice caps are located. Most of the major rivers in the region originate from these highlands or elsewhere in China. Altogether, China shares 110 international rivers and lakes with 18 neighboring countries (He et al. 2014: 1159). Among these rivers, 16 are of particular importance due to their geopolitical and economic influence on China and its riparian neighbors. These rivers, which can be grouped in four geographical sub-regions, are the Heilong/Amur River (Mongolia, China, and Russia), Suifen/Razdolnaya River (China and Russia), Tumen/Tumannaya River (China, North Korea, and Russia), and Yalu/Amrok River (China and North Korea) in the northeast; the Irtysh-Ob River (China, Kazakhstan, and Russia), Ili River-Lake Balkhash (Kyrgyzstan, China, and Kazakhstan), and Tarim River (China and Kyrgyzstan) in the northwest; Senge Zangbo-Indus (China, India, and Pakistan), Yarlung Zangbo/Brahmaputra River (China, Bhutan, India, and Bangladesh), and Ganges (China, Nepal, India, and Bangladesh) in the southwest; as well as the Irrawaddy River (China and Myanmar), Nu/Salween River (China, Myanmar, and Thailand), Lancang/Mekong River (China, Myanmar, Laos, Thailand, Cambodia, and Vietnam), Yuan/Red River (China, Vietnam, and Laos), Beilun/Ka Long River (China and Vietnam), and Pearl/North River (China and Vietnam) in the southeast (also see Map 1.1).[3] Altogether, these basins are inhabited by almost three billion people (He 2015: 313).

While some of these rivers, particularly in China's northeast, are border rivers (that is, they run along the borderline between two countries, in fact constituting the border), most of the major Chinese rivers flowing into Central, South, and Southeast Asia are successive in nature (that is, they are cross-border rivers). Due to the fact that China generally represents the most upstream country along its cross-border rivers, most countries along China's periphery are to varying degrees dependent on incoming water from China (Nickum 2008: 227, 230; also see Map 1.1 and Table 1.3). In fact, the amount of water flowing out of China is 28 times greater than the amount of water flowing into China (He 2015: 313). This, however, also implies that how China manages the water resources on its own territory has implications not only for Chinese people but also for China's neighboring countries. More precisely, Chinese actions – not only its infrastructure development, but also its increasing water demand in general – bear potential to further undermine the often already poor state of water security in many of its riparian neighbors because they might entail, among other things, less water, more polluted water

Map 1.1 China's shared river basins
Source: segment taken from Wolf et al. (1999: 400).

Table 1.3 Water dependency ratio of China and its riparian neighbors (2014) (%)

Country	Ratio
Afghanistan	28.72
Bangladesh	91.44
Bhutan	0
Cambodia	74.67
China	0.96
India	30.52
Kazakhstan	40.64
Kyrgyzstan	1.13
Laos	42.91
Mongolia	0
Myanmar	14.13
Nepal	5.71
North Korea	13.16
Pakistan	77.71
Russia	4.72
Thailand	48.81
Vietnam	59.35

Source: FAO (2016), Aquastat Main Country Database.

Note: Dependency ratio is the ratio of incoming water to total renewable water resources. Countries are not necessarily solely dependent on water resources coming in from China.

as well as greater and more frequent fluctuations in water levels downstream of China.

However, despite its pivotal – or because of its advantageous – geographical position, China was one of only three countries (with Turkey and Burundi) to vote against the 1997 United Nations Watercourse Convention (UNWC), seeking to regulate the non-navigational uses of international watercourses. China's reasons were that the UNWC (1) would not represent universal international agreement, (2) would fail to acknowledge the principle of territorial sovereignty, and thus, (3) would reveal a considerably imbalanced account on the respective rights and obligations of upstream and downstream countries in favor of the latter, and (4) would contain a compulsory nature towards dispute settlement (UNGA 1997). Even those who have argued that under closer scrutiny China has essentially endorsed the basic principles of the UNWC (e.g., Chen et al. 2013 and Wouters 2014) have likewise recognized that "[t]here is room for improvement" (Wouters and Chen 2015: 11) in this regard. What this, then, also means is that the role of international law remains limited when it comes to China's attitude towards its shared water resources. This, in turn, implies that the role of politics – hydro-politics, in fact – becomes all the more significant for how China seeks to manage its shared water resources and govern its international river basins.

Yet, just like other areas of politics in China, the country's hydro-politics is plagued by a phenomenon that has long been coined "fragmented authoritarianism" (Lieberthal and Oksenberg 1988). More specifically, "there is not a single lead agency responsible for all the issues relating to China's transboundary waters" (Feng et al. 2015: 331). Instead, alone under China's State Council, the Ministry of Foreign Affairs, the Ministry of Water Resources, the Ministry of Environmental Protection, the Ministry of Housing and Urban-Rural Development, the Ministry of Agriculture, the State Bureau of Forest, the State Power Group, the State Development and Reform Committee, the Ministry of Transport, the Ministry of Health, and the State Bureau of Tourism are all somehow in involved in matters of (international) river governance. The result is a hugely fragmented administration, where responsibilities overlap, interests diverge, communication is poor, and compromising remains protracted and difficult (Feng et al. 2015: 331–332).

This is the overall frame in which China's international hydro-politics takes place. The three key characteristics, once again, are: (1) China's advantageous geographical position; (2) China's very cautious approach to letting international law govern its shared water resources, thereby putting a premium on political processes; and (3) China's fragmented "hydro-polity." These three general characteristics have to be always taken into consideration when it comes to understanding the formulation and implementation of China's international hydro-politics in any of its shared rivers and lakes.

The Mekong

As previously stated, China shares alone 16 *major* international rivers with its neighboring countries. Roughly speaking, the specific conditions in these river basins certainly vary according to the four geographical sub-groupings outlined above. For example, some rivers are border rivers, while others are cross-border rivers. Likewise, in some basins, water quality may be an issue, whereas in others water quantity or infrastructure development may be of larger concern. As a result, some of the specificities of China's respective hydro-political approach are likely to vary as well. At the same time, however, we can also expect similarities across the different river basins. These should be driven by a few constants such as China's deteriorating domestic water situation as well as its advantageous geographical position in its cross-border rivers. While the final chapter of this book will include an extensive section on some of the key rivers in all of the four sub-regions respectively, seeking to bring out some of these overarching similarities, the focus of this book will be on China's hydro-politics in one river basin only, that is, the Mekong. Why the Mekong?

The Mekong is arguably the most interesting case amongst China's shared rivers to observe and analyze the country's international hydro-politics. This is for various reasons. First, China has been relatively active in the Mekong for a comparatively long time. More precisely, China has begun to build mainstream dams on the Lancang, the Chinese part of the Mekong, already in the late 1980s. Second, the Mekong is the river that is shared by the highest number of riparian countries among all of China's international rivers, that is, six, namely, China, Myanmar, Laos, Thailand, Cambodia, and Vietnam. What is more, the Mekong is China's only shared river where we find a multilateral governance body set up by China's riparian neighbors, that is, the Mekong River Commission (MRC) comprising Thailand, Laos, Cambodia, and Vietnam (henceforth called the Mekong downstream riparian countries, MDRCs).[4] Third, apart from the existence of the MRC, the Mekong River Basin is also relatively rich in NGOs, and activist groups in general, working on diverse issues related to environmental sustainability and human security. Dam building in the Mekong and its potential impacts have long been on their agendas. As dam building has coincided several times in the past with extreme water levels in the Mekong, river developers, above all China, have received a lot of blame. Fourth, and finally, the Mekong sub-region as part of mainland Southeast Asia is itself part of a bigger sub-region that, together with maritime Southeast Asia, forms Southeast Asia, or the "ASEAN region," which for its part is of critical importance for China's neighborhood diplomacy and beyond. Take the South China Sea into which the Mekong empties as an example. Due to overlapping maritime territorial claims between China and several of its maritime neighbors, the South China Sea has in recent years increasingly turned into one of the primary hot spots not only of regional affairs but has also drawn in external players such as the US. Also, Vietnam is not only a Mekong riparian country, but also a claimant in the South China Sea. This alone indicates how Mekong hydro-politics is potentially interlinked with other significant international relations issues. While some of these four aspects are to some extent comparable to others of China's shared rivers, it is only the Mekong that combines all of them.

As a result of this focus on the Mekong, this book poses the following concrete, while still broad, questions: What is China's hydro-political approach in the Mekong, what are its key characteristics, and how can these be explained, also with regard to China's overall foreign policy behavior? How far is China willing to cooperate over shared water resources in the Mekong and how far is China also ready for conflict? Under what conditions might China be more forthcoming to cooperate and what are the red lines China is reluctant to overstep? And, finally, is there an evolution in China's approach towards the Mekong and what might explain it?

The key argument of this book, in somewhat raw terms at this point, is that there is both conflict and cooperation, sometimes even at the same time, in China's Mekong hydro-politics. Basically, China has on the one hand unilaterally engaged in building large-scale infrastructure schemes in the Mekong and has sought to sell this to its neighbors as a form of joint development, thereby trying to steer the discourse away from more sensitive security-related issues. On the other hand, China has pursued quite a reactive approach, where piecemeal on-and-off cooperation has followed upon phases of criticism of Chinese behavior. From the Chinese perspective, this reactive approach has created a "passive dynamism" towards gradually more cooperation, as China is not interested in receiving blame from its neighbors – blame that has the potential to tarnish China's image abroad, sow distrust between China and its neighbors, and run counter some of China's overall foreign policy objectives such as continued economic development.

Theoretical lenses: realism, institutionalism, and securitization theory

From a theoretical angle, China's international hydro-politics, in the Mekong and elsewhere, has commonly been treated as a case for realism (e.g., Liebman 2005; Menniken 2007; Nickum 2008; Chellaney 2011; and Sinha 2012). While there are several different strands to the realist school of IR, it can be said that they are all skeptical about the prospects for international cooperation (also see above). This is especially the case when it comes to cross-border rivers. As Lindemann (2008: 119) has stated,

> chances for international cooperation are regarded to be even worse [than in other issue areas of international relations when applying the realist paradigm] given that upstream-downstream externalities involve asymmetric incentives to cooperation. Accordingly, power-based arguments point to the prevalence of a passive or active unilateralism in international river basins and consider it unrealistic, if not impossible to elaborate comprehensive basin-wide agreements that establish a mutually beneficial cooperative regime.

The only chance for international water cooperation and river regime formation recognized by realists is the presence of a hegemon, either benign or coercive, that possesses a preponderance of material resources. Literature in international hydro-politics has thus drawn on the theory of hegemonic stability; however, not without critical amendments. Most notably, Lowi (1993) has diverged from the original argument that the existence of a dominant power in any given basin will almost naturally lead to cooperation, due to this power taking the lead in forming and maintaining a water regime and also enforcing compliance with its rules. Instead, Lowi has come up with the distinction between upstream and downstream hegemons. According to this new rationale, it is – if at all – only the presence of a downstream hegemon that could enable water regime formation, because only the downstream hegemon might have both the interest in securing its water supply through international regime formation and the power to compel cooperation. By contrast, a hegemon in the upstream position generally does not have the incentive to engage in – let alone initiate – cooperative arrangements, as these would only be considered as a constraint to unlimited future action and discriminatory use of a river's resources (Lowi 1993: 10).

Those who have portrayed China's international hydro-politics relying on realist arguments have therefore started from China's vastly superior power capabilities, militarily and economically, vis-à-vis (most of) its riparian neighbors.[5] The Mekong case once again is a good example to make this point blatantly obvious. While China's GDP in official exchange rates was in 2016 estimated at US $10.73 trillion, the combined GDP of the four MDRCs was only around US $650 million. Consequently, the approximately 1.3 percent of its GDP that China in 2017 spent on military expenditure implies an absolute figure likewise extremely higher than what comes out of similar percentages for the MDRCs (CIA 2017). On top, realist accounts have added China's advantageous geographical position as an upstream state, thus making China an "upstream hegemon" generally disinclined to cooperate. The previously stated fact that China was one of only three countries to veto the UNWC has moreover bolstered this reasoning. At the same time, however, realist argumentation is faced with difficulties as soon as China, the upstream hegemon, *does* cooperate. These difficulties are aggravated because most strands of realism share a highly static conception of international relations (Brooks 1997: 455). This means that, while geography is a fixed factor anyways, changes in cooperative behavior cannot be explained if concomitant changes in economic and/or military capabilities among the actors involved fail to materialize.

As a consequence, others – albeit still a minority – have questioned the realist logic when it comes to China's international hydro-politics and have rather emphasized what they perceive as the cooperative element of China's behavior in its shared rivers (e.g., Onishi 2007, 2011; Zawahri and Hensengerth 2012; Lee 2014; and Han 2017). Generally speaking, Dinar (2009) has argued that rather than realist thinking on IR, institutionalism is better equipped to explain international hydro-politics. Considering the many historic agreements over water resources worldwide, he has claimed that even the stronger upstream riparian state may realize that benefits can accrue from coordination and joint action. The existence of international institutions is a key factor in explaining cooperation. They aim at creating the necessary incentives for cooperation and at achieving compliance with what has been agreed upon. Institutions are commonly defined broadly as "persistent and connected sets of rules (formal or informal) that prescribe behavioral roles, constrain activity, and shape expectations" (Keohane 1988: 383). What, however, happens when cooperation takes place outside of institutional frames, that is, for example, when cooperation is not based on persistent rules? In those cases, the explanatory power of institutionalism decreases. As later chapters will show, where China has cooperated, it has in fact mostly – although not exclusively – done so on a rather loose on-and-off basis. Institutions have (to date) only played a limited role in China's international hydro-politics.

As a result, two of the major IR theoretical approaches seem to be flawed as far as China's behavior in its shared rivers is concerned. While realism rejects the existence of cooperation in international river basins with an upstream hegemon, institutionalism overestimates the existence and extent of cooperation (through institutions). In particular, both theoretical approaches have problems to explain constellations in which conflict and cooperation *coexist*, although, as Zeitoun and Mirumachi (2008) have compellingly argued, this ambivalent state of affairs actually constitutes the hydro-political reality during most of the time and in the vast majority of cases (also see Mirumachi 2015). This book therefore applies a different approach to fathom China's international hydro-politics, namely, securitization theory designed by the so-called Copenhagen School of Security Studies. This theory has the advantage of being a dynamic approach that can account for phases of overlapping or consecutive cooperation and conflict in China's international hydro-politics. Securitization theory is also able to integrate contextual factors, thereby admitting important and necessary linkages of hydro-politics to other areas of China's foreign policy (also see Biba 2014: 22).

Structure of the book

The topics, questions, and arguments outlined above are spread over the next six chapters and make up the body of this book. What exactly securitization theory is and how it works is explored further in great detail in Chapter 2. The chapter explains key terminology and major concepts of the theory and shows how the approach can be applied to China's international hydro-politics. In particular, the chapter pays special attention to distinguishing politicization, securitization, and desecuritization as well as securitization moves, full securitization, and securitization failure from each other, also embedding a review on debates about the value of security. In addition, the chapter makes a conceptual contribution to the theory by introducing three behaviorally different strategies of how audiences faced with attempts at securitization can respond in order to reject those attempts, also resulting in different outcomes. All this is set against the backdrop that China is not interested in letting issues surrounding its international hydro-politics become securitized and, therefore, the chapter aims at illustrating China's options to prevent this. The chapter also discusses the theory's take on contextual factors.

After the theoretical foundations are laid, the book turns to empirical issues. As international hydro-politics is only one issue-area of China's foreign relations with its riparian neighbors and thus needs to be understood through contextual knowledge, Chapter 3 widens the focus of concern and looks at China's broader international relations environment in the Mekong as well as in Southeast Asia more generally. The chapter delineates China's overall foreign policy objectives and outlines the importance of Southeast Asia for achieving these very objectives. The chapter then examines China's political, economic, and security relations with the MDRCs and highlights the huge asymmetry in

Sino-MDRC relations working in China's favor. Since all MDRCs are likewise member states of ASEAN, the most important state grouping in Southeast Asia, the chapter also depicts a few facets of Sino-ASEAN relations. The focus is on some key events that time-wise framed the spring 2010 Mekong crisis, itself in the focus of later chapters detailing China's hydro-political approach in the Mekong. In a final step, the chapter briefly explores the US role in the Mekong and Southeast Asia, especially after in 2009 it announced its "back to Asia" policy, which also had an impact on China.

Chapter 4 narrows the focus again and zeroes in specifically on China's hydro-politics in the Mekong. The chapter gives a comprehensive overview of China's water resources-related behavior and actions in the Mekong and also takes into account downstream perspectives. After describing China's significant role for the hydrology of the river, the chapter elaborates on China's attitude towards Mekong governance. In particular, the chapter introduces the MRC, evaluates the organization's strengths and weaknesses, and explains China's reasons for not joining the Mekong's prime governance body. In the center of this chapter's attention, however, is the Mekong's most controversial development as of now, that is, mainstream dam building. The chapter reports on China's dam-building activities upstream and points to the various adverse effects downstream, which could result from China's activities. The chapter also shows that despite these potential negative impacts, downstream attitudes towards mainstream dam building and China's role in it are in fact highly ambivalent. Demonstrating how exactly this plays out, the chapter also expands on the events and interactions during a summer 2008 Mekong flooding, which at the same time functions as an interesting prelude to the analyses in the following chapters. In a final step, the chapter summarizes China's Mekong hydro-politics at the dawn of the spring 2010 Mekong crisis and links China's approach to its larger foreign policy objectives.

Having provided an enormous amount of significant background information, Chapters 5 and 6 jointly turn to presenting, in a very detailed way, a concrete case study of China's Mekong hydro-politics. This case is the spring 2010 Mekong crisis when water levels in the river had sunk to a record low, resulting in negative effects on people's livelihoods and stirring massive blame on the Chinese dams. As a whole, this crisis, the worst of its kind to date, triggered unprecedented interactions between China and various MDRC stakeholders, thereby constituting a rare opportunity to showcase in great detail the full range of China's Mekong hydro-politics. Methodologically, the empirical case study makes use of a wide set of primary sources in order to thoroughly trace the process of events. Most significant are English news articles from regional outlets. This use of English sources makes sense because the actors involved came from different countries. Through coverage of the crisis in English, regional and international news outlets made sure that everybody involved, or intended to be drawn in, would understand and get the messages directed at each other. This not only applied for news articles, but also for other primary sources issued in English by NGOs or the MRC, for instance.

In addition, more than 30 interviews conducted with local activists and NGO employees, journalists, university professors, experts from think-tanks, as well as MRC and government officials in China and the MDRCs during the summer and fall of 2012, helped fill in on some "dark spots" left behind where no official/public documents were available or traceable.

In Chapter 5, the MDRCs are in the focus. It is noteworthy at this point that in this chapter, as well as in previous and later chapters, the MDRCs will mostly be treated as a group. This is not to imply that these four countries represent an overly cohesive group, and the fact that they are not (always) will also be taken into consideration and acknowledged where necessary. At the same time, though, what allows for the MDRCs to be seen as a group, and as a "collective counterpart" to China in the Mekong in a sense, is their joint membership in the MRC. Having said that, Chapter 5 gives a thorough account of the spring 2010 Mekong crisis itself, especially delineating the impacts of the low water levels. Subsequently, the chapter traces the myriad of attempts on the part of various local and international activist and NGO groups as well as the media in the MDRCs and beyond to blame the Chinese dam building on the upper reaches of the Mekong for the situation and make it a matter of security by portraying it as an existential threat to people's livelihoods in the form of endangering their food security and economic security. Also, the chapter investigates what role the four MDRC governments and the MRC played during the crisis. The chapter reveals that while they had a different take on the reasons for the low water levels, they still sought to use the opportunity of the crisis, with its widespread criticism of the Chinese dams, to ask China for more cooperation on aspects related to joint Mekong governance.

Chapter 6 brings China back to the center of concern, as the chapter provides deep insight into China's behavior during and after the immediate crisis, analyzing the country's complex response to the blame its dams received as well as to the MDRC requests for more cooperation. The chapter divides China's response into four distinct, although partly overlapping, phases, showing how China's reaction moved (1) from completely ignoring the blame on its dams, (2) to rejecting it, (3) to accepting and making offers of enhanced cooperation, and (4) to even seeking to prevent similar criticism in the future. The chapter then dissects the characteristics of each of the four phases and explains China's motivation behind its multi-pronged response, bringing to light how China was in effect driven by MDRC criticism and the broader international relations context around the time in an effort to meet its overall foreign policy objectives.

Chapter 7, finally, returns to the questions set out at the beginning of this book and explores the wider implications of the findings. In doing so, the chapter determines how far China is willing to go in terms of conflict and cooperation over its shared water resources in the Mekong. Through incorporating a concise overview of China's hydro-political approach(es) towards its other major shared river basins around its periphery, the chapter moreover illustrates how China's behavior in the Mekong is representative of a more general pattern in China's hydro-politics. Before concluding with a few policy recommendations, the chapter looks at the more recent developments in Southeast Asia in general and the Mekong in particular. Above all, the chapter emphasizes China's establishment of the Lancang-Mekong Cooperation Mechanism in early 2016, asking in how far the spring 2010 events might, with the benefit of hindsight, have been a watershed event for China, making its hydro-politics gradually shift from a reactive to a much more proactive approach.

Notes

1 The European Union, if taken together, also has a larger economy than China.
2 Originally, the BRI was commonly referred to as "One Belt, One Road" (*yi dai, yi lu*). However, because it is not really *one* belt or road anymore, the term BRI is now more frequently used.
3 In brute geographical terms, China's southeast is facing the sea and there are no shared rivers. However, as the countries with which China shares international rivers such as the Mekong are usually called the countries of mainland Southeast Asia, it makes sense – also with regard to consistency with later chapters – to also speak of China's shared rivers in its southeast.
4 While Myanmar is a Mekong riparian country, it has – like China – not been a member of the MRC. In addition to its passive political role to date, several other indicators, such as flow distribution, basin land area and country territory in basin (also see Chapter 4), make Myanmar a negligible actor in Mekong hydro-politics. As a result, Myanmar will not subsumed to the group of the four MDRCs. As a matter of fact, Myanmar will hardly play any role throughout this book.
5 Russia may be an exception in terms of military capabilities. But then China and Russia mostly share border rivers without upstream-downstream constellations.

References

Arends, B. (2014) "It's Official: America Is Now No. 2," *Market Watch*, 4 December, www.marketwatch.com/story/its-official-america-is-now-no-2-2014-12-04.
Atkins, R. (2009) "China Overtakes Germany in Race to Be 'Export Champion'," *Financial Times*, 25 August, www.ft.com/cms/s/0/70542f2e-910d-11de-bc99-00144fea bdc0.html#axzz4Jkd3cvbU.
Biba, S. (2012) "China's Continuous Dam-building on the Mekong River," *Journal of Contemporary Asia*, 42(4), 603–628.
Biba, S. (2014) "Desecuritization in China's Behavior towards its Transboundary Rivers: The Mekong River, the Brahmaputra River, and the Irtysh and Ili Rivers," *Journal of Contemporary China*, 23(85), 21–43.
Biba, S. (2016a) "It's Status, Stupid: Explaining the Underlying Core Problem in US-China Relations," *Global Affairs*, 2(5), 455–464.
Biba, S. (2016b) "The Goals and Reality of the Water-Food-Energy Security Nexus: The Case of China and Its Southern Neighbours," *Third World Quarterly*, 37(1), 51–70.
British Petroleum (BP) (2008) *Statistical Review of World Energy, June 2008*, London: BP.
British Petroleum (BP) (2017) *Statistical Review of World Energy, June 2017*, London: BP.

Brooks, S. (1997) "Dueling Realisms," *International Organization*, 51(3), 445–477.
Central Intelligence Agency (CIA) (2017) "The World Factbook," www.cia.gov/library/publications/the-world-factbook/.
Chang, G. (2001) *The Coming Collapse of China*, New York: Random House.
Chellaney, B. (2011) *Water: Asia's New Battleground*, Washington, DC: Georgetown University Press.
Chen, H., A. Rieu-Clarke, and P. Wouters (2013) "Exploring China's Transboundary Water Treaty Practice through the Prism of the UN Watercourse Convention," *Water International*, 38(2), 217–230.
De Stefano, L., P. Edwards, L. de Silva, and A. Wolf (2010) "Tracking Cooperation and Conflict in International Basins: Historic and Recent Trends," *Water Policy*, 12(6), 871–884.
Dinar, S. (2009) "Power Asymmetry and Negotiations in International River Basins," *International Negotiation*, 14(2), 329–360.
Dupont, A. (1998) "The Environment and Security in Pacific Asia," *Adelphi Paper*, 319, Oxford: Oxford University Press.
Economy, E. (2004) *The River Runs Black*, Ithaca, NY: Cornell University Press.
Economy, E. (2007) "The Great Leap Backward?," *Foreign Affairs*, 86(5), 38–59.
Economy, E. (2013) "China's Water Challenge: Implications for the U.S. Rebalance to Asia," *Council on Foreign Relations*, 24 July, httwww.foreign.senate.gov/imo/media/doc/Economy_Testimony.pdf.
Elhance, A. (1999) *Hydropolitics in the 3rd World: Conflict and Cooperation in International River Basins*, Washington DC: United States Institute of Peace Press.
Energy Information Administration (EIA) (2015) "China," 14 May, www.eia.gov/beta/international/analysis.cfm?iso=CHN.
Fan, H., D. He, and H. Wang (2015) "Environmental Consequences of Damming the Mainstream Lancang-Mekong River: A Review," *Earth Science Reviews*, 146, 77–91.
Feng, Y., D. He, and W. Wang (2015) "Identifying China's Transboundary Water Risks and Vulnerabilities – A Multidisciplinary Analysis Using Hydrological Data and Legal/Institutional Settings," *Water International*, 40(2), 328–341.
Food and Agriculture Organization (FAO) (2016), *Aquastat Main Country Database*, www.fao.org/nr/water/aquastat/dbase/index.stm.
Ford, E. (2013) "28,000 Rivers Wiped Off the Map of China," *The Times*, 30 March, www.theaustralian.com.au/news/world/rivers-wiped-off-the-map-of-china/story-e6frg6so-1226609139591.
Gleick, P. (1993) "Water and Conflict: Freshwater Resources and International Security," *International Security*, 18(1), 79–112.
Gleick, P. (2009) "China and Water," in P. Gleick (ed.) *The World's Water 2008–2009. The Biennial Report on Freshwater Resources*, Washington, DC: Island Press, 79–100.
Gurtov, M. (2013) *Will This Be China's Century? A Skeptic's View*, Boulder, CO: Lynne Rienner.
Han, H. (2017) "China, an Upstream Hegemon: A Destabilizer for the Governance of the Mekong River?" *Pacific Focus*, 32(1), 30–55.
He, D., R. Wu, Y. Feng, Y. Li., C. Ding, W. Wang, and D. Yu (2014) "China's Transboundary Waters: New Paradigms for Water and Ecological Security through Applied Ecology," *Journal of Applied Ecology*, 51(5), 1159–1168.

He, Y. (2015) "China's Practice on the Non-navigational Uses of Transboundary Waters: Transforming Diplomacy through Rules of International Law," *Water International*, 40(2), 312–327.

Ho, S. (2014) "River Politics: China's Policies in the Mekong and the Brahmaputra in Comparative Perspective," *Journal of Contemporary China*, 23(85), 1–20.

Ho, S. (2017) "China's Transboundary River Policies towards Kazakhstan: Issue-linkages and Incentives for Cooperation," *Water International*, 42(2), 142–162.

Hofstedt, T. (2010) "China's Water Scarcity and Its Implications for Domestic and International Stability," *Asian Affairs: An American Review*, 37(2), 71–83.

Holslag, J. (2011) "Assessing the Sino-Indian Water Dispute," *Journal of International Affairs*, 64(2), 19–35.

Hughes, C. (2011) "Reclassifying China's Nationalism: the Geopolitk Turn," *Journal of Contemporary China*, 20(71), 601–620.

Ikenberry, G. (2008) "The Rise of China and the Future of the West," *Foreign Affairs*, 87(1), www.foreignaffairs.com/articles/asia/2008-01-01/rise-china-and-future-west.

International Rivers (2016) "China," www.internationalrivers.org/programs/china.

Keohane, R. (1988) "International Institutions: Two Approaches," *International Studies Quarterly*, 32(4), 379–396.

Kuenzer, C., I. Campbell, M. Roch, P. Leinenkugel, V. Q. Tuan, and S. Dech (2013) "Understanding the Impact of Hydropower Developments in the Context of Upstream-Downstream Relations in the Mekong River Basin," *Sustainability Science*, 8(4), 565–584.

Lee, S. (2014) "Benefit Sharing in the Mekong River Basin," *Water International*, 40(1), 139–152.

Li, M. (2011) "Rising from Within: China's Search for a Multilateral World and Its Implications for Sino-US Relations," *Global Governance*, 17(3), 331–351.

Li, Z., and F. Wu (2017) "China and Shared Water Resources: Geopolitics, Domestic Institutions and Global Governance," in F. Wu and H. Zhang (eds.), *China's Global Quest for Resources: Energy, Food and Water*, London and New York: Routledge, 59–78.

Li, Z., D. He, and Y. Feng (2011) "Regional Hydropolitics of the Transboundary Impacts of the Lancang Cascade Dams," *Water International*, 36(3), 328–339.

Lieberthal, K., and M. Oksenberg (1988) *Policy Making in China: Leaders, Structures, and Processes*, Princeton, NJ: Princeton University Press.

Liebman, A. (2005) "Trickle-down Hegemony? China's 'Peaceful Rise' and the Dam Building on the Mekong," *Contemporary Southeast Asia*, 27(2), 281–304.

Lim, Y. (2015) "How (Dis)Satisfied Is China? A Power Transition Theory Perspective," *Journal of Contemporary China*, 24(92), 280–297.

Lindemann, S. (2008) "Understanding Water Regime Formation – A Research Framework with Lessons from Europe," *Global Environmental Politics*, 8(4), 117–140.

Lowi, M. (1993) *Water and Power: The Politics of a Scarce Resource in the Jordan River Basin*, Cambridge: Cambridge University Press.

Magee, D. (2012) "The Dragon Upstream: China's Role in Lancang-Mekong Development," in J. Öjendal, S. Hansson, and S. Hellberg (eds.), *Politics and Development in a Transboundary Watershed. The Case of the Lower Mekong Basin*, Heidelberg, London and New York: Springer, 171–193.

Mearsheimer, J. (2006) "China's Unpeaceful Rise," *Current History*, 105(690), 160–162.

Mearsheimer, J. (2014) "Can China Rise Peacefully?" *National Interest*, 25 October, http://nationalinterest.org/commentary/can-china-rise-peacefully-10204.
Menniken, T. (2007) "China's Performance in International Resource Politics: Lessons from the Mekong," *Contemporary Southeast Asia*, 29(1), 97–120.
Mirumachi, N. (2015) *Transboundary Water Politics in the Developing World*, London and New York: Routledge.
Nickum, J. (2008) "The Upstream Superpower: China's International Rivers," in O. Varis, C. Tortajada, and A. Biswas (eds.), *Management of Transboundary Rivers and Lakes*, Berlin: Springer-Verlag, 227–244.
Noble, J. (2014) "China's Foreign Exchange Reserves near Record $ 4tn," *Financial Times*, 15 April, www.ft.com/intl/cms/s/0/4768bd3c-c461-11e3-8dd4-00144feabdc0.html.
Onishi, K. (2007) "Interstate Negotiation Mechanisms for Cooperation in the Mekong River Basin," *Water International*, 32(4), 524–537.
Onishi, K. (2011) "Reassessing Water Security in the Mekong: The Chinese Rapprochement with Southeast Asia," *Journal of Natural Resources Policy Research*, 3(4), 393–412.
Organization for Economic Co-operation and Development (OECD) (2007) "Environmental Performance Reviews: China (2007)," www.oecd.org/china/environmentalperformancereviewschina2007.htm.
Pearse-Smith, S. (2012) "'Water War' in the Mekong Basin?" *Asia Pacific Viewpoint*, 53(2), 147–162.
Räsänen, T., J. Korponen, H. Lauri, and M. Kummu (2012) "Downstream Hydrological Impacts of Hydropower Development in the Upper Mekong Basin," *Water Resources Management*, 26(12), 3495–3513.
Ren, X. (2015) "A Reform-minded Status Quo Power? China, the G20, and Reform of the International Financial System," *Third World Quarterly*, 36(11), 2023–2043.
Sinha, U. (2012) "Examining China's Hydro-behaviour: Peaceful or Assertive?" *Strategic Analysis*, 36(1), 41–56.
Smil, V. (1998) "China's Energy and Resource Uses: Continuity and Change," *The China Quarterly*, 156, 935–951.
Starr, J. (1991) "Water Wars," *Foreign Policy*, 82, 17–36.
Stockholm Environment Institute (SEI) (2011) "Understanding the Nexus," Bonn 2011 Conference on The Water, Energy and Food Security Nexus: Solutions for the Green Economy, Bonn, 16–18 November.
Stockholm International Peace Research Institute (SIPRI) (2016) "Trends in World Military Expenditure, 2015," *SIPRI Fact Sheet*. April, 2016, http://books.sipri.org/files/FS/SIPRIFS1604.pdf.
Swaine, M. (2015) "Chinese Views and Commentary on the 'One Belt, One Road' Initiative," *China Leadership Monitor*, 47.
United Nations General Assembly (*UNGA*) (1997) "Official Records of the General Assembly," 51(99). 21 May
Water Technology (2016) "South-to-North Water Diversion Project, China," www.water-technology.net/projects/south_north/.
Wolf, A., J. Natharius, J. Danielson, B. Ward, and J. Pender (1999) "International River Basins of the World," *Water Resources Development*, 15(4), 387–427.
Wouters, P. (2014) "The Yin and Yang of International Water Law: China's Transboundary Water Practice and the Changing Contours of State Sovereignty," *Review of European Community and International Environmental Law*, 23(1), 67–75.

Wouters, P., and H. Chen (2015) "Editors' Introduction," *Water International*, 40(1), 1–20.

Yahuda, M. (2013) "China's New Assertiveness in the South China Sea," *Journal of Contemporary China*, 22(81), 446–459.

Yan, X. (2001) "The Rise of China in Chinese Eyes," *Journal of Contemporary China*, 10(26), 33–39.

Yeophantong, P. (2014) "China's Lancang Dam Cascade and Transnational Activism in the Mekong Region: Who's Got the Power?," *Asian Survey*, 54(4), 700–724.

Zawahri, N., and O. Hensengerth (2012) "Domestic Environmental Activists and the Governance of the Ganges and Mekong Rivers in India and China," *International Environmental Agreements*, 12(3), 269–298.

Zeitoun, M., and N. Mirumachi (2008) "Transboundary Water Interaction I: Considering Conflict and Cooperation," *International Environmental Agreements*, 8(4), 297–316.

Zhang, H. (2016) "Sino-Indian Water Disputes: The Coming Water Wars?" *WIRE's Water*, 3, 155–166.

Zhao, S. (2010) "The China Model: Can It Replace the Western Model of Modernization?" *Journal of Contemporary China*, 19(65), 419–436.

Zhao, S. (2011) "China's Approaches toward Regional Cooperation in East Asia: Motivations and Calculations," *Journal of Contemporary China*, 20(68), 53–67.

Zhao, S. (2013) "Foreign Policy Implications of Chinese Nationalism Revisited: The Strident Turn," *Journal of Contemporary China*, 22(82), 535–553.

2 Securitization theory and China's international hydro-politics

Introduction

For reasons explained in the previous chapter, and also at the end of this chapter, this book choses neither realism nor institutionalism as theoretical frames to grasp China's international hydro-politics. Instead, it makes the case for securitization theory. Securitization theory has been hailed as one of the most promising developments in the field of post-Cold War security studies. It is therefore a rather recent, yet promising, approach to theorizing in International Relations (IR). But what exactly is securitization theory and, most significantly, how does it work? The first part of this chapter answers these rather general questions, albeit with keeping the specific area of this book, that is, (fresh) water-related issues as the focal point of hydro-politics, in mind. Consequently, the first part of this chapter primarily introduces and explains key terminology and major concepts of securitization theory. It also includes criticism of the theory and amendments to it by other authors, as long as their points are important for later analyses. However, while these quite general aspects about securitization theory are expedient, and even necessary, to understand many of the events surrounding the spring 2010 Mekong crisis to be the focus of later chapters, an introductory discussion of securitization theory is not sufficient to fathom in detail China's international hydro-politics through the prism of this very theory. To make the latter possible, a more detailed knowledge about securitization theory is required. Above all, we need to learn about the outcomes of various securitization processes as well as about China's outcome preferences and its options to realize them. These aspects are therefore in the center of the second part of this chapter.

Securitization theory – explaining the key concepts

Securitization theory was designed by the so-called Copenhagen School (CS) of Security Studies. Within the CS, securitization theory has been associated most closely with the name Ole Wæver. His first major writing on the topic came out as a book chapter titled "Securitization and Desecuritization" in 1995. Developing his theory, Wæver borrowed from several intellectuals from diverse fields, particularly from John L. Austin, the British founder of speech act theory, the French literary theorist Jacques Derrida, the German philosopher Carl Schmitt, as well as Kenneth Waltz, the father of neorealism (Floyd 2010: chapter 1). Having so many different intellectual ancestors, the classification of the theory into the spectrum of IR theories has not always been straightforward. Wæver himself has described his approach as one of "post-structural realism" (Floyd 2010: 9). Judged from the outside, the theory has been localized within the context of both classical realist and constructivist approaches to IR (Williams 2003: 512). It is constructivist as threats are seen as socially constructed and inter-subjective; it is realist due to its focus on existential threats as well as the fact that security still is about survival (Buzan et al. 1998: chapter 2).

The most comprehensive work of the CS on securitization theory to date is Barry Buzan, Ole Wæver and Jaap de Wilde's 1998 book *Security: A New Framework for Analysis*. In it, the authors argue that:

> any public issue can be located on a spectrum ranging from non-politicized (meaning the state does not deal with it and it is not in any other way made an issue of public debate and decision), through politicized (meaning the issue is part of public policy, requiring government decision and resource allocation or, more rarely, some other form of communal governance) to securitized (meaning the issue is presented as an existential threat, requiring emergency measures and justifying actions outside the normal bounds of political procedure).
> (Buzan et al. 1998: 23–24)

Importantly, this spectrum of escalation stages is not only one way. This means, apart from the process of, for example, moving an issue from politicized to securitized (securitization), it is also possible to bring a previously securitized issue back into the realm of politics (desecuritization; also see below). However, securitization has been the concept in the focus of CS deliberations. Securitization may be defined as when "an actor declares [through speech acts] a particular issue [...] to be an 'existential threat' to a particular referent object" (McDonald 2008a: 69). The following sections will, in turn, look at the various concepts mentioned in this definition of securitization so as to present a comprehensive picture of how the theory works.

Actors of securitization: states and beyond

Securitizing actors (also called securitizers) are those "actors who securitize issues by declaring something – a referent object – existentially threatened" (Buzan et al. 1998: 36). Securitizing actors are not usually the same as the referent objects of securitization (compare below); rather, the former (are supposed to) act on behalf of the latter. The most critical exception to this is with regard to the state. The state, for example in the form of its government, has the right to speak on its own behalf (Buzan et al. 1998: 40–41). More frequently, however, actors cannot argue to defend their own survival, but rather seek to securitize a "larger community, principle, or system" (Buzan et al. 1998: 40). While actors such as the state can generally be disaggregated down to the level of individuals, the CS maintains that it is usually more adequate to "see as the 'speaker' the collectivities for which individuals are designated authoritative representatives (e.g., parties, states, or pressure groups)" (Buzan et al. 1998: 40–41).

The CS has stated that, generally speaking, many different actors can assume the role of the securitizer. However, its members also hold that different actors are placed in different "positions of power by virtue of being generally accepted voices of security" and that these positions impact on the chances to act as securitizer (Buzan et al. 1998: 31). States have therefore often been considered the most critical actors of securitization, whereas for the individuals threatened it is usually deemed hard to speak security and be heard. However, not all scholars have bought into this state-centric logic. For example, Floyd (2010: 22–23) sees in this argumentation a potential neorealist reduction to the distribution of material capabilities, such as resource endowment or economic and military capabilities, which she rejects. Instead, referring to Pierre Bourdieu's concept of capital, Floyd argues for the incorporation of cultural capital (knowledge and skills) as well as symbolic capital (authority) into the CS concepts of power and capabilities. In her view, the relevance of the different sources of capabilities depends on the respective security sector: "For example, whilst strong green credentials are a source of symbolic power in the environmental security sector, they are of little use in the societal sector of security" (Floyd 2010: 23).

Buzan et al. (1998: Chapter 4) have conceded that particularly in the environmental sector of security[1] – under which water-related issues may fall as well – there are a number of actors seeking their say in securitization other than the state. The CS does not explicitly refer to them as securitizing actors, though. On the one hand, there are so-called "lead actors" that have a strong commitment to effective action on environmental issues. Lead actors can refer to epistemic communities as far as scientific agendas are concerned, or, with regard to political agendas, to activist and lobbying groups. Their strategies especially include raising awareness by informing public opinion in the locales concerned (Buzan et al. 1998: 77). On the other hand, "support actors" may support lead actors, for example when the latter lack the resources. Support actors are not necessarily located at the danger spots (Buzan et al. 1998: 78–79). While Buzan et al. (1998) do not make this specific connection, the media could be regarded as an important example of a support actor.

Issues, existential threats, and referent objects

Securitization also requires an "issue" representing an "existential threat" to a particular "referent object." First of all, the CS has stated that in principle, any issue that can be intensified to the point where it is presented as an existential threat is capable of securitization (Buzan et al. 1998: 23). This is certainly true as well for water-related issues that are at the center of hydro-politics. Fresh water is essential to human existence. It is necessary for economic activities (agriculture, industry, energy production, and transportation), human development (consumption, food production, public health), and ecological services (preservation of ecosystems on which human life and economic activity depend) (Gurría 2009: 396). Generally speaking, these critical tasks, however, can come under threat through water scarcity,[2] changes in water availability (not necessarily leading to scarcity, but to steep declines), problems regarding the safe access to or supply of water (i.e., water availability is principally sufficient, but either distribution is not guaranteed and/or equitable, or prices are not affordable), and water pollution (i.e., problems in water quality, no longer in quantity) (Grey and Sadoff 2007: 548).

According to the CS, any threats moreover need to be "existential." This implies that if the problem is not tackled, "everything else will be irrelevant" (Buzan et al. 1998: 24). In other words, the issue is "dramatized and presented as an issue of supreme superiority," creating the need for "extraordinary means" outside the bounds of normal politics to be taken (Buzan et al. 1998: 26). However, it should be noted that the difference between "normal politics" and "emergency action" may be hard to establish. Consequently, Abrahamsen (2005: 59) has militated against a sharp distinction and instead held that "rather than emergency action, most security politics is concerned with the much more mundane management of risk." Also seeking to clarify the distinction between "normal" and "emergency," Jutila (2006: 172) has maintained that "'emergency politics' and securitizing acts might be understood as initiatives made in the name of a collective in order to save it from future disaster and extermination." These clarifications are important in helping qualify to some extent the absolute necessity for emergency action and indicate that political actions taken to manage risk and avoid future disaster can be a sufficient means.

The referent object for which the various issues may constitute an existential threat has traditionally been the state. Also being the primary securitization actors, this means that states used to, and still do, protect themselves. However, similar to what has been said about securitizing actors before, the CS has held that in theory, "anything can be constructed as a referent object" while in practice, securitization is "more likely to be successful with some types of referent objects than with others" (Buzan et al. 1998: 36). For the CS, it still is the "middle scale of limited collectivities," such as states and nations, which has shown the highest degree of successful securitization. In contrast, so the CS, micro level referent objects, such as individuals and small groups, have faced bigger obstacles in making a claim to survival while at the other end of the spectrum, macro referent objects like all humankind so far have mostly lost out to middle scale referent objects (Buzan et al. 1998: 36).

Transferred specifically to water-related issues in international rivers, Goh (2004: 12) has already identified several possible options how states as securitizers seeking to protect themselves in light of water insecurity resulting from one of the above-mentioned causes could frame their attempts at securitization. These framing options are: first, as a threat to sovereignty and autonomy (when one state is able to control transboundary watercourses); second, and related, as an impetus to diplomatic tensions between states; third, as a threat to the popularity and stability of a governing regime (national or local); fourth, as a threat to socio-political stability due to subsequent migration or resettlement; and, fifth, as a threat to a country's economic base (when water shortages, pollution, or flooding prevent economic growth) (here, see Barnett 2010). For individuals and local communities confronted with water insecurity, the perspective is different. Acting as securitizing actors, individuals and local communities primarily, but not exclusively, seek to sustain their livelihoods (with livelihoods meaning to gain access to as well as use and exercise control over any number of resources that are identified as important for well-being, including water resources; see Goh 2004: 12). Apart from livelihoods, questions of health, identity, and culture, for example, may also play a role (see Petersen-Perlman et al. 2017: 108). Importantly, it is possible that individual and local concerns for the sustaining of livelihoods may either be congruent with or run counter state concerns for survival and legitimacy.

Speech acts and their audiences

The CS has furthermore stipulated that threat declarations come in the form of "speech acts" (Wæver, 1995: 55). This means that security is orally invoked on behalf of a particular referent. However, the CS has not been entirely clear about whether to regard those speech acts as illocutionary (i.e., "doing something in saying something") or as perlocutionary (i.e., "doing something by saying something"; also see Austin 1962). In case of the illocutionary act, an action is performed at the moment of speech. Securitization would then be a "self-referential" practice (Buzan et al. 1998: 24). In case of the perlocutionary act, in turn, the speech act only enables particular actions. That is to say, the perlocutionary speech act is one that "gets someone else to do something" (Floyd 2010: 52). In this case, securitization is no longer self-referential but it becomes "intersubjective" (Buzan et al. 1998: 31). The problem, however, as Balzacq (2005) has correctly found, is that securitization cannot be both self-referential *and* intersubjective at the same time.

At least two major aspects are indicative that speech acts should be treated as perlocutionary and that securitization, therefore, constitutes an intersubjective process. First, security speech acts are generally not regarded as being synonymous with instances of actual – that is, successful – securitization. Rather, the CS has incorporated the differentiation between full "securitization" and a "securitization move" preceding successful securitization (Buzan et al. 1998: 25). Second, the CS has also included a non-negligible role for what it has termed "audience" and whose task it is to receive securitization moves and decide whether to accept or reject them (Buzan et al. 1998: 25).[3] The latter entails so-called "securitization failure" (Buzan et al. 1998: 25; also see below). The former opens the door for full securitization. However, as Roe (2008: 632) has posited, even then is "speaking security [...] not the same as doing security." Roe has therefore advanced a conceptual distinction comprising two stages of securitization: first, identification, that is, rhetorical securitization, and second, mobilization, meaning active securitization.[4]

Despite bringing the concept of the audience into being, generally speaking, however, the CS has not been very detailed on the specifics of this concept. Particularly, the question of how to identify the relevant audience at all has lacked clarity. Among the first to think about the audience in more conceptual ways was Balzacq (2005, 2011). For him, the audience is whoever has a direct causal relationship with the issue and the ability to enable the securitizing actor to take measures to cope with the threat (Balzacq, 2011: 9). Moreover, Balzacq (2005: 185) has argued that "actors seek to convince as broad an audience as possible." Whether this claim is correct or not, it has certainly opened the door for thinking about multiple audiences. The most valuable attempt in this context comes from Salter (2008), whose understanding of the different audiences possibly involved in receiving securitization moves is the most nuanced. Drawing on dramaturgical analysis, Salter differentiates between four different audiences. These are the popular, the (political) elite, the technocratic, and the scientific audiences. Every securitization move can address several, but does not have to address all of these audiences, and can be successful with some yet fail with others (Salter 2008: 322). Important for the success and failure of securitization moves is, according to Balzacq (2005: 174), also the power speaker and listener bring to the table, thus implying that huge power differentials can influence the outcome of a particular securitization move in favor of the more powerful party.

Context

Context is not really part of how the CS originally designed securitization theory. Apparently, Wæver feared that the inclusion of context would be too far-reaching and change the character of the theory (see Floyd 2010: 21). Therefore, the closest the CS has come to integrating contextual matters into its thinking is in the form of what Buzan et al. (1998: 31–33) have termed "facilitating conditions" for the success of the speech act. These are, first, the demand that the speech act follows the "grammar of security"; second, the social conditions with respect to the authority of the securitizing actor; and, third, the characteristics associated with a threat (Buzan et al. 1998: 33). However, these conditions have been criticized compellingly, both for being too imprecise and too narrow. As a matter of fact, several authors have opined that securitization processes do not happen *in vacuo*, but are context-dependent (e.g., Balzacq 2005, 2011; Stritzel 2007; McDonald 2008b; Salter

2008; and Ciuta 2009). More precisely, McDonald (2008b: 573), for instance, has held that the facilitating conditions are too "amorphous" and that the construction of security must be mindful as well of the "social, political, and historical contexts" in which discourses of security occur. Similarly, Salter (2008: 331) has argued that "formal syntax" and "informal social context" do not suffice to understand the success and failure of securitization. Instead, "different sociological, political, bureaucratic, and organizational contexts" need to be incorporated into the analysis, just as well as factors that predate the actual securitization process (Salter 2008: 326). Importantly in this regard, context itself is prone to change and thus in constant flux (Derrida 1982: 322).

Securitization and its "derivatives" – China's preferences and options

While this chapter has so far elaborated on the general workings of securitization, it is, however, the case that China – as we will see in later chapters of this book and as I have also shown elsewhere (see Biba 2014) – has not been interested, to say the least, in making, or in letting others make, its behavior in its shared rivers a matter of security. This clearly has to do with what successful, that is, full, securitization (possibly) entails (see below). Instead, China has consistently sought to keep its international hydro-politics on the escalation stages of non-politicization or, at the most, politicization. At the same time, however, China's reluctance towards securitization has not meant that China's riparian neighbors have not at times tried to confront China with securitization moves, for instance, with regard to Chinese dam-building activities. As a result, China has followed various strategies to prevent securitization, depending on the specific situation. The following sections delve into these matters more comprehensively.

The outcomes of securitization

As a matter of fact, when it comes to the outcomes of securitization, a controversial debate has been going on. This debate has been framed by the more general question about the ethics of security. While scholars of traditional security studies do not usually reflect on the concept of security itself, this issue has been a central aspect for so-called "critical security studies." Two main schools of thought have emerged: on the one hand, the Welsh School which regards security as emancipation[5] and highlights its positive value; on the other hand, the CS, studying security as securitization (as outlined above) and attributing inherently negative value to the concept of security.

It is somewhat striking that although securitization has been the focus of the CS and its securitization theory, in the larger debates about the value of security the CS has taken the position that security is a negative concept and thus also regards securitization as something that should be avoided. Precisely, the CS has contended that "security should be seen as a negative, as a failure to deal with issues of normal politics" (Buzan et al. 1998: 29). Other scholars have supported this stance. Williams (2003: 523), for instead, has held that security should always "be invoked with great care and, in general, minimized rather than expanded." Similarly, Emmers (2010: 142) has underlined the dangers of securitization in that it could "be abused to legitimize and empower the role of military or special security forces in civilian activities," especially in non-democratic settings.

As a result, the CS has voiced a preference for the "twin concept" of securitization, that is, desecuritization. Desecuritization has most clearly been defined by Williams (2003: 523) as "moving issues off the security agenda and back into the realm of … political discourse and 'normal' political dispute and accommodation." Wæver (1995: 57) has posited that desecuritization is "more effective than securitizing problems." Buzan et al. (1998: 29) have seconded that desecuritization is the "optimal long-range option," for it moves issues out of the "threat-defense sequence." As a corollary, it also becomes clear that the CS has favored politicization over securitization, or "normal" over "extraordinary" politics.

Meanwhile, it should not go by the board that the CS has also been criticized for its rationale. While Aradau (2004: 389), for example, has argued that securitization produces categories of "us" versus "them," she has likewise opined that, "as its mirror image, desecuritization suffers from the same contradictions that plague the concept of securitization." Taking a different view, Floyd (2007: 342–343) has maintained that there might be something such as "positive securitization," which deals with a security problem "faster, better and more efficiently" than politicization in terms of process, and benefits the many, rather than the few, in terms of outcome. Likewise, there might also be something such as "negative desecuritization" if an issue completely disappears from public policy. In a similar vein, albeit against a different background, Roe (2012: 250) has stated that the "lack of openness and deliberation" in processes of securitization has been "overexaggerated," and that the "mode of extraordinary politics" may also "serve to reveal more non-divisive referents and cooperative practices."

In sum, the theoretical debates about the positive/negative value of securitization are still in full swing. However, irrespective of these different "camps," most scholars working on securitization theory agree that successful securitization at least *can* lead to negative outcomes. That is, securitization *can* create friends and enemies. The problem, then, however, is that neither the success/failure of securitization moves nor the actual outcomes of successful securitization can really be predicted. Moreover, successful securitization lends a lot of weight and urgency to the issue of concern and additionally means that this issue is likely to attract a high degree of public attention. Together, these points can explain, at least from a (for now) quite general perspective, why China has shown no interest in the securitization of its international hydro-politics, namely, because securitization could openly inflame, or increase, tensions between China and its riparian neighbors, with China blamed as the "bad guy."

China's preference: non-securitization

As China has been reluctant towards the securitization of its behavior and actions in its international rivers, China's preference has thus been that attempts at securitization from its riparian neighbors do not arise in the first place. This preference could be termed "non-securitization." Non-securitization, however, has not entered the official jargon of securitization theory. Instead, non-securitization has, rather implicitly, been seen as one of the variants of desecuritization (see Roe 2004: 285).

Desecuritization, to repeat, has been referred to as moving issues off the security agenda and back into the realm of politics. Wæver (2000: 253) has offered three possible options of doing desecuritization. The first option is the "pre-emptive strategy." This option implies that there is no talk about issues in terms of security to begin with. The second option is the "management strategy." Here, previously securitized issues are managed in ways that do not spawn security dilemmas and vicious circles. Third, there is the "transformation strategy," where securitized issues are brought back into the realm of normal politics. However, as Roe (2004: 285) has compellingly argued, two out of Wæver's three strategies do not actually meet the key desecuritization criterion of moving issues out of the security realm and back into the arena of politics. As he aptly finds, in the case of the first strategy, issues never enter the stage of securitization in the first place. Therefore, this option might better be described as "non-securitization." As for the second strategy, managing securitized issues might bring some "normalization," but it also leaves (some of) the discourse in the realm of security and does not imply a (full) return to normal politics. Consequently, it is only Wæver's transformation strategy that actually lives up to the definition of desecuritization. At the same time, though, it is the pre-emptive strategy that Wæver seems to favor the most.

More recently, Hansen (2012: 529) has taken up the issue of desecuritization and identified four different modes: first, "change through stabilization" (when an issue is framed in terms other than security, but where the overarching conflict still looms); second, "replacement" (when one issue is removed from being securitized, while another securitization takes its place); third, "rearticulation" (when an issue is moved from being securitized to being politicized due to a resolution of the threats and dangers which underpinned the original securitization); and, fourth, "silencing" (when desecuritization takes the form of a depoliticization which sidelines those potentially threatened). On the one hand, Hansen's conceptualization suffers from similar weaknesses as does Wæver's. More precisely, Hansen's first two modes resemble Wæver's management strategy, particularly in that they leave parts of the relevant discourse in the realm of security. Therefore, they do not fully qualify as desecuritization. Her third mode, meanwhile, is equivalent to Wæver's transformation strategy and may therefore be seen as actual desecuritization. On the other hand, what is particularly interesting with regard to the notion of non-securitization is Hansen's fourth mode that does not seem to be reflected by any of Wæver's options.

However, as Hansen is not entirely clear about whether silencing really refers to issues that were previously securitized successfully, silencing could also be interpreted as another pre-emptive strategy. The difference, to be sure, would be that while Wæver's pre-emptive strategy seeks to have issues in the realm of politics, Hansen's silencing goes further than this and pushes issues out of public debate and decision so that they become non-politicized (see above).

China's non-securitization[6] preference therefore means that of the above-mentioned desecuritization options, China has been particularly interested in Wæver's pre-emptive and even Hansen's silencing strategies (the latter only for issues not previously securitized). While the pre-emptive strategy, generally speaking, allows for water-related cooperation between China and its riparian neighbors to occur, the silencing strategy carries a clearly negative connotation and does not open a window for cooperation, as China here (implicitly) signals disinclination to cooperate. This is critical: non-securitization does not always imply that China necessarily is a cooperative partner. It could actually be the opposite, but it would not arouse much stir because it is the character of silenced and hence non-politicized issues that nobody talk about them – much in contrast to successfully securitized issues. As will be shown in Chapter 4, for instance, China has generally been inclined to cooperate with its Mekong riparian neighbors on some water-related issues, while it has been reluctant to do so on other water-related issues. In any case, however, what it takes for China to incessantly and successfully pursue a strategy of non-securitization is a high degree of discursive power vis-à-vis its riparian neighbors so as to be able to steer the hydro-political discourse away from sensitive issues with possible security connotations in the first place (also see Biba 2014).

China's Plan B: causing securitization failure

Not surprisingly, as will be revealed, China has not at all times succeeded in actually steering the hydro-political discourse with its riparian neighbors completely away from security connotations. In other words, and as we will also see in later chapters, China has in the past also been confronted with attempts from its riparian neighbors at securitizing certain Chinese actions in their shared international river basins. In accordance with what has been stated earlier in this chapter, though, securitization moves are not conceptually tantamount to successful securitization. Rather, it is the audience(s) of securitization moves that determine whether those moves succeed or fail. This means that China, which usually also functions as one audience to attempts from its riparian neighbors at securitizing Chinese dam building, for instance, can reject those attempts, thereby causing securitization failure.

In a sense, securitization failure can be considered as being still in line with China's preference for non-securitization because in the securitization failure scenario full securitization is not established. However, this scenario also differs from China's preferred options (i.e., pre-emptive and silencing) because with the launch of securitization moves, an initial security framing of a certain issue nevertheless takes place. This framing not only raises public awareness of the issue at hand, but also puts the blame on the party that is accused of being responsible for the perceived threat. That is to say, if others perceive Chinese dams, for example, as a threat, then China is also the party receiving the blame for having created this threat. Obviously, this is not as much in China's interest as preventing securitization moves, and concomitant accusations, in the first place. If securitization moves occur nonetheless, then China, again, has a few options for rejection available. Before looking at those options as well as their (dis)advantages, it is helpful, though, to learn more about how, in terms of securitization theory, securitization moves fail and what such failures entail.

Wæver (2000: 252–253) has argued that securitization moves can fail because, first, the securitizing actor does not follow the "grammar of security"; second, the securitizing actor is not in a position of authority; or, third, the "conditions historically associated with a threat" are absent. The most significant option, however, also acknowledged by the CS, is that non-acceptance of securitization moves on the part of the audience(s) also leads to securitization failure (Buzan et al. 1998: 25; also see above). Aside from these rather preliminary deliberations on securitization failure on the part of the CS, Salter (2008, 2011) has shown that through carving out different stages of the securitization process, different securitization failures become possible – and thus, as I have added (see Biba 2016), different outcomes as well.

More precisely, for desecuritization, Floyd (2007) has argued that it can lead to either the politicization or the depoliticization of an issue (also see what has been said about Wæver's pre-emptive and Hansen's silencing strategies above). That is to say, following desecuritization, the issue in question either re-emerges on the political agenda (desecuritization as politicization), or it disappears from the political discourse altogether (desecuritization as depoliticization). With regard to securitization failure, nothing stands in the way of suggesting that the same logic is generally possible. On the one hand, securitization moves that fail may, as a consequence, lead to the issue of concern completely losing momentum and therefore dropping out of the political sphere altogether (securitization failure as depoliticization). On the other hand, it is likewise conceivable that failed securitization moves find themselves on the escalation stage of politicization, as they cannot make it to full securitization but nevertheless remain part of public policy and are debated and decided upon in a rather open and non-exclusive way (securitization failure as politicization).[7] The questions following from this fact are, first, who decides which outcome materializes and, second, for what reasons may one outcome be preferred over another. This also brings us back to China's options for rejecting securitization moves.

The role of the audience in determining the outcomes of securitization failure

When securitization failure is generally possible as depoliticization and (re)politicization and when audiences are key to securitization failure in the first place, it stands to reason that audiences also make for the respective outcome of securitization failure. So far, however, questions of audience behavior *beyond* the point of a very straightforward acceptance-versus-rejection dichotomy have not been tackled. Therefore, I have introduced three behaviorally different rejection strategies, from which audiences can choose and which also lead to different outcomes on the securitization spectrum (see Biba 2016: 424–425).

The first outcome, depoliticization, can be reached through two distinct rejection strategies. One option can be termed the *passive recipient strategy*. Confronted with securitizing moves, this strategy is simply to ignore these moves until they abate and eventually stop. But how to make sure that ignoring securitization moves is not tantamount to silent consent and thus acceptance of the moves? Here, it is useful to remember the arguments presented earlier about perlocutionary speech acts. It has been held, for example, that securitization is best described as the "process whereby an issue is understood as urgent, is placed onto the political agenda ... *and* subsequent action is taken" (Jackson, 2006: 315; emphasis in original). As for indicators of whether action was actually taken, Caballero-Anthony and Emmers (2006: 7) have mentioned aspects such as resource allocation trends, legislation, and institutionalization. Following this rationale, it should be possible to determine whether ignoring securitization moves is tantamount to silently accepting or rather rejecting them. That is, only if subsequent action is taken could ignoring securitization moves be interpreted as silent consent. The second option entailing depoliticization can be referred to as the *blocking strategy*. With this second strategy, in contrast to the first one the audience does make a reply, but also makes it very clear that it does not consider the issue a security matter and, additionally, does not see the need to discuss the issue any further. Sooner or later, this takes the wind out of the securitization actor's sails and the securitization attempts peter out. To some extent, these two strategies are similar to Hansen's silencing outlined above, at least as far as the results are concerned. However, to be sure, Hansen has placed her strategy in the context of desecuritization, not in the context of securitization failure.

Another possible outcome of securitization failure is (re)politicization. This occurs when the audience rejects the securitization moves by means of a *reshaping strategy*. On the one hand, the audience pursuing this strategy still does not consider the issue a matter to be securitized and also communicates this attitude clearly in a first step, thereby establishing a securitization failure. On the other hand, however, and crucially, the audience subsequently seeks to ease (at least some of) the securitizing actor's concerns and/or brings in its own ideas on how to deal with, mitigate, or even solve, a given issue. The result is that during and after the reshaping, the issue in question loses its security connotation and (again) becomes a matter of politics to be discussed in a rather open and non-exclusive manner. This strategy can, in some ways, be compared to Wæver's transformation strategy. Again, however, this is only in terms of outcomes. Like Hansen's silencing strategy, Wæver's transformation mode was designed to explain desecuritization, not securitization failure.

One caveat, though, is in order at this point. Not every audience is likely to be always able to reject securitization moves in the three different strategies presented. As previously indicated, the effectiveness of any given audience to determine the result of incoming securitization moves is dependent on the power (Balzacq 2005: 174) as well as on the authority and knowledge (Salter 2008: 330) this audience has vis-à-vis the actor of securitization moves. One example to illustrate this relationship could be that an audience far less powerful than a securitizing actor might not be able to simply ignore incoming securitizing moves long enough for the issue to simply disappear from the scene again.

That said, a final question is, what might make an audience, which has all rejection options at its disposal, prefer one of them to the others? Here, it is important to realize what the different outcomes of securitization failure entail. That is, in cases where audience behavior results in securitization failure as depoliticization, this means that the underlying root cause of the issue in question continues to exist. Atland (2008: 306) has convincingly argued that threats may reappear. In fact, no status on the securitization spectrum is ever set in stone; changes in the escalation stages are always possible. Therefore, if an issue is depoliticized without "adequate treatment," it is quite likely that this issue will re-emerge if a similar crisis or threat recurs in the future. Conversely, in cases where the audience reshapes securitization moves and thus is open to discussing and debating the issue at hand, the probability is much higher that the issue will be solved, or at least be improved. In potential future crises, this issue might then as a result be handled differently from the beginning, that is, without, or at least with less severe, security connotations. Audiences that have faced securitization attempts regarding the same issue for more than one time and are likely to face them again in the future may thus at some point consider the reshaping of the issue – particularly if the intensity of securitization moves grows with every new crisis.

Securitization theory: making the co-existence of conflict and cooperation in China's hydro-politics analytically tangible

As Zeitoun and Mirumachi (2008: 297, emphasis in original) have argued in a seminal article,

> [M]ost work [...] situates transboundary water conflict and transboundary water cooperation at opposing ends of a continuum. The examination of *either* conflict *or* cooperation [however] refutes the reality of the vast majority of contexts where cooperation and conflict actually co-exist.

This is not only a very important argument as regards hydro-politics in general. It has already been stated – and will further be shown in great detail throughout later chapters this book – that the usually found co-existence of conflict and cooperation in water politics is also a significant feature of China's behavior in its international rivers. A problem arises, however, when trying to capture, frame, and analyze this co-existence theoretically. As previously outlined in the introductory chapter, two of the major schools of IR theorizing that have frequently been applied in the field of hydro-politics as well, that is realism and institutionalism, tend to reproduce the misleading categories of *either* conflict (realism) *or* cooperation (institutionalism). In contrast, securitization theory is at an advantage here as it is well equipped to account for *both* conflict *and* cooperation in a dynamic inter-state environment. This has become quite obvious throughout this chapter. More precisely, the various concepts attached to securitization theory open more than one avenue for China to steer its hydro-politics vis-à-vis its riparian neighbors in an either more, or less, cooperative direction, while also retaining the possibility for China to choose a conflictive attitude. At the same time, the theory likewise allows China's riparian neighbors to take action, engage, or confront China, and try to push it towards more cooperation, while simultaneously facing the risk of alienating it and driving it into conflict mode. The result of these theoretical possibilities that securitization theory offers is a dynamic and inter-subjective setting where phases of overlapping or consecutive cooperation and conflict become possible and can be analyzed and explained.

Furthermore, Zeitoun and Mirumachi (2008: 309) have also maintained correctly that "transboundary water interaction is besought by the interests, power games, illusions and distrust that accompany all political processes." In other words, this means that hydro-politics does not occur *in vacuo*, but is always part of bigger political contexts. As mentioned above, the understanding of (de)politicization, (de)securitization and the like processes similarly relies on the inclusion of a potentially multi-faceted set of contextual factors. Here, again, securitization theory contrasts sharply with realist and institutionalist rationales that tend to disregard contextual features and rather stick with a narrower set of power-based or institution-based variables, respectively. In a next step, let us look at some of the contextual aspects that play a particularly important role for China's hydro-politics in the Mekong.

Notes

1 Members of the CS, in particular Barry Buzan, have also been leading in developing and conceptualizing different sectors of security, differentiating between military, environmental, economic, societal, and political. Each sector is basically concerned with sets of different threats and referent objects. The lines between the various sectors, though, are not always very straightforward, as the focus of securitization may shift from one sector into another and as a multi-sectoral approach to security is generally possible. Apart from Buzan et al. (1998), see above all Buzan (1983) for a comprehensive study on this topic.
2 Hydrologists typically assess scarcity by looking at the population-water equation. In concrete numbers, an area is experiencing water stress when overall annual water supplies drop below 1,700 m^3 per person. When overall annual water supplies drop below 1,000 m^3 per person, the population faces water scarcity, and below 500 m^3

absolute scarcity (UN 2017). It is noteworthy that these thresholds do not, however, depict seasonal variations of water availability. Moreover, when talking about scarcity, it should not go unmentioned that the exact opposite, namely flooding, may equally pose a threat to water security.
3 Some authors have nevertheless questioned the need for an audience in securitization theory (see, for example, Floyd, 2010). A vivid illustration of an indeed insignificant audience role in securitization processes might be found in the 2003 invasion of Iraq that was carried out despite large demonstrations against it – that is, without the acceptance of the (popular) audience. While Floyd may have a point – namely, that the political elite as securitizing actor frequently do what they like regardless of audience input – it seems a different matter in instances where the securitizer is *not* the state but represented by non-state actors. Non-state actors must be considered far less likely to successfully securitize an issue without the consent of governments, which are usually the ones to exercise the emergency actions then required. Therefore, the role of the audience cannot easily be dismissed across the board (also see Biba 2016: 424).
4 The debate about stages of securitization has also led to a slight "erosion" of the paramount role of speech acts in securitization theory as well as to a greater emphasis on the processes, instead of the outcomes, in instances of securitization. Prominently, Wilkinson (2007) has doubted the rigid and linear sequencing of "rhetoric first, action second," and, in doing so, she has also questioned the centrality of the speech act for securitization vis-à-vis other forms of expression in the first place. Also, Hansen in 2000 already described what she called a "silent security dilemma," referring to situations "when insecurity cannot be voiced, when raising something as a security problem is impossible or might even aggravate the threat being faced" (Hansen 2000: 287).
5 One of the leading advocates of the Welsh School, Ken Booth (1991: 319) has defined emancipation as "the freeing of the people [...] from those physical and human constraints which stop them carrying out what they would freely choose to do." The concept of emancipation is of no further importance for this study, though.
6 Note that in one of my previous publications on this topic, I still used the official CS term of desecuritization to analyze and explain China's international hydropolitics (see Biba 2014). While it remains technically correct, at least according to official CS jargon, to speak of desecuritization as a kind of "umbrella term," the approach chosen here is more nuanced conceptually.
7 Salter (2011: 120) has argued that "every securitization requires a prior politicization." If this is correct, it means that securitization moves that fail to succeed, and therefore leave an issue in the domain of politics, never actually see this issue change its escalation stage. Hence, it might actually be more appropriate to speak of securitization failure as *re*politicization (also see Biba 2016: 423).

References

Abrahamsen, R. (2005) "Blair's Africa: The Politics of Securitization and Fear," *Alternatives: Global, Local, Political*, 30(55), 55–80.

Aradau, C. (2004) "Security and the Democratic Scene: Desecuritization and Emancipation," *Journal of International Relations and Development*, 7(4), 388–413.

Atland, K. (2008) "Mikhail Gorbachev, the Murmansk Initiative, and the Desecuritization of Interstate Relations in the Arctic," *Cooperation and Conflict*, 43(3), 289–311.

Austin, L. (1962) *How to Do Things with Words*, Oxford: Clarendon Press.
Balzacq, T. (2005) "The Three Faces of Securitization: Political Agency, Audience and Context," *European Journal of International Relations*, 11(2), 171–201.
Balzacq, T. (2011) "A Theory of Securitization: Origins, Core Assumptions, and Variants," in Balzacq, T. (ed.), *Securitization Theory. How Security Problems Emerge and Dissolve*, London and New York: Routledge, 1–30.
Barnett, J. (2010) "Environmental Security," in Collins, A. (ed.), *Contemporary Security Studies*, Oxford: Oxford University Press, 218–238.
Biba, S. (2014) "Desecuritization in China's Behavior towards Its Transboundary Rivers: The Mekong River, the Brahmaputra River, and the Irtysh and Ili Rivers," *Journal of Contemporary China*, 23(85), 21–43.
Biba, S. (2016) "From Securitization Moves to Positive Outcomes: The Case of the Spring 2010 Mekong Crisis," *Security Dialogue*, 47(5), 420–439.
Booth, K. (1991) "Security and Emancipation," *Review of International Studies*, 17(4), 313–326.
Buzan, B. (1983) *People, States, and Fear: The National Security Problem in International Relations*, London: Harvester Wheatsheaf.
Buzan, B., Wæver, O. and de Wilde, J. (1998) *Security: A New Framework for Analysis*, London: Lynne Rienner.
Caballero-Anthony, M., and Emmers, R. (2006) "Understanding the Dynamics of Securitizing Non-traditional Security," in Caballero-Anthony, M., Emmers, R. and Acharya, A. (eds.), *Non-Traditional Security in Asia: Dilemmas in Securitization*, Singapore: Ashgate, 1–12.
Ciuta, F. (2009) "Security and the Problem of Context: A Hermeneutical Critique of Securitization Theory," *Review of International Studies*, 35(2), 301–326.
Derrida, J. (1982) *Margins of Philosophy*, Chicago, IL: University of Chicago Press.
Emmers, R. (2010) "Securitization," in Collins, A. (ed.), *Contemporary Security Studies*, Oxford: Oxford University Press, 136–151.
Floyd, R. (2007) "Towards a Consequentialist Evaluation of Security: Bringing Together the Copenhagen and Welsh Schools of Security Studies," *Review of International Relations*, 33, 327–350.
Floyd, R. (2010) *Security and the Environment: Securitisation Theory and US Environmental Security Policy*, Cambridge: Cambridge University Press.
Goh, E. (2004) "China in the Mekong River Basin: The Regional Security Implications of Resource Development on the Lancang Jiang," *Working Paper No. 69*, Singapore, Institute of Defence and Strategic Studies.
Grey, D., and Sadoff, C. (2007) "Sink or Swim? Water Security for Growth and Development," *Water Policy*, 9, 545–571.
Gurría, A. (2009) "Sustainably Managing Water: Challenges and Responses," *Water International*, 34(4), 396–401.
Hansen, L. (2000) "The Little Mermaid's Silent Security Dilemma and the Absence of Gender in the Copenhagen School," *Millennium – Journal of International Studies*, 29(2), 285–306.
Hansen, L. (2012) "Reconstructing Desecuritisation: The Normative-Political in the Copenhagen School and Directions for How to Apply It," *Review of International Studies*, 38(3), 525–546.
Jackson, N. (2006) "International Organizations, Security Dichotomies and the Trafficking of Persons and Narcotics in Post-Soviet Central Asia: A Critique of the Securitization Framework," *Security Dialogue*, 37(3), 299–318.

Jutila, M. (2006) "Desecuritizing Minority Rights: Against Determinism," *Security Dialogue*, 37(2), 167–185.
McDonald, M. (2008a) "Constructivism," in P. Williams (ed.), *Security Studies: An Introduction*, London and New York: Routledge, 59–72.
McDonald, M. (2008b) "Securitization and the Construction of Security," *European Journal of International Relations*, 14(4), 563–587.
Petersen-Perlman, J., Veilleux, J., and Wolf, A. (2017) "International Water Conflict and Cooperation: Challenges and Opportunities," *Water International*, 42(2), 105–120.
Roe, P. (2004) "Securitization of Minority Rights: Conditions of Desecuritization," *Security Dialogue*, 35(3), 279–294.
Roe, P. (2008) "Actor, Audience(s) and Emergency Measures: Securitization and the UK's Decision To Invade Iraq," *Security Dialogue*, 39(6), 615–635.
Roe, P. (2012) "Is Securitization a 'Negative' Concept? Revisiting the Normative Debate over Normal versus Extraordinary Politics," *Security Dialogue*, 43(3), 249–266.
Salter, M. (2008) "Securitization and Desecuritization: A Dramaturgical Analysis of the Canadian Air Transport Security Authority," *Journal of International Relations and Development*, 11, 321–349.
Salter, M. (2011) "When Securitization Fails: The Hard Case of Counter-Terrorism Programs," in Balzacq, T. (ed.), *Securitization Theory. How Security Problems Emerge and Dissolve*, London and New York: Routledge, 116–131.
Stritzel, H. (2007) "Toward a Theory of Securitization: Copenhagen and Beyond," *European Journal of International Relations*, 13(3), 357–383.
United Nations (UN) (2017) "International Decade for Action 'Water for Life' 2005–2015," www.un.org/waterforlifedecade/scarcity.shtml.
Wæver, O. (1995) "Securitization and Desecuritization," in Lipschutz, R. (ed.), *On Security*, New York: Colombia University Press, 46–86.
Wæver, O. (2000) "The EU as a Security Actor: Reflections from a Pessimistic Constructivist on Post-sovereign Security Orders," in Kelstrup, M. and Williams, M. (eds.), *International Relations Theory and the Politics of European Integration: Power, Security and Community*, London and New York: Routledge, 250–294.
Wilkinson, C. (2007) "The Copenhagen School on Tour in Kyrgyzstan: Is Securitization Theory Useable Outside Europe?" *Security Dialogue*, 38(5), 5–25.
Williams, M. (2003) "Words, Images, Enemies: Securitization and International Politics," *International Studies Quarterly*, 47(4), 511–531.
Zeitoun, M., and Mirumachi, N. (2008) "Transboundary Water Interaction I: Considering Conflict and Cooperation," *International Environmental Agreements*, 8(4), 297–316.

3 China and Southeast Asia

Introduction

China's international hydro-politics constitutes only one issue-area in the wide field of China's foreign policy. Similarly, China's relations with the Mekong downstream riparian countries (MDRCs) of Laos, Thailand, Cambodia, and Vietnam are only one mosaic in China's regional diplomacy around its vast periphery. Before delving into the details of China's hydro-politics in the Mekong as the central theme of this book, it is therefore expedient to be familiar with the overarching frame(s) in which this specific topic is set. In other words, in order to fully understand China's freshwater politics in the Mekong, it is important first to learn more about the broader context in which these politics have taken place. Besides, as mentioned in the previous chapter, context also represents a significant factor for securitization theory, that is, for analyzing the emergence, processes, and outcomes of (de)politicization and (de)securitization attempts.

As a result, the primary task of this chapter is to prepare and facilitate the examination of China's Mekong hydro-politics in later chapters. In doing so, this chapter presents a two-fold overview: first, of China's overall foreign policy objectives as well as of the role of Southeast Asia for China to achieve these very objectives; and, second, of China's relations with the MDRCs apart from specifically water-related aspects, that is, in terms of broader political, economic, and security aspects in particular. As regards this second overview, two more things are noteworthy and will therefore be taken into consideration. On the one hand, the MDRCs, situated in mainland Southeast Asia, are intimately tied to their maritime Southeast Asian neighbors through the Association of Southeast Asian Nations (ASEAN) in which they are all member states. China's foreign policy vis-à-vis Southeast Asia therefore always has to consider both the mainland and maritime dimensions. In addition, the paramount role of the United States (US) in Southeast Asia ever since the end of World War II must also be acknowledged, for it has had an impact on Chinese behavior, too. On the other hand, a time component comes into play. As the major empirical event to be studied in this book happened in spring 2010, it is particularly relevant to delineate the key foreign relations trends that could be witnessed in the region in the run-up to and during this event. Hence, one major goal of this chapter is to illustrate that China's diplomacy vis-à-vis Southeast Asia had – after years of broadly positive developments in the 1990s and early-to-mid 2000s – entered a general rough patch, primarily in economic and security terms, in the months before and during the Mekong crisis. More recent developments in terms of China's broader relations with Southeast Asia will, as far as they are relevant, be taken up in the concluding chapter of this book.

China's overall foreign policy goals

China's leaders have tended to put the country's overarching foreign policy goals into rather vague formulations. On the global level, one of the key catchphrases in the early 2000s used to be "peaceful rise" (*heping jueqi*). However, as this concept did not help alleviate the perception of a "China threat" among other states, it was soon replaced by "peaceful development" (*heping fazhan*). This notion resembled very much the older idea of "peace and development" (*heping yu fazhan*) that had risen to prominence under Deng Xiaoping in the 1980s. In more recent years, other thoughts have been added by each leadership generation, such as the claim under Hu Jintao in the late 2000s to build a "harmonious world" (*hexie shijie*) or the intention to create a "new type of great power relations" (*xinxing daguo guanxi*) as proposed by Xi Jinping in 2012. Also, building a "community of common destiny" (*mingyun gongtongti*), previously announced under Hu, has increasingly become *en vogue* under Xi as well. But what is behind all these official and abstract concepts?

As a matter of fact, despite the vagueness of China's official foreign policy vocabulary, the objectives behind such government-articulated rhetoric are nowadays rather clear and widely understood. The top priority of China's foreign policy since the founding of the People's Republic of China in 1949 has been regime preservation, referring to the continued leadership of the Chinese Communist Party (CCP) (F. Wang 2005: 676). Consequently, it may be said that, as a general rule, domestic politics have been given priority over foreign politics, or, to put it differently, the achievement of foreign policy goals is to be seen as the "extension" of the CCP's domestic agenda (also see Lai 2010). To guarantee political preservation, the CCP's primary concern is the permanent generation of legitimacy for its rule, as this legitimacy has to some extent become contested at home, for example due to corruption scandals or environmental degradation. As a result, the question is what China's foreign policy can do to support and strengthen the legitimacy of the CCP. Three issues in particular have served as critical avenues in this regard and must therefore be considered as the key enduring and long-term priorities of China's foreign policy. These are, with varying relative emphasis over time, sovereignty and territorial integrity, economic development, and international respect and status (Medeiros 2009: 13; also see Figure 3.1).

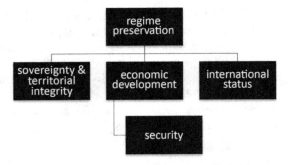

Figure 3.1 China's overall foreign policy goals

The protection of China's sovereignty and territorial integrity has been a core national interest for the People's Republic (e.g., Carlson 2008). Several aspects are important for this objective. First is securing China's borders. This is a tremendous task given that China shares land borders with 14 countries and has a 14,500 kilometer long coastline. In addition, China has long perceived internal threats to its territorial integrity, especially from "separatist groups" such as Muslim Uighurs in Xinjiang and the Dalai Lama in Tibet. More recently, student-led protests in Hong Kong, demanding less interference from Beijing, have also sparked concerns for the CCP. A second aspect is the reunification with Taiwan, which is still seen by Beijing as a "renegade province," not as a country of its own. Taiwan is widely considered in China to be the most significant missing piece on the road for the complete restoration of China's sovereignty and territorial integrity, which it lost during the "century of humiliation" (see below). China's 2005 Anti-Secession Law, which formalized the use of "non-peaceful means" in the event of a Taiwanese declaration of independence, made it very obvious what the stakes are for the Chinese leadership when it comes to Taiwan. Moreover, China has constantly worked on reducing Taiwan's international space – be it in regional and global international organizations or in bilateral state-to-state relations with third parties. For example, all countries that seek to enter into diplomatic relations with China have to obey the so-called "One China policy" (*yi ge Zhongguo zhengce*) that stipulates to sever official ties with Taiwan. Third, China has sought to limit external threats to its territory. Apart from Taiwan, China has faced a number of territorial disputes with the majority of its neighboring countries at some point since 1949 (see, for example, Fravel 2005). Most land disputes have been settled, but many maritime disputes remain unsolved. In particular, China continues to have overlapping territorial claims with some of its neighbors in the East and South China Seas. China's diplomacy has been geared towards lending substance to its own claims while at the same time preventing foreign incursions. A fourth aspect, finally, is China's intention to minimize external interference in its domestic development and politics. With the collapse of the Soviet Union, China became the largest remaining Communist country in the world and, inevitably, turned into the focus of Western criticism. Western reactions in the wake of the *Tian'anmen* Square incident further proved in Chinese eyes that the West was trying to exert pressure in order to promote Eastern-Europe style liberalization in China (Wang 2014: 93). China's strategy has primarily aimed at condemning Western criticism of China's authoritarian political system and human rights record.

Economic development has, since the reform and opening period launched in 1978 and expedited since the end of the Cold War, become the central foreign policy avenue for China to maintain political stability at home. Here, Beijing has sought "political preservation through performance" (F. Wang 2005: 682), also in light of the fact that the ideological basis of the CCP rule has eroded. The logic is that the Chinese leadership provides greater economic opportunities for an increasing number of the Chinese people so as to generate a sufficient amount of "output legitimacy" that helps the CCP to "deserve" to stay in power. Besides, it is believed that a rich country makes for a strong military (*fuguo qiangbin*) and rich people make for a strong nation (*fumin qiangguo*) (F. Wang 2005: 683). Apart from domestic aspects, a host of international conditions need nowadays be met in order for China to be able to continue its economic growth path. They include China's unrestrained participation in global economic governance and a more resilient global financial architecture; the continued access to natural resources, in particular fossil fuels and minerals; and the free access to export markets worldwide as well as the sustained inflow of high amounts of foreign direct investment (FDI), simultaneously promoting the continuous acquisition of foreign (high) technology. What is more, China's economic development also requires a secure external environment that can underwrite and facilitate the formerly mentioned conditions in the first place (see Sutter 2008a: 30). Security, in this regard, implies that a few essential factors be given. Most broadly speaking, and as much as possible, China needs to alleviate fears of its rise in general and of its economic clout in particular. To do so, it is important for China to have at least workable relationships with all major powers in the world and, flowing from this, to prevent any anti-China blocs and alliances that seek to actively contain China's rise. Moreover, China needs to create and maintain a peaceful and stable periphery, which in addition is at best free from dominant influences of other major powers.

International status is the third pillar of China's foreign policy goals, with status implying an actor's specific rank within a social hierarchy. Status is of intrinsic value for a state because, generally speaking, the higher its rank, the more privileges a state can enjoy. As a result, states tend to seek a high status, just as they require this status to be recognized by others. However, not every state can have a high status, because then none does (Larson et al. 2014: 7–9). For China, achieving a high international status is, in effect, a two-pronged goal. F. Wang (2005) has therefore correctly referred to this aspect as China's strife for power and prestige. In other words, it is a core objective of

China's foreign policy to be a great power in the international system and to be treated and respected as such by others. In addition to the intrinsic motivation of a state for a high international status, China's impetus has also had to do with the fact that China used, or at least perceived itself, to be what is nowadays called a great power, or even a superpower, throughout most of its long history. However, the period from the First Opium War in 1839 to the foundation of the People's Republic of China in 1949, during which China became semi-colonized, tarnished this self-image. Today, the Chinese consider this "century of humiliation" (*bainian guochi*) at the hands of Western and Japanese intervention and imperialism as a "historical mistake" to be corrected. Many Chinese therefore tend to not speak of China's rise, but of the country's "rejuvenation" (*zhenxing* or *fuxing*) (Yan 2001: 33–34). As a result, China has on the one hand striven for comprehensive national power (*zonghe guoli*) and has, for example, already made it to the world number two in terms of military expenditure and nominal GDP (SIPRI 2016: 2; Statistics Times 2016). On the other hand, China has sought to be granted an international status equivalent to its vastly increased power resources. In doing so, China has, for instance, joined all the major global and regional international institutions and has shown interest in playing an active role in many of them so as to be perceived as a "responsible major power" (*fuzeren de daguo*) in the international community (Medeiros 2009: 17). Generally speaking, China has attached increasing importance to building, and in fact polishing, its national image (H. Wang 2005: 76), hoping that a positive image abroad would help earn China respect and appreciation.

The role of Southeast Asia for China's foreign policy goals

The Chinese leadership has long realized that apart from its relationship to the world's great powers, it is the relations with its mostly smaller neighboring countries that – alone due to the geographical proximity – are crucial for the achievement of China's long-term foreign policy priorities. Consequently, China has been very active in formulating foreign policy strategies for engaging with its neighborhood. In the late 1980s already, China first announced its "periphery policy" (*zhoubian zhengce*) or "good-neighborly policy" (*mulin zhengce*), which served as a precursor to the 2002 regional diplomacy guideline of "building good-neighborly relationships and partnerships with our neighbors" (*yulin weishan, yilin weiban*) (Zhao 2011: 54). This guideline, in turn, was later supplemented by the policy of "amicable neighbor, secure neighbor, and prosperous neighbor" (*mulin, anlin, fulin*) to foster increased "cooperation and coordination" (*hezuo yu xietiao*) (Medeiros 2009: 126–127). In addition, China has sought to frame its inter-state relations with the non-Western world, including its neighborhood, in the United Nations concept of "South-South cooperation," that is to say, in the Chinese case, to highlight the equality between China and its smaller peripheral countries as well as to emphasize common development objectives and thus foster so-called "win-win" (*shuangying*) situations (MOFA 2003). Clearly, these various strategies have aimed at supporting China's key foreign policy goals. That is, these strategies have been designed to in particular create a stable periphery conducive for domestic economic development, foster a positive image of China, and play down territorial disputes and other potential contentious issues.

Southeast Asia, consisting of its mainland and maritime parts, nowadays certainly is one of the most critical peripheral regions for China's foreign diplomacy. Consequently, as later sections of this chapter will show in more detail, China has reached out to Southeast Asia in very profound ways. This is simply because Southeast Asian countries have an important role to play with regard to all of China's primary foreign policy objectives outlined above. In terms of questions of sovereignty and territorial integrity, Southeast Asia is one of the regions where China still has unresolved territorial disputes with its neighbors. More precisely, the protracted South China Sea issue (also see below) has been a recurring irritant both for China's bilateral relations with the other Southeast Asian claimants (i.e., Brunei, Malaysia, Philippines, and Vietnam), ASEAN as a regional organization in which all Southeast Asian claimants in the South China Sea are member states, and the US which has been interested in maintaining maritime security and upholding freedom of navigation in the disputed waters. Against this backdrop, Southeast Asia has also turned into one of the main litmus tests for Chinese status seeking as a respected responsible great power, as China still has to prove to the world that it is a benevolent neighbor and that it can (continue to) rise peacefully (also see Biba 2016). Economically, Southeast Asia is a region that is significant for China particularly in order to diversify its access to natural resources. For example, Malaysia and Indonesia are major Chinese import sources of liquefied natural gas (EIA 2015). Also, Southeast Asian countries represent important markets for China's import and export, particularly for those Chinese provinces directly bordering Southeast Asian neighbors. Accordingly, Medeiros (2009: 126) has neatly summarized that China's approach towards Southeast Asia has chiefly been driven by Beijing's desire

> to expand China's access to markets and investment, to reassure regional nations that China's rise does not threaten them economically or militarily, to broaden access to natural resources and technologies for further development, and to undermine any and all efforts, U.S.-led and otherwise, to constrain China's economic, diplomatic, and military influence.

The following sections will now dig deeper into China's relations with Southeast Asia, detailing China's more concrete behavior, particularly until 2010, in order to achieve its overarching goals, at least as far as this specific region is concerned. In doing so, critical contextual information for China's hydro-politics in the Mekong will also be revealed.

China's relations with the Mekong downstream riparian countries

China and the MDRCs are neighboring states in close proximity to each other. With two of them, Laos and Vietnam, China even has joint borders. As a result, China shares a history of long-standing, intense, and volatile bilateral relations with all of them. In more recent decades, particularly since the 1990s, China-MDRC relations have, bumps aside, all in all seen a largely friendly and positive development, as the Mekong has turned into a critical sub-region for China and its neighborhood diplomacy. As a result, whether MDRCs like it or not, China today is among the key players in the foreign relations of all four MDRCs. While MDRCs are in the following mostly treated as a group, it is certainly also true that China's relationship with each one of them has been characterized by distinct political trajectories, respectively.

China and Thailand have forged a very close relationship already since the 1970s. This may be ascribed to several factors. First, both sides formed a *de facto* strategic alliance when China became Thailand's most important security partner during the Vietnamese invasion of Cambodia in the late 1970s. Thailand, in reverse, became the first of ASEAN's founding members to tighten its One China policy directed at isolating Taiwan internationally. Second, both countries have shared economic synergies. Implicitly, this could also be witnessed during the Asian financial crisis in 1997–1998. When the Thai currency collapsed rapidly, Beijing proved a reliable partner to Bangkok, as the latter opted not to take advantage of the crisis and did not depreciate its own currency, which would likely have had dramatic consequences for Thailand. Third, in contrast to other Southeast Asian countries such as Indonesia, Thailand's ethnic Chinese community has been completely assimilated and has subsequently advanced politically and economically. Fourth, Sino-Thai relations are absent of territorial disputes. Beijing has thus long valued its close relations to Thailand highly, as Bangkok is among the most influential players in Southeast Asia. Regarding Cambodia, China's relations witnessed a tremendous boost only in the late 1990s. China's diplomatic, monetary, and military support helped Cambodia's still incumbent Prime Minister Hun Sen assume power in 1997. Since then, Cambodia has not only returned the favor by backing China on several domestic and international issues. Also, Phnom Penh gradually made China its prime external partner and the dominant player in modernizing Cambodia's economy. China has thus gained a very close, maybe even its closest, partner in Southeast Asia. Consequently, China has also established good military ties with Cambodia, as Beijing has, for example, educated and trained Cambodian military officers and delivered patrol boats to the Cambodian navy. By contrast, 2000 years of Chinese overlordship over Vietnam and frequent violent encounters – the most recent of which was China's brief "pedagogical war" on Vietnam from February to March 1979 after Hanoi had invaded Cambodia in late 1978 – have made the Sino-Vietnamese relationship the most complex and conflict-prone among the four bilateral China-MDRC relations. Certainly, a normalization process was launched in the late 1980s and also produced a few results such as treaties on the Sino-Vietnamese land border in 1999 and the Gulf of Tonkin in 2000. However, China and Vietnam have so far ruled out a particularly close bilateral relationship. Above all, sovereignty disputes, combined with frictions over fishing grounds and offshore energy fields, that have led to recurring tensions in the South China Sea, have troubled bilateral relations until today. Additionally, China and Vietnam have vied for influence in Laos. While Hanoi might still enjoy an edge over Beijing as far as political and security ties are concerned, Beijing has overtaken Hanoi's influence in economic matters, as Beijing has rapidly developed huge economic interests in Laos, including the country's rich natural resources, its hydropower and agricultural sectors as well as its transportation infrastructure as a connection between China's Yunnan Province and Thailand. Facilitating Chinese economic involvement in Laos certainly was that then Lao President Kaysone was the first foreign leader to visit China after the *Tian'anmen* Square incident and that the Lao government openly praised China's 2005 Anti-Secession Law (Storey 2011: chapters 4, 5, 7, and 8).

From China's perspective, the largely positive trajectory in China–MDRC relations, together with China's strongly increased interest in this sub-region since the 1990s, has above all resulted in soaring trade and investment volumes. The figures from 1990 to 2010 paint a very clear picture. From 1990 to 2007 (before the temporary impacts of the global financial crisis materialized), the combined exports and imports between China and the MDRCs increased more than 30-fold, from US $1.6 billion to US $53 billion. While most of the growth in absolute numbers accounted for Sino-Thai trade and, to a lesser extent, also for Sino-Vietnamese trade, percentage increases were equally large for all four countries (see Table 3.1). Consequently, China in 2009 – that is, the year before the spring 2010 Mekong crisis – was the second and third largest world market for exports originating from Vietnam and Thailand. The US and, in the case of Vietnam, also Japan were still ahead, albeit not very far. In Laos, China was itself already ahead of its non-MDRC competitors. On the import side, China's key role for the MDRCs could be felt even more. It was only trailing Thailand in Laos, accounting for 14.3 percent of Lao global imports. In Thailand, China again ranked second with 12.7 percent, this time only behind Japan. For Cambodia and Vietnam, China was by far the single most important source of imports, with numbers running up to 22.6 percent and 23.5 percent, respectively. Meanwhile, none of the MDRCs belonged to China's main trading partners. Besides, except for Thailand, all MDRCs ran a trade deficit with its northern neighbor (IMF 2011 and Biba 2012: 618; also see Table 3.1 and Table 3.2).

In terms of China's outbound FDI into the MDRCs, the strong upward trend was the same, albeit not yet as pronounced. China had around 2010 begun to make palpable headway, particularly into the less developed

Table 3.1 China's trade with the MDRCs (various years in US $ million)

	1990	1995	2000	2005	2007	2009
China's Imports						
Laos	6.436	6.449	6.422	25.544	84.991	336.572
Thailand	385.619	1,610.760	4,380.190	13,993.700	22,652.500	24,845.800
Cambodia	0.177	5.724	59.491	27.305	51.082	36.346
Vietnam	0.854	332.008	929.100	2,549.350	3,214.420	4,741.070
China's Exports						
Laos	14.477	47.766	34.419	105.336	177.409	376.280
Thailand	854.427	1,752.280	2,243.410	7,818.550	11,978.600	13,326.200
Cambodia	3.010	51.614	164.081	536.109	881.250	904.984
Vietnam	1.683	721.747	1,537.290	5,639.330	11,905.600	16,303.000
China's Balance						
Laos	8.041	41.317	27.997	79.792	92.418	39.708
Thailand	468.808	141.520	-2,136.780	-6,175.150	-10,673.900	-11,519.600
Cambodia	2.833	45.890	104.590	508.804	830.168	868.638
Vietnam	0.829	389.739	608.190	3,089.980	8,691.180	11,561.930
Total	480.511	618.466	-1,396.003	-2,496.574	-1,060.134	950.676

Source: IMF (2011).

Table 3.2 China's position in the MDRC's world trade in 2009

	Percentage of Overall Trade	Rank
MDRCs Imports from China		
Laos	14.3	2. (after Thailand)
Thailand	12.7	2. (after Japan)
Cambodia	22.6	1.
Vietnam	23.5	1.
MDRCs Exports to China		
Laos	20.1	2. (after Thailand)
Thailand	10.6	2. (after US)
Cambodia	0.3	–
Vietnam	8.6	3. (after US and Japan)

Source: IMF (2011).

MDRCs of Laos and Cambodia, leaving non-MDRC competitors such as Japan or Western countries far behind. This led to a situation where Laos and Cambodia became increasingly dependent on Chinese FDI. The total MDRC-wide volume of China's FDI increased more than six-fold from almost US $93 million to above US $580 million from 2003 to 2009. The sectors in which Chinese investments were flowing concentrated on energy, transport, agribusiness and tourism (MOFCOM 2009 and Biba 2012: 618; also see Table 3.3). Apart from FDI, China in this period also expanded its use of official development assistance, including grants, interest-free loans, and concessional loans. Such assistance has been aimed at the poorer Mekong countries. Cambodia was the primary MDRC benefactor of Chinese aid. Reilly (2012: 79) states that China provided Cambodia with US $204 million in grants and US $500 million in concessional loans between 2003 and 2009, with most of the money going into large-scale projects for

Table 3.3 China's outbound FDI flows to the MDRCs (2004–2009 in US $ mil.)

	2004	2005	2006	2007	2008	2009
Laos	3.56	20.58	48.04	154.35	87.00	203.24
Thailand	23.43	4.77	15.84	76.41	45.47	49.77
Cambodia	29.52	5.15	9.81	64.45	204.64	215.83
Vietnam	16.85	20.77	43.52	110.88	119.84	112.39

Source: MOFCOM (2009).

infrastructure development. Laos, in the meantime, received another US $46.5 million in Chinese development aid by 2009 (Reilly 2012: 82).[1]

Summing up, then, China has "emerg[ed] as the top trader, investor and donor in the region [i.e., in the Mekong]" (Chheang 2010: 362). In other words, China in the 2000s made large headway towards achieving its foreign policy goals of expanding its access to MDRC markets and increasing its investments in the sub-region. On the one hand, growing trade and investment ties have been mutually beneficial to a large extent. On the other hand, however, these trends have also been asymmetric in the sense that China's superior material resources have clearly drawn the MDRCs into China's orbit much closer than vice versa.

China and the Greater Mekong Subregion

Asymmetric relations also entail that the bigger power is likely in a position to transform its economic superiority into political influence vis-à-vis the smaller states. A good way to do so – while at the same time managing the asymmetric relationship in a reasonable way – is "multilateral buffering" of the bilateral relations (Womack 2010: 31). In accordance with this strategy, China has been a leading actor in a key multilateral grouping of Mekong riparian countries, namely, the Greater Mekong Subregion (GMS). What exactly is the GMS and why has China been so actively engaged in it?

The GMS is a 1992 initiative of the Asian Development Bank (ADB); members are all the six Mekong riparian countries, that is, China, the four MDRCs, and Myanmar. In fact, China participates at two levels, central government and provincial (with Yunnan and Guangxi). The GMS was originally established to facilitate sub-regional economic development and political rapprochement in the aftermath of the Cambodian conflict. According to Dosch (2011: 19), the GMS has the "ultimate objective of promoting the development of GMS markets and the movement of goods and people across the common borders." To realize this objective, the initiative has in particular sought to strengthen infrastructure linkages, facilitate cross-border trade, investment, and tourism, enhance private sector participation and competitiveness, develop human resources as well as protect the environment and promote the sustainable use of shared natural resources (GMS 2011: 2). In organizational terms, the GMS is a project-driven mechanism with a rather loose structure, primarily featuring sectoral working groups supplemented by national coordination committees. All decisions are made by annual ministerial meetings. Every three years since 2002, there has been a summit of prime ministers. The ADB continues to function as the GMS secretariat and provides technical assistance and consultation for diverse GMS projects (Will 2010: 25–26).

The GMS claims to have achieved substantial progress in several areas of cooperation since 1992, particularly in transport infrastructure. Dosch and Hensengerth (2005: 272) argue that GMS projects can be seen as "multidimensional confidence-building measures." According to a study of the UN sub-organization Economic and Social Commission for Asia and the Pacific, GMS projects have moreover contributed to some economic successes. The average GDP per capita in GMS countries (excluding China) almost doubled from US $664 to US $1042 between GMS inception in 1992 and 2006. This growth rate was slightly higher than that of all ASEAN members as a group. Besides, the percentage of intra-GMS trade of all GMS countries grew from 2 to 5 percent between 2002 and 2006 – a rate above what the other (i.e., non-GMS) ASEAN countries achieved over the same period (Will 2010: 26). At the same time, however, a closer look also reveals growing disparities among GMS countries, which stand in stark contrast to the idea of an integrated and flourishing sub-region. As a matter of fact, the gaps in GDP per capita as well as between the rich and the poor have widened among and within GMS countries respectively. Furthermore, intra-GMS trade growth has primarily benefited China and Thailand only (Will 2010: 26–27).

All that said, China's role in the GMS is particularly interesting, as the country has turned from beneficiary to benefactor (Lim 2008: i). Underlining its bilateral trade and investment policies, China has especially focused on developing the transport sector of the so-called "North-South Corridor," which includes its provinces of Yunnan and Guangxi and stretches southward in two different sectors to Bangkok and Hanoi, respectively. After hosting the 2005 GMS Summit, China created a US $20 million poverty reduction fund in the ADB and spent around US $4 billion constructing highways that connect Kunming, the provincial capital of Yunnan, with different parts of the GMS. In 2006, China also started, unilaterally, removing tariffs for more than 200 items from Cambodia, Laos, and Myanmar and pushed private and state-owned Chinese companies to invest in GMS countries (Lim 2008: 4). The result of these measures, as outlined above, included rapidly increasing trade and investment volumes with the MDRCs.

On a different page, the GMS has also become an important venue for Chinese policy-makers to voice and circulate Beijing's overarching objectives in the Mekong sub-region, wrapped in official and assuaging neighborhood rhetoric. During a speech at the 2008 Summit in Vientiane, for instance, China's then Premier Wen Jiabao promoted the idea that regional states should "keep to the path of pursuing common development and prosperity." In doing so, a list of priority items ranked infrastructure development, transport and trade facilitation, rural development, and health cooperation before ecological and environmental protection. While remarks on water resources management were completely missing, Wen instead stressed China's "path of peaceful development" and the adherence to a "win-win strategy" (Wen 2008).

Meanwhile, however, China's actions are certainly not as altruistic as they might seem at first sight. In fact, Beijing has also had its own strong domestic interests in developing the GMS. For example, Menniken (2007: 111) contends that "the GMS goals match the Chinese efforts to transform remote Yunnan into the 'Gateway to Southeast Asia'." Hensengerth (2009: 339–340) puts it more sharply, stating that

> [t]he GMS both benefits and suffers from the power of China, which views mainland Southeast Asia chiefly as an export market for products from its southwest provinces. Beijing and the two provincial governments [of Yunnan and Guangxi] are set to develop the GMS to this end. Their engagement in cross-border infrastructure building and improved Mekong navigation therefore develops the countries of the GMS, but it is motivated by the self-interest to create the domestic public good of poverty reduction that can only be achieved through cross-border development: while China helps the developing countries of the GMS, it also develops its own southwestern economy. Beijing therefore has a strong national interest in ensuring GMS cooperation occurs, but on its own terms.

Indeed, the GMS agenda has suited China's interests. A focus on aspects of economic development – and gradually non-traditional security threats such as illegal migration and drug trafficking as well – is quite to Beijing's gusto, as it reflects China's domestic policy goals in its southwestern provinces as well as an important factor in its foreign policy strategy towards the sub-region. Moreover, China is the most powerful player in the GMS and is thus usually able to dominate the agenda. Indicative of this is, for example, that Beijing has successfully prevented the GMS to put the issue of water resources management on the agenda (Hensengerth 2009: 331). Meanwhile, the GMS as a multilateral institution is also beneficial for bigger powers such as China in making power disparities more acceptable to the weaker parties, as multilateral venues give the latter a relatively bigger say (see Ikenberry 2008: 23–25). In other words, the GMS has been conducive for China to reassure its neighbors of its "good intentions" and to convey a positive image of itself, while at the same time subtly asserting Beijing's political influence in tandem with its increasing economic stakes in the Mekong region.

All in all, it can be argued that China's relations with the MDRCs as a group – albeit certainly more with Cambodia, Laos, and Thailand than with Vietnam (also see below) – were in a relatively good shape before the spring 2010 Mekong crisis. From Beijing's perspective, it was certainly positive that political and economic ties with the MDRCs had first been consolidated throughout the 1990s and were then strengthened and further intensified during the 2000s.

China's relations with ASEAN

Just as much as the MDRCs in mainland Southeast Asia belong to China's strategic and economic backyard, so do the countries of maritime Southeast Asia. Together, the countries of these two sub-regions have formed ASEAN, an intergovernmental organization that has long functioned as their primary institution for international relations amongst each other and vis-à-vis external players such as China. China's relations with the four MDRCs, thus, have to be thought in the bigger frame of China-ASEAN relations as well.

Established in 1967, ASEAN nowadays consists of ten member states, the four MDRCs, plus Brunei, Indonesia, Malaysia, Myanmar, Philippines, and Singapore. Even though ASEAN comprises a set of mostly smaller powers, which on top are very heterogeneous with regards to their political systems, development stages, and ethnic composition, for example, the organization has managed to largely remain in the driver's seat of growing trends of regionalism in Southeast Asia and even beyond. ASEAN and its values, primarily the so-called "ASEAN Way," which builds on "informality, organization minimalism, inclusiveness, intensive consultations leading to consensus and peaceful resolutions of disputes" (Narine 2008: 414), has been at the core of new regional mechanisms proliferating since the mid-1990s and including the ASEAN Regional Forum, the ASEAN Plus Three, and the East Asia Summit. This has rendered, or kept, the organization attractive to and important for powerful external players, such as the US, China, Japan, and India, which have all come to participate in (some of) the various ASEAN-driven regional mechanisms. ASEAN has welcomed the engagement of all these external powers as long as none of them seek domination in its "own" region. In fact, the organization has pursued a strategy of "omni-enmeshment," referring to a process of engaging with all the major states deemed important for ASEAN "so as to draw [them] into deep involvement into international or regional society, enveloping [them] in a web of sustained exchanges and relationships, with the long-term aim of integration" (Goh 2007: 121).

It is in this context that also China has found its relationship with ASEAN since the end of the Cold War when many diplomatic relations between Beijing and ASEAN capitals were restored. Especially during the 1990s and early-to-mid 2000s, China worked hard to intensify relations and counter fears of a "China threat." This certainly bore fruit. As a consequence of China's increasingly active and often seen as benevolent participation in ASEAN-led regional cooperation, a widely shared sentiment in Southeast Asia in the 2000s was that "China is clearly more popular and the target of less suspicion than in the past among many Asian governments, elites and popular opinion" (Sutter 2005: 10, cited in Zhao 2011: 58). In other words, Southeast Asian leaders largely reacted positively to China's diplomatic and political advances during the 2000s, which were described as a "charm offensive" (Kurlantzick 2007). At the same time, however, as both Chinese power and Sino-ASEAN ties continued to grow, the same leaders also showed disinclination to simply move under China's sway (Sutter 2008b: 91).

China's diplomatic charm offensive was accompanied, and in fact underlined, by growing efforts on the economic front. China–ASEAN economic relations took off alongside the overarching shift in the joint relationship in the late 1980s and early 1990s and then followed a similar steep upward trajectory as in the China–MDRC case. Beijing's key economic initiative aimed at ASEAN then clearly was the momentous proposal of a China-ASEAN free trade agreement (CAFTA) in 2000, in whose aftermath economic ties became the main driver of China-ASEAN relations. For ASEAN countries, China's proposal offered great economic opportunities. According to a research report by the ASEAN Secretariat, CAFTA, when completed in 2010, would raise ASEAN exports to China by 48 percent and ASEAN GDP by 0.9 percent (while China would have a 55.1 percent increase in its exports to ASEAN and a 0.3 percent GDP growth) (Men 2007: 254, 258). For China, its CAFTA proposal was as much an economic initiative as it was a political one, as leaders in Beijing were well aware, and also afraid, that China's rising economic power and WTO entry in 2001 might heighten concerns in ASEAN countries – a possible trajectory that China wished to counter actively (Men 2007: 257).

As a result, China sought to combine its economic and political agendas by looking for economic tools to reassure ASEAN states of Beijing's peaceful development path and to not let anti-China coalitions gain traction. For one thing, China allowed an (at times tremendous) overall trade deficit with ASEAN. China hoped that this could be a factor in fueling ASEAN countries' economies and, therefore, in helping alleviate fears of China.[2] For another thing, and related, China in January 2004 launched a so-called "early harvest program" for early liberalization of mainly agricultural products so that ASEAN countries could get early access to the Chinese market under the condition of cut tariff rates. Additionally, China made even more considerable concessions to the four newest ASEAN members, also the grouping's least developed countries (i.e., Cambodia, Laos, Myanmar, and Vietnam; equivalent to three of the four MDRCs), extending the "most favored nation" status to them and agreeing to give them five extra years, until 2015, to comply with CAFTA rules (Men 2007: 256).

Meanwhile, security relations between China and ASEAN have not developed in an equally positive direction. Even though Arase (2010) has emphasized the increasing institutionalization of China–ASEAN ties in the field of non-traditional security (e.g., piracy, smuggling, human trafficking, drug trade, transnational crime, illegal immigration, terrorism, subversion, and ethnic/religious movements), on an overarching scale, security relations have been overshadowed by the perennial disputes in the South China Sea, where China has overlapping maritime territorial claims with Brunei, Malaysia, Philippines, Taiwan, and Vietnam.[3]

Even though the disputed islands have little worth in themselves – many of them are just rocks hardly jumping out of the water – they are very attractive to their claimants, including China, for various reasons. First, the South China Sea area is estimated to be very rich in natural resources – be that fish, gas, or oil. Being a net energy importer since 1993, control of the fossil fuels in the South China Sea is a major interest for Beijing. Second, the South China Sea is of geostrategic importance. The area represents a major waterway for international trade, linking the oil fields of the Middle East and the factories of East Asia. The majority of China's oil imports, for instance, are shipped through the South China Sea. Third, and finally, the South China Sea issue carries a considerable nationalist element for Beijing. Territorial sovereignty is an aspect of crucial value for China's leaders, as it is closely linked to regime legitimacy and political preservation of the CCP (see above). Chinese claims in the South China Sea date back to the early 1950s. A sudden retraction of territorial claims after such a long time during which Chinese people have continuously been told that the South China Sea belongs to China could become very costly for leaders in Beijing (Emmers 2010: 243).

As a dispute between China and ASEAN, the South China Sea issue emerged not before the early 1990s. Since then, it has repeatedly heated up and cooled down again. The first wave of tensions occurred in the early-to-mid 1990s. In 1992, China first passed the Law of the People's Republic of China on the Territorial Waters and Contiguous Areas, reiterating its claims in the South China Sea and also stipulating the right to use force to protect islands there. On 8 February 1995, the Mischief Reef Incident happened, when China seized the first major piece of new territory after the Cold War, and this, for the very first time, from an ASEAN member (Philippines) that also claimed the reef. In the early 2000s, tensions then seemed to ease off a little, as China's charm offensive also included some symbolic gestures with relevance to the South China Sea disputes. Chief among them were Beijing's signing of the Declaration on the Code of Conduct of Parties in the South China Sea in November 2002 as well as China's accession to ASEAN's Treaty of Amity and Cooperation in October 2003. These actions were interpreted as signs for China's willingness to abide by ASEAN principles and norms, such as the peaceful resolution of territorial disputes and the building of trust and confidence between the parties involved. However, China never agreed to any legally binding or enforceable treaty. Therefore, for many ASEAN countries, China's behavior in the South China Sea has not really been helpful in allaying fears and dispelling mistrust of a possible increasingly assertive China. As a result, China's more positive advances in the economic field of its relations with ASEAN always have to be weighed against the frequently less positive situation in the South China Sea. However, while all ASEAN countries have been interested in strong and beneficial economic ties with China, not all of them are involved, or want to be involved, in the South China Sea disputes.

China–ASEAN relations around the time of the spring 2010 Mekong crisis

While China–ASEAN relations had generally developed in a rather optimistic direction in the early-to-mid 2000s, it is quite interesting and noteworthy that they underwent a loss of momentum in the months preceding the spring 2010 Mekong crisis. This was true both for the economic and security realms (see Storey 2010).

Less than one year before the spring 2010 Mekong crisis, China had pledged a huge aid package to help ASEAN countries cope wit the global financial crisis. According to Reilly (2012: 89), this package included a US \$10 billion contribution to launch a China–ASEAN Investment Cooperation Fund, a US \$15 billion line of commercial credit targeted at poorer ASEAN states, an extra US $39.7 million for "special aid" to Cambodia, Laos, and Myanmar, and US $5 million to the China–ASEAN Cooperation Fund. China moreover announced to raise scholarship funds, donate 300,000 tons of rice to an emergency East Asia reserve, and proposed a joint China–ASEAN project to create high-quality, high-yield crop demonstration farms in ASEAN countries.

However, despite China's 2009 aid package and the potential benefits to be derived from CAFTA, ASEAN states long harbored anxieties about whether they would be able to compete with China economically. More precisely, ASEAN states on the one hand worried about job and trade loss to China due to Chinese competition in their domestic markets, reliance on the same third-country markets (i.e., US, EU, and Japan) and the export of similar products (Ba 2003: 638–639). On the other hand, ASEAN states also feared China's great potential to divert FDI away from ASEAN (Ravenhill 2006: 653). In other words, even though China had gone to great lengths in trying to make CAFTA as agreeable to ASEAN as possible, Beijing did not fully succeed in reassuring its neighbors. This became once again apparent shortly before CAFTA was scheduled to come into effect in January 2010.

While concerns about the potential negative implications of CAFTA were still widespread in ASEAN, it particularly was critical voices from Indonesia, the largest ASEAN member state, that could be heard in late 2009 and early 2010. Indonesian manufacturers long feared that CAFTA would be a threat to domestic textile, garment, and footwear industries, as they predicted that the agreement would lead to cheap goods from China flooding the Indonesian market, thereby forcing enterprises out of business, causing job losses between one to two million and further worsening the trade deficit, which in 2009 stood at US $4.6 billion. Many Indonesian businessmen and trade associations therefore lobbied the government to renegotiate CAFTA or at least delay tariff removals on some 200 items. Indonesian Industry Minister M.S. Hidayat then in fact echoed the concerns. Consequently, in April 2010, Indonesia sought Chinese guarantees to set up a joint working group to settle issues resulting from CAFTA's implementation as well as commitments to pursue balanced trade (Storey 2010: 8). In essence, then, the coming into force of CAFTA in January 2010 had Beijing meet with a repeated wave of skepticism regarding its economic power and resulting political influence in (parts of) Southeast Asia.

Around the same time, several developments and a number of incidents (not all of them caused by China) indicated a marked deterioration of the overall situation in the South China Sea. For one thing, after years of positive engagement during the early 2000s, the Spratly dispute returned to dominate the agenda of Sino–Philippines relations. This was attributable to several events, such as the Filipino Congress approval in February 2009 of the Archipelagic Baselines Act confirming the country's territorial claims in the South China Sea and causing a row of angry diplomatic exchange between Beijing and Manila (Storey 2009: 7–8). For another thing, observers in the meantime began to speak of a generally increasing "Chinese assertiveness" in the South China Sea (e.g., Yahuda 2013). According to those observations, China, among other things, exerted pressure on British Petroleum and ExxonMobil already in April 2007 and June 2008, respectively, not to take part in offshore energy projects with Vietnam in waters claimed by Beijing and passed legislation in December 2007 that created a county level city on Hainan Island to administer its claims in the South China Sea. In March 2009, Chinese naval ships clashed with the US ocean surveillance vessel Impeccable along what China claims to be its Economic Exclusive Zone in the South China Sea. Through its behavior, China intended to deliver a message of strength, demonstrating its sovereignty over the area but simultaneously enhancing diplomatic tensions (Storey 2009: 8). In March 2010, China upped the ante as information was leaked that Chinese officials had told two visiting senior US officials that China had elevated its sovereignty claims in the South China Sea to becoming one of its "core interests" – a term previously used in connection with Taiwan, Tibet, and Xinjiang only (Hong and Jiang 2011: 7). Moreover, China's rapid naval build-up and the resultant changing power distribution in the South China Sea increasingly stirred concerns among ASEAN members that China could soon be in the position to resolve the sovereignty disputes militarily (Emmers 2009: 2).

The main target of Chinese activities in 2009 and 2010 was Vietnam. According to Vietnamese media reports, China detained or seized more than 30 Vietnamese fishing boats and over 400 crewmembers in 2009. Among this number were several Vietnamese fishing boats that were seized by China when they sought shelter in the Paracel Islands during storms in August and October 2009. In 2010, China continued this policy. During the first quarter of the year, there were again 30 cases when Chinese authorities seized Vietnamese fishing craft and detained more than 200 fishermen (Thayer 2010: 23). As a result, Vietnam, then chair of ASEAN, sought to forge a united front against China on the South China Sea. In a series of ASEAN-related meetings throughout the first half of 2010, Vietnam tried to launch diplomatic efforts that would involve China in a more binding code of conduct (Thayer 2010: 11–12). Those intentions, however, found little enthusiasm on the part of the Chinese who at that time seemed to generally backpedal from multilateral solution approaches in the South China Sea (e.g., the 2002 Declaration) and revert to its earlier policy of bilateral discussions with individual claimants (Goh 2011: 21).

To sum up, China's relations with ASEAN have, generally speaking, been more challenging for Beijing than China's relations with the MDRCs. Primarily, this has been due to the highly controversial South China Sea issue. Since Vietnam is the only MDRC claimant in the South China Sea territorial disputes, it can be maintained that these disputes have been of relatively less importance for China–MDRC relations. Also, Vietnam has mainly tried to work with its fellow Southeast Asian claimants to engage ASEAN and thus exert more pressure on China. That said, however, it also stands to reason that the rough patch through which China–ASEAN relations were going before and in early 2010 only enhanced the value China saw in its overall quite positive relationship with its Mekong neighbors (excluding Vietnam)

China and the US factor in Southeast Asia

While Southeast Asia is part of China's close neighborhood, ever since the end of World War II, the US has without doubt been the preponderant power in this sub-region and, in fact, in entire East Asia. Goh (2008) argues that the US has stood at the top of a hierarchical regional order since 1945. In that position, the US has had the ability to make war and peace, provide security, and generate wealth. In doing so, the US has made available public goods in the economic and security realms and shown its benignity and normative leadership, thereby also maintaining order in the region. Regional states have generally paid deference to the US, as underlined, among other things, by their lack of opposition and the great prioritization of their relationship with the US. In addition, for many countries in Southeast Asia, the US has long been the "least distrusted power" involved in regional affairs, as Washington does not have any territorial claims in the region and has for most of the post-World War II period acted as a reliable security guarantor (Sutter 2008b: 94).

In the 2000s, however, this US-led regional order increasingly came under challenge. One reason certainly was China's continued rise, which kept gathering speed at the time and was undergirded by China's charm offensive. Another reason, though, was of America's own making. For it was in the early 2000s that the US economy faltered and the country's political and security focus shifted almost entirely towards the Middle East in the wake of the terrorist attacks on 11 September 2001. Especially in Southeast Asia, many felt neglected by the Bush administration's war on terrorism in Iraq and Afghanistan at a time when China's presence in their region grew enormously.

On the one hand, the US managed to improve military-to-military relations, above all with the Philippines and Indonesia, as Southeast Asia had turned into the "second front" of the war on terrorism and Washington was looking for partners. On the other hand, though, most other areas did not see any positive development between 2000 and 2008. In particular, Southeast Asian elites blamed the US for a misguided militaristic and "one size fits all" approach towards fighting terrorism. The publics in the region, especially those with a large Muslim share, often perceived the US "war on terrorism" as a war against Islam *per se*, thus leading to a somewhat tarnished US image amongst Southeast Asian populations. One of the most frequently voiced points of criticism supposedly indicating Washington's disregard towards Southeast Asia moreover was that US leaders simply did not show up. Then US Secretary of State Condoleezza Rice decided to skip two out of three meetings of the ASEAN Regional Forum between 2005 and 2007 and then President George W. Bush in 2007 even cancelled a highly anticipated US-ASEAN summit that meant to celebrate the 30th anniversary of US-ASEAN relations (Ba 2009: 376–378).

As a result of this situation, the arrangement of the regional order in Southeast Asia seemed to enter a state of flux in the first decade of the new millennium, as it became an increasingly widely held belief that China was about to become the next regional hegemon. In this light, however, it soon turned out that the US was not affirmative of this prospect and instead began to show a re-emerging interest in Southeast Asia towards the end of the 2000s.

US efforts to re-engage Southeast Asia preceding the spring 2010 Mekong crisis

The Obama administration took office in January 2009, and soon afterwards the US announced its "return to Asia" policy, later to be followed by its "pivot/rebalance to Asia" strategy. With this new policy, the Obama administration changed the course of US diplomacy towards (South-)East Asian countries dramatically. Especially the aspects of physical presence and rhetoric, which carry high symbolic value in international relations in general and in East Asia in particular, returned prominently onto the US regional agenda.

The first signal came from then Secretary of State Hillary Clinton who chose Asia, including one Southeast Asian country, for her first official visit overseas, touring Japan, Indonesia, South Korea, and China in late February 2009 (DoS 2009a). In late July 2009, Clinton already came back to Southeast Asia, paying a three-day visit to Thailand. During this trip, Clinton not only made it clear that "the United States is back" and that "we are fully engaged and committed to our relationships in Southeast Asia" (DoS 2009b). More noteworthy even, Clinton signed the ASEAN Treaty on Amity and Cooperation, thus eventually making the US the last Pacific power to accede to the treaty and thereby simultaneously paving the way for a US entry into the ASEAN-led East Asia Summit (DoS 2009c). Finally, Clinton also attended the inaugural meeting of the Lower Mekong Initiative (LMI) (DoS 2009d), to which we will return in a moment.

Apart from Clinton, US President Barack Obama himself also signaled right from the start of his first term that he would concentrate his attention on the region more than his predecessor had done. During his first Asia trip in November 2009, Obama who had spent a few years of his childhood in Indonesia called himself "America's first Pacific president" and "pledged a renewed engagement with Asia Pacific nations" (CNN 2009). Additionally, Obama also announced that the US would engage with the Trans-Pacific Partnership, a regional free trade initiative, in an effort to enhance regional economic integration without China (USTR 2009) and attended the first-ever US-ASEAN leaders' meeting in Singapore. This event was labeled by ASEAN as a "seismic change" (ASEAN 2013) in the relationship, indicating that the US "return to Asia" was welcomed widely across the region.

However, within Southeast Asia, US attention in 2009 was not only redirected towards ASEAN as a group. Washington also showed increased interest in the countries of mainland Southeast Asia. Given that these countries, with the exception of Thailand, represent the newest ASEAN members and also those countries, which during the Cold War belonged to the antagonistic communist bloc, it was of high symbolic value that the Obama administration explicitly sought to also reach out to these states. The primary vehicle for the US to do so became the LMI.

The LMI was established in July 2009 on the sidelines of the yearly ASEAN Regional Forum and brought together the US and the four countries of the Lower Mekong Basin, that is, the MDRCs.[4] Convening annual ministerial meetings at the level of foreign ministers as well as several working group meetings, the official goal of the LMI has since its founding been "to create integrated sub-regional cooperation" (LMI 2017a). Several key pillars of common interest have been identified and include the areas of environment (including water), health, education, infrastructure development, and food and energy security (LMI 2017b). At the same time, as the joint press statement of the first LMI Ministerial Meeting in July 2009 made clear, for Washington, the LMI was also linked to the bigger regional picture: "U.S. Secretary of State Hillary Rodham Clinton underlined the importance of the Lower Mekong region and its individual countries to the United States and America's commitment to advancing peace and prosperity in the ASEAN region as a whole" (DoS 2009d).

As a result, it could be heard that while China did not officially oppose this new US initiative in its immediate backyard, Beijing privately expressed reservations over increased US involvement in the Mekong (Chang 2013: 298). This is certainly to be seen in light of the fact that the US made another effort to gain a somewhat stronger foothold in the Mekong, namely, by pursuing a sister river partnership between the Mississippi River Commission and the Mekong River Commission (which also has the four MDRCs as members; also see next chapter). This idea was first made public in the joint press statement of the first LMI ministerial meeting held upon the grouping's establishment (DoS 2009d). The partnership, in the form of a memorandum of understanding, was then inked in May 2010. The intention has been to "share research, expertise and experiences" in areas such as climate change adaptation of river systems, water resource management, flood and drought management, hydropower, navigation, food security, and maintaining water quality (DoS 2010).

Finally, it did not go unnoticed in Beijing that bilateral security and defense ties between the erstwhile enemies Washington and Hanoi were strengthened remarkably around 2010. While Vietnam is one of China's prime adversaries in the South China Sea, for the US, bilateral relations with Vietnam had improved to a point where the 2010 Quadrennial Defense Review issued in February that year stated the intention to develop a "new strategic partnership" with Hanoi (DoD 2010: 59).

In sum, therefore, within the first year of the Obama administration, the US had made a tremendous "comeback" to Southeast Asia. To be sure, the US had never actually left Southeast Asia, but the new verve with which key figures such as the president himself as well as his state secretary paid attention to this sub-region, in tandem with very concrete measures to enhance US presence there, was certainly striking. In how far China's charm offensive of the 2000s was the actual reason for the US policy shift has been debated. Clearly, though, China itself was worried by these developments (e.g., Lieberthal 2011 and Wang and Yin 2014).

The sum of China's southeast diplomacy in early 2010

Southeast Asia, mainland and maritime, is without doubt one the most important regions for the pursuit of China's overarching foreign policy objectives and represents a critical litmus test for the functioning of China's neighborhood diplomacy. After many bilateral ties between China and Southeast Asian countries had normalized only in the wake of the Cold War, China's Southeast Asia policy experienced almost two decades of largely positive developments. Trade and investment between both sides boomed, the China image in the region became much more friendly, Beijing's political influence grew through its active participation in several multilateral mechanisms, and even regional security affairs seemed to enter more shallow waters at times. In other words, China seemed to be successful in creating an ever more stable Southeast Asian backyard, conducive for promoting China and its neighbors' economic development as well as for fostering China's image of a benevolent and responsible rising great power that seeks to solve territorial disputes peacefully.

However, at least since 2009, dark clouds emerged on the horizon that put the further achievement of China's foreign policy objectives in the region at risk. First, the coming into effect of CAFTA in January 2010 raised concerns in some ASEAN countries about China's increasing economic power and the possible political leverage to result from this power. Second, the South China Sea issue saw a new and sustained round of heightened tensions and, in particular, it was China that was perceived to act increasingly assertive in the disputed waters. Third, the Obama administration taking office in 2009 reshifted its focus towards Southeast Asia, thereby challenging China's growing role in the region and rejecting Chinese hopes to replace the US. In sum, China's charm offensive had lost its momentum and all that had worked relatively well for Beijing during much of the early-to-mid 2000s suddenly met with growing resistance. As a result, China was increasingly put on the defensive in regional affairs in Southeast Asia. Shambaugh (2013: 37) has put it like this: "[m]uch of the progress made during the decade from 1998 to 2008 unraveled almost overnight during 2009–10 with a sudden spike in Chinese nationalism and assertiveness in the region."

That said, however, it is also true that preceding the spring 2010 Mekong crisis, MDRCs, with the notable exception of Vietnam, maintained a generally more positive image of China than the rest of Southeast Asia did. This was mainly because Laos, Thailand, and Cambodia are not (directly) involved in the South China Sea disputes. Moreover, CAFTA did not yet become effective for Laos and Cambodia (and Vietnam) in 2010. However, the fact that the MDRCs (minus Vietnam) remained favorable of China at a time when many other states in Southeast Asia rather emphasized the contentious issues vis-à-vis China also meant that the former countries were becoming relatively more important for China's foreign policy goals in the region, as the MDRCs could potentially play the role of Chinese "advocates" in Sino-ASEAN relations.[5] This, in turn, implied that China must have had an increased interest in keeping the MDRCs happy.

Notes

1 Myanmar has also received Chinese aid in considerable numbers (see Reilly 2012: 86–88). However, as stated in the Introduction to this book, Myanmar does not really play a role in this study.
2 However, China's overall trade deficit with ASEAN did not mean that every single ASEAN country ran a trade surplus vis-à-vis China.
3 More precisely, Brunei, China, Malaysia, Philippines, Malaysia, Taiwan, and Vietnam all claim sovereignty over (some of) the Spratly Islands. In addition, China, Taiwan, and Vietnam also claim the Paracel Archipelago. In total, therefore, there are six claimants, with China, Taiwan, and Vietnam claiming (more or less) the entire South China Sea area and Brunei, Malaysia, and Philippines laying claim to only parts of it. Indonesia does not raise claims, but in 1993 equally retracted neutrality in the face of Chinese claims to the waters above the Natuna gas fields currently exploited by Jakarta. With the exception of Brunei, all other claimants have meanwhile established physical presence on some of the islands concerned. Besides, each party has shown reluctance to make any concessions on their sovereignty claims respectively. While China, Taiwan, and Vietnam have made their claims based on historical reasons of discovery and occupation, Brunei, Malaysia, and Philippines have built their cases on the extension of sovereign jurisdiction under interpretations of the provision of the United Nations Convention on the Law of the Sea including the extension of the continental shelf. Beijing has not provided a legal explanation for, nor given specific delimitations to, its territorial claims (Emmers 2010: 242–243).
4 Myanmar also joined the LMI in 2012.
5 As a matter of fact, a situation like this should occur in July 2012 when ASEAN failed to reach an agreement on the South China Sea issue mainly because Cambodia stepped in on China's behalf (BBC 2012).

References

Arase, D. (2010) "Non-Traditional Security in China-ASEAN Cooperation: The Institutionalization of Regional Security Cooperation and the Evolution of East Asian Regionalism," *Asian Survey*, 50(4), 808–833.
Association of Southeast Asian Nations (ASEAN) (2013) "Overview of ASEAN-US Dialogue Relations," www.asean.org/news/item/overview-of-asean-us-dialogue-relations.
Ba, A. (2003) "China and ASEAN: Renavigating Relations for a 21st Century Asia," *Asian Survey*, 43(4), 622–647.

Ba, A. (2009) "Systemic Neglect? A Reconsideration of US-Southeast Asia Policy," *Contemporary Southeast Asia*, 31(3), 369–398.

BBC (2012) "ASEAN Nations Fail to Reach Agreement on South China Sea," 13 July, www.bbc.com/news/world-asia-18825148.

Biba, S. (2012) "China's Continuous Dam-building on the Mekong," *Journal of Contemporary Asia*, 42(4), 603–628.

Biba, S. (2016) "It's Status, Stupid: Explaining the Underlying Core Problem in US-China Relations," *Global Affairs*, 2(5), 455–464.

Carlson, A. (2008) "Chinese Views of Sovereignty and Methods of Access Control," *U.S.-China Economic and Security Review Commission*, 27 February.

Chang, F. (2013) "The Lower Mekong Initiative & U.S. Foreign Policy in Southeast Asia: Energy, Environment and Power," *Orbis*, 57(2), 282–299.

Chheang, V. (2010) "Environmental and Economic Cooperation in the Mekong Region," *Asia Europe Journal*, 8(3), 359–368.

CNN (2009) "Obama Vows Renewed Ties with Asia," 14 November, www.cnn.com/2009/WORLD/asiapcf/11/13/obama.asia/.

Department of Defense (DoD), United States (2010) "Quadrennial Defense Review Report, February 2010," www.defense.gov/qdr/images/QDR_as_of_12Feb10_1000.pdf.

Department of State (DoS), United States (2009a) "Former Secretary Clinton: 2009 Travel. Asia, February 15–22," www.state.gov/secretary/trvl/2009/116166.htm.

Department of State (DoS), United States (2009b) "Remarks by Secretary Clinton: July 2009. Remarks With Thai Deputy Prime Minister Korbsak Sabhavasu," www.state.gov/secretary/rm/2009a/july/126271.htm.

Department of State (DoS), United States (2009c) "United States Accedes to the Treaty of Amity and Cooperation in Southeast Asia," www.state.gov/r/pa/prs/ps/2009/july/126294.htm.

Department of State (DoS), United States (2009d) "Joint Press Statement of the U.S.-Lower Mekong Ministerial Meeting," www.state.gov/r/pa/prs/ps/2009/july/126377.htm.

Department of State (DoS), United States (2010) "Mississippi River Commission Agreement Creates Unique Partnership a World Apart," www.state.gov/p/eap/mekong/143272.htm.

Dosch, J. (2011) "Reconciling Trade and Environmental Protection in ASEAN-China Relations: More than Political Window Dressing?," *Journal of Current Southeast Asian Affairs*, 30(2), 7–29.

Dosch, J., and O. Hensengerth (2005) "Sub-regional Cooperation in Southeast Asia: The Mekong Basin," *European Journal of East Asian Studies*, 4(2), 263–286.

Emmers, R. (2009) "The Changing Power Distribution in the South China Sea: Implications for Conflict Management and Avoidance," RSIS Working Paper No. 183 (September), www.rsis.edu.sg/publications/WorkingPapers/WP183.pdf.

Emmers, R. (2010) "Maritime Security in Southeast Asia," in Ganguly, S., Scobell, A. and Liow, J. (eds), *The Routledge Handbook of Asian Security Studies*, London and New York: Routledge, 241–251.

Energy Information Administration (EIA) (2015) "China," Analysis, 14 May, www.eia.gov/beta/international/analysis.cfm?iso=CHN.

Fravel, T. (2005) "Regime Insecurity and International Cooperation: Explaining China's Compromises in Territorial Disputes," *International Security*, 30(2), 46–83.

Goh, E. (2007) "Great Powers and Hierarchical Order in Southeast Asia: Analyzing Regional Security Strategies," *International Security*, 32(3), 113–157.

Goh, E. (2008) "Hierarchy and the Role of the United States in the East Asian Security Order," *International Relations of the Asia-Pacific*, 8(3), 353–377.

Goh, E. (2011) "Rising Power… To Do What? Evaluating China's Power in Southeast Asia," *RSIS Working Paper No. 226* (30 March), www.rsis.edu.sg/publications/WorkingPapers/WP226.pdf.

Greater Mekong Subregion (GMS) (2011) "The Greater Mekong Subregion Economic Cooperation Program Strategic Framework 2012–2022," www.adb.org/sites/default/files/gms-ec-framework-2012-2022.pdf.

Hensengerth, O. (2009) "Transboundary River Cooperation and the Regional Public Good: The Case of the Mekong River," *Contemporary Southeast Asia*, 31(2), 326–349.

Hong, N., and Jiang, W. (2011) "Chinese Perceptions of U.S. Engagement in the South China Sea," *China Brief*, 11(12), 7–9.

Ikenberry, J. (2008) "State Power and International Institutions: America and the Logic of Economic and Security Multilateralism," in Bourantonis, D., Ifantis, K. and Tsakonas, P. (eds.), *Multilateralism and Security. Institutions in an Era of Globalization*, London and New York: Routledge, 21–42.

International Monetary Fund (IMF) (2011) "Data of Trade Statistics (DOTS)," (various years), http://elibrary-data.imf.org/FindDataReports.aspx?d1/433061&e1/4170921.

Kurlantzick, J. (2007) *Charm Offensive: How China's Soft Power is Transforming the World*, New Haven, CT: Yale University Press.

Lai, H. (2010) "Internal Sources of External Policy: An Analytical Framework," in Lai, H. (ed.), *The Domestic Sources of China's Foreign Policy*, London and New York: Routledge, 19–41.

Larson, D., Paul, T.V., and Wohlforth, W. (2014) "Status and World Order," in Paul, T.V., Larson, D. and Wohlforth, W. (eds.), *Status in World Politics*, Cambridge: Cambridge University Press, 3–29.

Lieberthal, K. (2011) "The American Pivot to Asia: Why President Obama's to the East Is Easier Said Than Done," *Foreign Policy*, 21 December, www.foreignpolicy.com/articles/2011/12/21/the_american_pivot_to_asia?page=0,0.

Lim, Tin Seng (2008) "China's Active Role in the Greater Mekong Sub-Region: A 'Win-Win' Outcome?," *East Asia Institute, Background Brief*, 397, Singapore, National University of Singapore, www.eai.nus.edu.sg/BB397.pdf.

Lower Mekong Initiative (LMI) (2017a) "LMI Overview," http://lowermekong.org/about/lower-mekong-initiative-lmi.

Lower Mekong Initiative (LMI) (2017b) "LMI Plan of Action," http://lowermekong.org/about/lmi-plan-action.

Medeiros, E. (2009) "China's International Behavior," *RAND Corporation*, Monograph Series, www.rand.org/content/dam/rand/pubs/monographs/2009/RAND_MG850.pdf.

Men, J. (2007) "The Construction of the China-ASEAN Free Trade Area: A Study of China's Active Involvement," *Global Society*, 21(2), 249–268.

Menniken, T. (2007) "China's Performance in International Resource Politics: Lessons from the Mekong," *Contemporary Southeast Asia*, 29(1), 97–120.

Ministry of Commerce (MOFCOM), China (2009) "2009 Statistical Bulletin of China's Outward Foreign Investment," http://chinainvests.files.wordpress.com/2010/12/2009-mofcom-investment-report1.pdf.

Ministry of Foreign Affairs (MOFA), China (2003) "China's Stand on South-South Cooperation," http://www.fmprc.gov.cn/eng/wjdt/wjzc/t24884.htm.

Narine, S. (2008) "Forty years of ASEAN: A Historical Review," *The Pacific Review*, 21(4), 411–429.
Office of the United States Trade Representative (USTR) (2009) "Increasing U.S. Exports, Creating American Jobs: Engagement with the Trans-Pacific Partnership," 13 November, www.ustr.gov/about-us/press-office/blog/2009/november/increasing-us-exports-creating-american-jobs-engagement-tra.
Ravenhill, J. (2006) "Is China an Economic Threat to Southeast Asia?" *Asian Survey*, 46(5), 653–674.
Reilly, J. (2012) "A Norm-Taker or a Norm-Maker? Chinese Aid in Southeast Asia," *Journal of Contemporary China*, 21(73), 71–91.
Shambaugh, D. (2013) *China Goes Global. The Partial Power*, Oxford: Oxford University Press.
Statistics Times (2016) "List of Countries by Projected GDP," 21 October, http://statisticstimes.com/economy/countries-by-projected-gdp.php.
Stockholm International Peace Research Institute (SIPRI) (2016) "Trends in World Military Expenditure, 2015," http://books.sipri.org/files/FS/SIPRIFS1604.pdf.
Storey, I. (2009) "Impeccable Affair and Renewed Rivalry in the South China Sea," *China Brief*, 9(9), 7–10.
Storey, I. (2010) "China's 'Charm Offensive' Loses Momentum in Southeast Asia [Part I]," *China Brief*, 10(9), 7–10.
Storey, I. (2011) *Southeast Asia and the Rise of China: The Search for Security*, London and New York: Routledge.
Sutter, R. (2005) *China's Rise in Asia: Promises and Perils*, Lanham: Rowman & Littlefield Publishers.
Sutter, R. (2008a) *Chinese Foreign Relations*, Lanham: Rowman & Littlefield Publishers.
Sutter, R. (2008b) "China's Rise, Southeast Asia, and the United States," in Goh, E. and Simon, S. (eds.), *China, the United States, and Southeast Asia: Contending Perspectives on Politics, Security, and Economics*, New York and London: Routledge, 91–106.
Thayer, C. (2010) "Recent Developments in the South China Sea: Grounds for Cautious Optimism?" *RSIS Working Paper* 220 (December), www.rsis.edu.sg/publications/workingpapers/wp220.pdf.
Wang, F. (2005) "Preservation, Prosperity and Power: What Motivates China's Foreign Policy?" *Journal of Contemporary China*, 14(45), 669–694.
Wang, H. (2005) "National Image Building and Chinese Foreign Policy," in Deng, Y. and Wang, F. (eds.), *China Rising: Power and Motivation in Chinese Foreign Policy*, Boulder: Rowman & Littlefield, 73–102.
Wang, Z. (2014) *Never Forget National Humiliation*, New York: Colombia University Press.
Wang, D., and Yin, C. (2014) "Mainland China Debates U.S. Pivot/Rebalancing to Asia," *Issues & Studies*, 50(3), 57–101.
Wen, J. (2008) "Build a Bond of Cooperation and a Common Homeland," Third GMS Summit, Vientiane, Laos, 31 March, www.china-embassy.org/eng/zt/768675/t476515.htm.
Will, G. (2010) "Der Mekong: Ungelöste Probleme regionaler Kooperation," *SWP-Studie*, www.swp-berlin.org/fileadmin/contents/products/studien/2010_S07_wll_ks.pdf.
Womack, B. (2010) *China Among Unequals: Asymmetric Foreign Relationships in Asia*, Singapore: World Scientific.

Yahuda, M. (2013) "China's New Assertiveness in the South China Sea," *Journal of Contemporary China*, 22(81), 446–459.
Yan, X. (2001) "The Rise of China in Chinese Eyes," *Journal of Contemporary China*, 10(26), 33–39.
Zhao, S. (2011) "China's Approaches toward Regional Cooperation in East Asia: Motivations and Calculations," *Journal of Contemporary China*, 20(68), 53–67.

4 China and the Mekong

Introduction

After the previous chapter has outlined China's overarching foreign policy goals as well as China's foreign relations with its Southeast Asian neighbors in broader and more general terms, this chapter zeroes in on a much more specific area of those foreign relations, also the focus of this book, that is, China's hydro-politics in the Mekong. As previously defined (see Chapter 1), (international) hydro-politics refers to "the systematic study of conflict and co-operation between states over water resources that transcend international borders" (Elhance 1999: 3). In other words, hydro-politics is about what states do with their shared water resources (in terms of the various functions of those resources such as food production, energy generation, transportation, or environmental preservation) and about what consequences their actions have (eventually in terms of conflict and cooperation). Moreover, keep in mind that one state's hydro-politics feeds into its overall foreign relations with other countries and that this one state's overarching foreign policy objectives likewise play a role for its hydro-politics.

With approximately 4,900 km, the Mekong is the tenth-longest river in the world and the most important watercourse in mainland Southeast Asia. Its riparian countries include – from upstream to downstream – China, Myanmar, Laos, Thailand, Cambodia, and Vietnam (also see Map 4.1 and Table 4.1). The basin of the Mekong drains a total land area of 795,000 km^2, reaching from the eastern watershed of the Tibetan Plateau to the Mekong Delta in southern Vietnam (MRC 2017a). Of the 65 million of basin inhabitants (60 million of which are in the lower basin), about 85 percent makes a living directly from the river, particularly through fishing and irrigated rice production (Jacobs 2002: 356). However, the Mekong has increasingly turned into a rapidly changing river basin, primarily because of large-scale development projects, especially hydropower dams. This trend, among others, has caused Yoffe et al. (2003) to define the Mekong as one of the world's high-risk basins for future water conflicts.

As its most upstream and most powerful country, China has the key role to play in Mekong hydro-politics. Conversely, the Mekong and its resources are

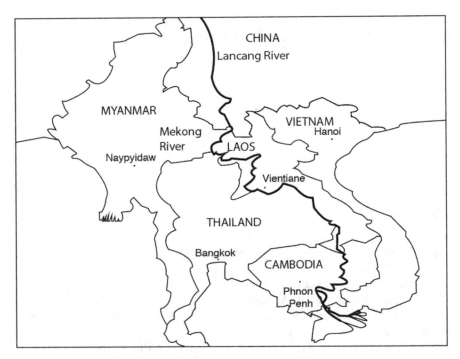

Map 4.1 The Mekong River and its riparian countries
Source: Biba (2012: 604).

Table 4.1 The Mekong River Basin and its riparian countries

	China	Myanmar	Laos	Thailand	Cambodia	Vietnam
Flow contribution (%)	16	2	35	18	18	11
Basin land area (%)	12	2	26	23	20	8
Country territory in basin (%)	3	4	97	36	86	20
Basin population (%)	16	1	7	34	14	28
Country population living in basin (%)	n.a.	n.a.	89	36	81	24

Source: adapted from Goh (2001: 471), Backer (2007: 39–44), and MRC (2011: 13).

also significant for China and its sustained development. To expose those interdependencies, how they translate into politics on water resources, and what corollaries they bring along are main tasks of this chapter. Consequently, the chapter expands on China's role for the hydrology of the Mekong, China's attitude towards joint governance of the Mekong, and China's activities, particularly its dam building, in the Mekong. While the focus is on China, the (potential) consequences of its behavior for the river and the downstream riparian countries as well as the latter's attitude to China's behavior all figure prominently as well. This includes the description and analysis of a summer 2008 flooding in the Mekong, serving also as a prelude to the spring 2010 crisis that will gain center stage in later chapters. Two major goals of this chapter are, first, to show how both conflict and cooperation co-exist in China's Mekong hydro-politics and, second, how this conflict-cooperation trade-off is related to China's overall foreign policy goals.

China and Mekong hydrology

The Mekong's hydrology is an important aspect to understand first in order to evaluate the need for governance and the risks of infrastructure development on the river later. In particular, tributaries in the upper basin are generally small, whereas from Laos downstream, larger tributaries join the Mekong (MRC 2017a). This constellation entails that the upstream flow of the Mekong contributes only a relatively small portion to the river's overall annual runoff. As a result, China accounts for what has often been portrayed as "only" 16 percent of the Mekong's entire flow (MRC 2017b; also see Table 4.1).[1] In fact, this number has frequently been used by China to downplay its influence on the river's hydrology, for example, when it comes to its dam building on the Mekong (see below). However, "the importance of upstream flow should not be underestimated as dry-season snow melt from China contributes to over 24% of the total flow" (MRC 2017b). Goh (2004: 2–3) has furthermore emphasized that the figure of China's 16 percent understates two points. First, the total flow is measured for the whole basin and ignores the fact that at the Lao capital Vientiane, still around 60 percent of the Mekong water comes from China; second, during the critical dry season, China's discharge amounts to most of the mainstream of the Mekong in Laos and Thailand, and contributes to almost 45 percent of the average flow as far downstream as in Cambodia.

All this is no trivial matter because the continued existence of clearly determined flood and dry seasons is critical for the Mekong. During the flood season, which lasts from June to November, 80 to 90 percent of the total annual discharge occurs. While annual floods have the potential to cause damage to riparian communities, they are essential for the Lower Mekong Basin. First, many of the Mekong's diverse ecosystems have developed as a result of seasonal flow fluctuations. The basin's extensive wetland habitats, for example, would not exist without annual floods. Wetlands constitute a productive environment for agriculture, aquaculture, capture fisheries, non-fish aquatic goods, and tourism revenue. Moreover, they provide equally significant indirect benefits, such as flood mitigation, water storage, and wastewater treatment. Second, the life cycles of many Mekong fish species are dependent on the change of the seasons. Fish migrate to deep pools in the mainstream to survive the dry season; later, during the flood season, they return to spawning and nutrient-rich feeding grounds on floodplains. Therefore, the flood pulse also sustains the immense productivity of Mekong freshwater fisheries. Third, the seasonal floods deposit nutrients and sediments on to the natural flood plains, thereby improving soil fertility and in the end raising agricultural output (MRC 2017b, 2017d and 2017h).

At the same time, however, the Mekong has been characterized as a "drought-prone" (Adamson and Bird 2010) area, thus putting the Mekong's flood pulse at risk. The problem is that droughts can result in water and food shortages, loss of income, and higher levels of disease. Droughts are furthermore damaging to agriculture, especially rice, and can cause an overall loss of crops, livestock, and fisheries. In addition, the Mekong is also considered one of the world's regions most vulnerable to climate change. Both droughts and climate change will likely affect the Mekong's sensitive ecosystems and its high agricultural productivity in considerable ways (MRC 2017c and 2017f).

China and Mekong governance

An international river and highly sensitive ecosystem like the Mekong needs a governing body to bring the riparian countries together and coordinate their various interests while at the same time protecting the river's resources. In the post-World War II era, the Mekong has already seen various attempts at joint governance. Since 1995, the prime organization for this task has been the Mekong River Commission (MRC), which includes Laos, Thailand, Cambodia, and Vietnam as members. The Mekong therefore represents a special case among China's shared rivers because it is the only major basin where China is confronted with a multilateral water governance body established by its riparian neighbors. China itself (like Myanmar) has only been a dialogue partner of the MRC since 1996.

Institutionally, the MRC functions as follows.[2] On top of the organization structure is the Council, a policy-making body, which is comprised of four members – each with the rank of a minister or equivalent – from each of the four members and which usually convenes once a year. Under the Council, the Joint Committee is the MRC's operational decision-making unit. Members of the Joint Committee are senior officials at no less than head of department level of their respective ministries in the four member countries. Moreover, the MRC has a Secretariat based in Vientiane, Laos, as its operational arm for technical and administrative functions. The Secretariat is managed by a Chief Executive Officer and includes several topical programs funded by various international donors. In parallel with the MRC structure, there are the

National Mekong Committees (NMCs) of each member state. They are intended to link the MRC regional programs with the development plans and policies of the sectoral ministries at the national level. Like the MRC, NMCs are equipped with a permanent secretariat respectively. Last but not least, there is a Donor Consultative Group, consisting primarily of European countries, Australia, and Japan as well as the World Bank and the Asian Development Bank. At least until recently (see below), the MRC has largely depended on this group for funding (MRC 2017i and Suhardiman et al. 2012: 575–576).

Article One of the MRC founding document, the "Agreement on the Cooperation for the Sustainable Development of the Mekong River Basin" (also called "Mekong Agreement"), outlines the areas of cooperation and thus refers to the objectives of the MRC, namely,

> [t]o cooperate in all fields of sustainable development, utilization, management and conservation of the water and related resources of the Mekong River Basin […] in a manner to optimize the multiple-use and mutual benefits of all riparians and to minimize the harmful effects that might result from natural occurrences and man-made activities.
>
> (MRC 1995)

Initially, the Mekong Agreement was lauded by some observers as "a milestone in international water resources management due to its emphasis on joint development, ecological protection, and a dynamic process of water allocation" (cited in Jacobs 2002: 360). Today, it might be more correct to say that the MRC has played a considerable role as a cooperation platform between its members, as it has gathered and shared information between members and provided a dialogue forum for the governments (Keskinen et al. 2008: 90). In particular, the MRC Secretariat has, through its donor-funded programs, gained enormous amounts of information and technical and scientific knowledge on the basin and its resources (Backer 2007: 45).

At the same time, the MRC has long been confronted with several points of criticism. To begin with, one important aspect that has been criticized is that the 1995 Mekong Agreement highlights the sovereign equality and territorial integrity of its signatory states (Art. 4). The MRC thus is a strictly intergovernmental organization. Particularly, the agreement features virtually no restrictions on what a country is allowed to do within its own territory. The assumption is that MRC members have the right to control the river within their own national boundaries. Besides, the agreement only requires notification in case of tributary development – which is in contrast to mainstream development which requires consultations. It goes without saying, though, that water from the Mekong mainstream cannot be separated in any way from water of the tributaries (Fox and Sneddon 2007: 255). These regulations have therefore gravely curtailed the "enforcement power" of the MRC (Keskinen et al. 2008: 90). Hirsch and Jensen (2006: 113) have even come to the conclusion that the MRC is a governed organization, instead of a governing organization – a coordinator at best, rather than a controller.

In essence, this situation is rooted in the following two aspects. First, the weak bindingness of the Mekong Agreement pays tribute to the political culture in Southeast Asia. All MRC members are likewise members of the Southeast Asia's primary inter-state organization, the Association of Southeast Asian Nations (ASEAN), whose key principles include sovereignty and non-interference (Hirsch and Jensen 2006: 75–80). Second, the MRC has frequently been sidelined simply because national interests have prevailed over regional interests in the Mekong (Hirsch and Jensen 2006: 45). The crux is that all in all, "[e]ach country tries to capitalise on its river location by exploiting the river's resources as much as possible for its own interests and needs, regardless of the consequences pending further downstream or the overall health of the hydraulic system" (Kuenzer et al. 2013: 578).

What is more, though, there are, strictly speaking no unitary national interests in any of the four MRC member countries. Instead, as Suhardiman et al. (2012: 574) have pithily described, power interplay at the national level dominates the scenery, as bureaucratic competition, particularly between relevant sectoral ministries in charge of matters such as environment, energy, agriculture, fishery etc., and fragmentation has become common practice within government bureaucracies.

As a result of those diverse interests, most members have generally preferred the MRC to be a "rather toothless organization that identifies development projects and attracts external funds, whilst control of the development remains with the states themselves" (Backer 2006: 38). This fact has also created problems for the MRC Secretariat, which sits awkwardly between the diverse national interests and the international donors of the MRC. With Integrated Water Resources Management, the MRC Secretariat pursues a concept, which partly goes against the recent development drive of its members (Suhardiman et al. 2012: 577–578).[3] While the Secretariat has the task to implement MRC policies and programs in a way that balances the various interests, as of now it does not have the capacity to accommodate all these interests simultaneously.

Another significant point of criticism has targeted the MRC relationship with the public. As the MRC has frequently shown open disregard for public participation, the body has gravely constrained its own ability to properly evaluate the needs of the people living in the Mekong. By not seeking public input in its projects, the MRC has opened the door for NGO and civil society protest against the perceived opaque decision-making processes in the MRC, which are believed to primarily benefit actors other than local communities (Ha 2011: 131).

Finally, however, the MRC's lack of inclusiveness has been regarded as possibly the most critical weak spot of the organization. For the MRC, the problem lies in the fact that without all Mekong riparian countries united in a joint Mekong governance regime, integrated basin-wide development is virtually impossible. This brings us back to China. Although the MRC has at several occasions shown interest in admitting China, Beijing has so far rejected to becoming a full member. Apart from its dialogue partner status mentioned before, China in 2002 only signed the "Agreement on the Provision of Hydrological Information on the Lancang/Mekong River," under which China has provided water level data in the flood season from two stations on its territory (MRC 2017j). This agreement was inked after a round of talks in the aftermath of a 2000 flooding, when some 800 people in the Mekong Delta were killed and flood forecasting became an important issue for the downstream riparian countries (Asia Times Online 2008).

But why has China declined to become a full MRC member? At first sight, the MRC focus on the national sovereignty of its members as well as its exclusion of public stakeholders, for example, might seem attractive for China. In fact, however, there are several substantial reasons why China is not a member of the MRC (also see Backer 2007: 43–44). First, as outlined in Chapter 1, China shares many international rivers all around its vast periphery. Therefore, the Mekong could possibly be turned into an unwanted precedent for China. That is to say, if China joined the MRC and gave concessions to its riparian neighbors in the Mekong, other riparian countries in other shared river basins might well make similar demands. In addition, China's powerful upstream position and, as a result, its low vulnerability to the river makes it hard for China to find incentives to be restricted in its freedom of action by any multilateral cooperation agreement. This aspect is also related to a second reason. The entire MRC is often viewed in China as having quite a narrow agenda, with its focus solely on water resources management. Instead, China has preferred broader cooperation frameworks, which more clearly speak to the country's pivotal goal of fostering socio-economic development. Therefore, in contrast to the MRC, China has joined, and in fact soon afterwards driven, the Greater Mekong Subregion, which emphasizes the enhancement of economic relations between the Mekong countries and, at the same time, does not touch upon more sensitive questions of water resources management (also see Chapter 3).

A third reason is that joining the MRC would imply for China to enter into an arrangement with predefined rules. In the 1995 Mekong Agreement, it is clearly stipulated that additional parties have to abide by the rights and obligations under the agreement (Art. 39). However, this rather strict approach is not acceptable to China because in Chinese eyes, the Mekong Agreement does not really serve the interests of upstream riparian countries in that it does not acknowledge the services that the upstream reaches of the Mekong provide to downstream areas, such as sediment accumulation. China therefore fears that it would unduly pay for MRC membership without being properly compensated. Fourth, it also needs to be taken into consideration that from a Beijing perspective, the Mekong is located at a far corner of China. At least until the recent crises occurred (see below and later chapters), this has made it relatively harder for Mekong issues to reach the top of the agendas of central policy and decision makers. Finally, and apart from China-focused reasons for its non-membership in the MRC, it has also been suggested that MRC interest in letting China in has in fact been rather lukewarm, too. Some Western donor agencies as well as some MRC member countries themselves might actually be apprehensive that as a full member, China could try to seize the reins in a way unfavorable to the current members.

Lately, the MRC has increasingly struggled to maintain its relevance – and the reason has not really been China. Dore and Lazarus (2009: 360) have long implied that the MRC has been marginalized from the planning and decision-making processes regarding the big questions, most prominently hydropower construction. This trend has only intensified in recent years, that is, particularly since Laos in fall 2010 started building the first Mekong mainstream dam (Xayaburi) downstream of China, meanwhile followed by two more (Don Sahong and Pak Beng). The MRC has not been able to play a central and effective role in managing the decision-making processes surrounding these highly controversial projects. Instead, the four member countries have been repeatedly at each other's throat, and there has been "financial mismanagement and political bullying" (Hunt 2016a). As a consequence, the MRC donors have dropped their funding and effectively abandoned the organization. Bereft of the largest part of its financial resources, the MRC "has [at least for now] been reduced to a shell of its former self" (Hunt 2016b; also see Hunt 2016c and 2017; more on these and related developments in Chapter 7).

China and Mekong mainstream dam building

The Mekong is a vital resource for its riparian countries and basin inhabitants in many respects. Among other things, it provides water for consumption, irrigation, and fisheries, and represents a vital transportation route for trade and tourism. Since the 1990s, however, it is its potential for hydropower generation that has increasingly gained center stage. The Mekong River Basin's total hydropower potential, including tributaries, is estimated at 59,000 MW (30,000 MW in the lower basin, mostly Laos, and 29,000 MW in the upper basin).[4] Until today, not even 20 percent of this potential has been exploited; in the lower basin, this percentage is still under 10 percent. Yet, the mountainous parts of the basin as they are found in China, Myanmar, Laos, and Thailand are – geographically speaking – ideal locations for the construction of large hydropower dams (Kuenzer et al. 2013: 568 and MRC 2011: 81).

China, the Mekong's most upstream country, has been the frontrunner in this development. In the late 1980s, China began to unilaterally launch a dam cascade project on the middle reaches of the Lancang (as the Mekong is called in China). This cascade was originally supposed to comprise a series of eight consecutive dams that takes advantage of a 700-meter drop within a 750 km stretch of the river in order to mainly generate hydropower. Altogether, these dams were supposed to have a maximum installed capacity of over 15,000 MW, roughly equivalent to 80 percent of China's Three Gorges Dam, the presently largest dam in the world in terms of installed capacity. Construction of the cascade began in 1986. The first dam went operational in 1993. At present, six dams have been completed and one is still in its planning stage, while the most downstream dam has meanwhile been cancelled. A key characteristic of the dam cascade moreover is that two of the dams, Xiaowan and Nuozhadu, possess large water storing reservoirs with multi-season regulating capacity (Biba 2012: 607; Habich 2016: 73; and Song 2010; also see Map 4.2 and Table 4.2).[5]

China's dam building on the Mekong is to be seen against the backdrop of various domestic drivers (also see Chapter 1). First, China has been faced with a surging energy demand in order to maintain its high economic growth rates. Especially during the hot and humid summer months in southern and southeastern China, primarily in the densely populated and economically vibrant province of Guangdong, blackouts have already produced problems for the provincial economy. Electricity generated from the Mekong dams and then fed into the China Southern Power Grid is therefore meant to supply the heartland of China's economy with much needed power. Second, Mekong

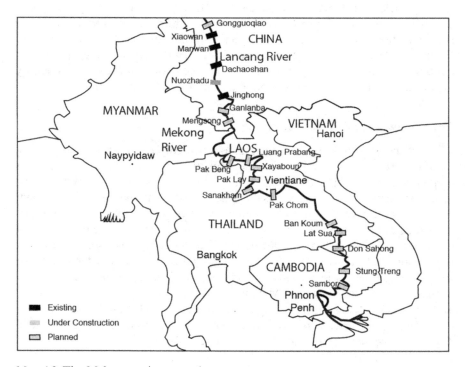

Map 4.2 The Mekong mainstream dams
Note: This map is no longer fully up to date. The Nuozhadu and Gongguoqiao Dams have by now been completed, the Mengsong Dam has been cancelled. The Xayaburi, Don Sahong, and Pak Beng Dams in Laos are under construction.
Source: author, first used in Biba (2012: 621).

Table 4.2 China's dam cascade on the Mekong River

	Elevation (m above sea level)	Dam height (m)	Installed capacity (MW)	Reservoir volume (billion m³)	Status
Gongguoqiao	1,319	130	900	0.51	Existing
Xiaowan	1,240	292	4,200	15.13	Existing
Manwan	994	132	1,500	1.06	Existing
Dachaoshan	899	120.5	1,350	0.88	Existing
Nuozhadu	812	260	5,850	22.74	Existing
Jinghong	602	107	1,750	1.23	Existing
Ganlanba	533	60.5	155	0.072	Planned
Mengsong	519	n.a.	600	n.a.	Cancelled

Source: adapted from Biba (2012: 608) and Magee (2012: 175).

dam building is likewise intended to promote rural electrification across Yunnan Province, which until today has many poor and undeveloped regions. In that sense, the dams are considered to be a tool to balance out regional disparities and support poverty alleviation. Third, China's dam building speaks to the country's important objective to cut total carbon emissions. As China in 2009 surpassed the United States as the world's biggest carbon emitter, China increasingly emphasizes the need for a low-carbon economy during the next phase of its economic development (Magee 2012: 178–183).

Possible impacts of China's dams

Large-scale dam building has been an often highly contentious undertaking worldwide (see Biswas 2012). In the Mekong case, the general arguments emphasizing the positive and negative impacts of China's dam building can be summarized as follows. On the positive side, as just mentioned, the development of a renewable energy course and the reduction of carbon and sulphur dioxide emissions can be noteworthy.[6] A more direct, and thus more frequently noted (particularly by the Chinese side) potential effect is that dams can help with flood control in the wet season and an increased downstream water supply for irrigation and navigation during the dry season, thus balancing the flood and drought patterns of the lower Mekong. This, in turn, could reduce the social and economic damage inflicted by excessive floods and droughts (Biba 2012: 609). Moreover, increased navigation capacity and enhanced regional economic development by providing a new source of energy have been mentioned (Li et al. 2011: 330).

By contrast, the list of possible negative impacts for the Mekong downstream riparian countries (MDRCs, including the four MRC member countries) is much longer. Beginning with ecological aspects, first, the weight of water impounded after the construction of large dams might lead to an increased frequency and magnitude of landslides and earthquakes, especially since China's southwest sits along the fault lines of various tectonic plates. Second, the filling of large reservoirs easily takes up several years. During this period, water is held back, resulting in massive falls in water levels during the dry season. Third, the flood and drought control capacity of China's dams is not entirely clear. As the chief purpose of (at least some of) these dams is the storage of water to generate electricity, China is likely to withhold water in the dry season to maintain its output, while it is probable that it will release water to protect the dams when huge floods occur. Consequently, the evening-out of floods and droughts mentioned before as positive might also be reversed, leading to adverse ramifications. Fourth, flow regulation also means fewer seasonal floods downstream during normal years. Seasonal floods, as noted previously, however, are critical in more than one respect. For one thing, they sustain wetlands and deposit nutrients and sediments on to the natural floodplains. Their reduction likely leads to a decline in soil fertility over wide areas of rice cultivation in the Lower Mekong Basin and, more dramatically even, may put whole ecosystems at risk. For another thing, agriculture and salinity are also affected by flow regulation. Floods usually provide a natural constraint to salt water intrusion from the sea into the delta. Fifth, and related, aquatic life adapted to the ecosystems could be seriously endangered by the alteration of the flow regime, as fish migration, for instance, could be blocked due to dam building. If the Mekong's biodiversity declined, this would likely be accompanied by falling productivity in the wild fisheries. As with soil fertility, this issue would bear a salient economic component since fishing directly affects both the region's food supply and its economic viability. Lastly, there are potential negative ramifications in the political realm. Technically speaking, China's dams on the upper Mekong enable Beijing to control the quantity of water released to the downstream countries. The dams thus represent a potentially powerful tool to exercise influence over the MDRCs and could pose a possible diplomatic threat, particularly in the absence of any formal agreements that bind China to a reasonable international water policy (Biba 2012: 609–610; Freeman 2009: 458, 462–463; Goh 2004: 3–6; and Li et al. 2011: 330).

Downstream attitudes to (China's) Mekong mainstream dam building

Given the potentially grave adverse impacts of the Chinese dams on its downstream neighbors, one might think that the latter should be opposed to Chinese dam building. This is even more the case when taking into consideration that Mekong-dependent fisheries and agriculture account for more than 50 percent of GDP in both Laos and Cambodia and employ 85 and more than 90 percent of their entire populations, respectively. In Vietnam, the Mekong Delta produces 50 percent of the country's agricultural output (including 80 percent of the its rice crops and 90 percent of its rice exports) and accounts for 50 percent of its seafood exports. For Thailand as a whole, the Mekong is relatively unimportant as compared to the other MDRCs when it comes to agriculture and fisheries. As a source for irrigating and thus for developing the country's dry and underdeveloped northeast, the Mekong's potential has more recently been recognized, though (Schmeier 2009: 34–38).

But do the MDRCs *actually* oppose China's upstream dam building? As a matter of fact, the picture is rather ambivalent and multi-faceted. In somewhat simplified terms, the fault line runs between the political and economic elites, particular the energy bureaucracies, on the one side and the common people on the other. Mehtonen (2008: 161) has fittingly summarized that

> [i]t is often argued that China builds dams on the upstream Mekong despite the opposition of the downstream countries. Particularly the media have reported the situation as if the downstream nations wished China to stop the damming. However, the opposing voices represent mostly the civil society and the NGOs,[7] and not the national governments. Actually, all of the Mekong countries are involved in the plans for regional power trade, in which the Yunnan province of China will be a net exporter.

Current energy requirements, and even more so expected future demand, particularly in the form of electricity, appear to make MDRC governments – that is, as far as they can be regarded as a monolithic bloc (compare Chapter 3) – primarily see the positive effects of China's dams. Annual growth rates in electricity demand in a period from 2000 to 2020 are expected to range from 6.3 percent in Thailand, 8.5 percent in Laos, and 9.7 percent in Vietnam to 12.1 percent in Cambodia (Kuenzer et al. 2013: 577). Therefore, Thailand has since the outset of China's hydropower planning shown great interest in electricity imports from China's upstream dams. A memorandum of understanding signed by Thailand and China specifies Thailand's purchase of annually up to 3,000 MW generated by Chinese dams by 2017 (Menniken 2007: 108). Furthermore, Thailand was said to plan on funding hydropower projects on Chinese stretches of the Mekong, although this plan failed in the end. In addition, Vietnam – depending up to 40 percent on hydropower – imports hydroelectricity largely from China, and increased these imports in 2006 in order to avoid shortages during the dry season (Mehtonen 2008: 165–166; also see Eyler 2014).

In the MDRCs themselves, hydropower development has been under consideration since the 1950s, but due to several reasons such as wars, a lack of finance, political risk, difficult geography, and environmental concerns, very little has actually been materialized (Matthews 2012: 393). All this has begun to change, though. Apart from growing electricity requirements, it has also seen better opportunities to proceed with large-scale development due to decreasing dependence on multilateral funding provided by international institutions (such as the World Bank and the Asian Development Bank) in the light of potent private investors which has led the MDRCs to nowadays find themselves on the verge of heralding the start of a whole new era of dam building in the lower basin, too (Grumbine et al. 2012: 4).

China has played a considerable two-fold role in lower Mekong dam building as well. For one thing, China's dam building upstream has set an important precedent for the MDRC governments, true to the motto: "When you build mainstream dams, why can't we?" For another thing, Chinese companies have been among the very key investors in downstream development projects. According to estimates, up to 40 percent of the proposed mainstream and tributary hydropower schemes in coming years in the MDRCs will be implemented by Chinese companies. These schemes include four mainstream dams – three in Laos (Pak Beng, Pak Lay, Sanakham) and one in Cambodia (Sambor) (Hirsch 2011 and International Rivers 2014; also see Map 4.2).

As a result of the initiated trend, eight dams are currently planned on the lower Mekong mainstream and three, the Xayaburi, Don Sahong, and Pak Beng Dams in Laos, have even begun their initial construction phases. Additionally, apart from the nearly 40 dams already built on the lower Mekong tributaries, another 89 dams are in their planning or construction stages (Kuenzer et al. 2013: 567, 573). While the two poorer MDRCs of Laos and Cambodia are the ones who seek to rush ahead with large-scale dam building (Laos in particular seeks to become the "Battery of Southeast Asia"), Thailand and Vietnam are the key energy consumers in the sub-region (accounting for 96 percent of the projected MDRC power demand by 2025) and are therefore estimated to buy almost 90 percent of the power to be produced by the mainstream projects in Laos and Cambodia (ICEM 2010: 8). In fact, large power trade deals among the MDRCs (plus China and Myanmar) have already been signed in the background. Frequently, big companies in Thailand and Vietnam now also get involved in financing dam projects in the export market of Laos primarily, with the latter then selling the electricity back to the former, thereby earning a lot of foreign exchange for itself and providing the former with the power needed (Kuenzer et al. 2013: 577).

Meanwhile, this beginning downstream dam-building era is at least questionable. From 2009 to 2010, the MRC commissioned the International Centre for Environmental Management (ICEM), an independent technical service center assisting governments and the private sector with sustainable development, to conduct a Strategic Environmental Assessment (SEA) of the planned lower Mekong mainstream dams in order to, among other things, evaluate their impacts, costs, and benefits. The SEA, which is publicly accessible, found that the proposed mainstream dams would likely present economic benefits for the regional power sector as well as provide stimuli for economic development in the host countries. At the same time, however, the dams would entail permanent losses in aquatic and terrestrial biodiversity, also resulting in increasing food insecurity for millions of people. The livelihoods of at least 2.1 million would be degraded, more than 100,000 people would have to be resettled. Consequently, and most significantly, the SEA has recommended postponing all mainstream dam building for at least ten more years (ICEM

2010). ICEM has thus been very much at odds with the Lao government, which has obviously rejected ICEM's recommendations, while the SEA itself has contributed to fueling tensions between the four MRC members. What this entire situation moreover demonstrates is a deeply embedded and hard-to-resolve conflict in the MDRCs between the imperative of economic development on the one hand, and the demand of social and ecological sustainability on the other hand when it comes to harnessing the Mekong's resources.

In general, the basin population, particularly the 52 million living in rural areas (Babel and Wahid 2009: 11), can be considered as rather poor. Indicators include the low proportion of children of primary and secondary school age actually enrolled in primary and secondary school respectively as well as the low sanitation and electricity rates. While this is not so much true for Thailand, Vietnam and particularly Laos and Cambodia still reveal great deficits in these regards (MRC 2011: 27, 31, 33, 35). In the lower basin, where more than 20 percent of the population is considered to live below the poverty line, and 15 percent is undernourished, agriculture provides food security and livelihoods for approximately 60 percent of the basin population. As a second mainstay besides agriculture, the inland fisheries of the Mekong basin, among the largest in the world, are a main occupation for the basin population and supply most people with their primary source of protein. Fisheries not only provide food security, though, they also support tens of thousands of businesses, ranging from the shops and food stalls that supply fishing families to boat builders and fishing gear suppliers (MRC 2017e and 2017g). However, the population of the lower basin has already grown by 14 percent in just about 10 years around the turn of the millennium and is predicted to grow to over 100 million by 2025 (MRC 2011: 13). This population growth will put additional pressure on the Mekong's resources in the future.

While MDRC elites tend to argue that dam building will also benefit the poor, local communities supported by civil society and NGOs have vividly countered these claims through slogans like: "I want to eat fish. I cannot eat electricity" (Earth Rights International 2009). By and large, however, the winners in this conflict – as the sheer number of current hydropower development projects in the Mekong proves – are more and more represented by powerful actors favoring the economic side of the equation; the losers, particularly local livelihoods and the environment, by contrast, are increasingly left behind.

An illustrative example of this situation is related to Thai energy investments in Laos. The state-owned Electricity Generating Authority of Thailand (EGAT), both entrenched in Thai politics and involved in the funding of Mekong dams in Laos, has an organizational structure that champions investment over politically more challenging alternatives such as energy savings. In its dual and almost monopolistic role as both key supplier and single distributor of electricity in Thailand, EGAT has a vested interest in high energy demand to generate revenues, thus driving hydropower development. Strong domestic civil society, however, is deflecting Thailand's hydropower investment towards Laos. There, Thai investments are enabled by Laos' week enforcement of laws, a lack of capacity to regulate development, the existence of corruption, and a tightly controlled state without strong civil society. As a result, dams are being constructed rapidly and without regard to long-term water resources planning and potential multi-use benefits (e.g., irrigation and reservoirs that support fisheries and tourism). In such an environment, in reverse, it can be quite hard for critics of the dams, such as NGOs, to garner enough political support to stop dam building or, at least, to push for adequate impact assessments, correct hydrological assessments, safe engineering, sufficient compensation and support for relocated people, and consideration of the effects of the dams on the fisheries, biodiversity, and livelihoods in the region (Matthews 2012).

Importantly, China has led in setting this entire machinery going through its upstream dams built first. China's financial engagement in, and moral support for, several downstream dams further contributes to tipping the scales in favor of hasty economic development at the likely expense of local livelihoods and environmental sustainability.

China and Mekong rock blasting

China's dam-building activities have clearly constituted the country's main thrust in its Mekong hydro-politics. One more aspect is also worth mentioning, though. China in the early 2000s engaged in blasting rocks and rapids in the Mekong, even outside its own territory, in order to clear the way for its trading vessels to reach new markets in the MDRCs, thereby also promoting the development of its southwestern provinces of Yunnan and Guangxi (also see previous chapter). Initially, this happened with Myanmar, Laos, and Thailand's consent as the four countries also signed an "Agreement on Commercial Navigation on the Mekong-Lancang River" in 2000 (Schmeier 2009: 32). Yet, after Thai fishermen protested against the Chinese blasting of rapids between Thailand's northern ports of Chiang Saen and Chiang Khong, the Thai government stepped in and Beijing eventually stopped its actions – at least on Thai territory (Perlez 2005). Additionally, Cambodia and Vietnam asserted that they were not consulted or even properly informed about the others' agreement, although they are the two countries in several ways most affected by upstream actions (Keskinen et al. 2008: 93). More recently, plans to dynamite Mekong rocks have been revived between China and Thailand (RFA 2017). The idea still is to make the Mekong more navigable for commercial shipping. In this regard, it also fits that China has been pushing hard for enhanced law enforcement through joint river patrols on the Mekong in recent years, as the river has seen increasing security problems related to extortion, robbery, drug smuggling and people trafficking (*China Daily USA* 2016; also see Chapter 7).

What follows next is a first concrete example of the controversial role played by the Chinese actions along the Mekong River.

The 2008 Mekong flooding

While activist groups and NGOs seem to be mostly on the losing end in their struggle against large-scale dam building in the Mekong, this does certainly not mean that they did not try to at least raise awareness of the potentially negative impacts of dam building in the basin. Consequently, activist groups and NGOs in the MDRCs have also differed from their governments in so far as they have repeatedly criticized Chinese dam building on the Mekong mainstream. As a matter of fact, these non-state circles have maintained that the coming online of China's first four mainstream dams between 1992 and 2010 has every time coincided with extreme water levels in the river (SMC 2010: 2). While the events in spring 2010, constituting the most severe crisis to date, will be in the focus of the following two chapters, the events surrounding a Mekong flooding that occurred in summer 2008 after the completion of the Chinese Jinghong Dam represent a demonstrative prelude to what would happen two years later.

In August 2008, flood conditions in the Lower Mekong Basin were among the most extreme ever recorded. As usual, floods did not occur in the entire lower basin, but were this time confined to its northern parts in Laos and Thailand. While conditions in the south were even below average, the north recorded water levels on the mainstream that were the highest since 1966 – and for some areas even higher. In Laos, where in particular the area between Luang Prabang and Vientiane was concerned, more than 32,000 households were affected (e.g., evacuations and electricity cuts) and 28,500 hectares of rice and other crops were damaged. Moreover, livestock losses were considerable, as was damage to infrastructure, particularly roads, bridges, and irrigation systems. The monetary loss was estimated at US $56 million, by far the highest figure since systematic damage assessments began in the early 1990s. In northern Thailand, where at least seven provinces were hit, financial loss remained modest (around US $6.5 million); farmland was nevertheless damaged. Besides, some 2,300 villages were afflicted by the high water levels, disaster zones had to be established and thousands of medical aid kits were distributed (*Asia Times Online* 2008; *Nation* 2008; and MRC 2009: 37–8, 58, 60, 62).

In this situation, local communities and environmental activists, mostly through and often at least indirectly supported by regional media outlets, started to blame Chinese dams for at least worsening the flood situation. After all, the flood hydrology in the northern lower basin is largely determined by water out of China and China's Jinghong Dam on the Mekong mainstream had begun generating hydropower only in late June the same year (*Xinhua* 2008). The Thai newspaper *Bangkok Post* was leading the coverage skeptical of the Chinese dams and reported extensively. On 16 August, an article referred to a campaign coordinator with the Bangkok-based NGO Towards Ecological Recovery and Regional Alliance (TERRA), saying that "the current flooding was proof that Chinese dams could not prevent flooding downstream as the Chinese government had claimed." Later, the article reached the conclusion that "[a]lthough it can't be said for sure if the Chinese dams were to blame for the inundation, they are certainly contributing to the ecological and hydrological changes in the river" (*Bangkok Post* 2008a).

This interpretation was more or less repeated two days later, on 18 August, when another article read that "[e]nvironmentalists say the construction of dams on the river in China and the clearing of reefs to allow navigation by large cargo vessels have also contributed to the flooding" (*Bangkok Post* 2008c). On 21 August, the newspaper then published a piece headlined "Chinese dams still blamed for floods." In it, several Thai farmers and fishermen reported that the 2008 floods had been different from previous seasonal flooding, as fluctuations in water levels had occurred very fast and had not always been in line with rainfall patterns – something unprecedented and likely caused by China's dams (*Bangkok Post* 2008e). Were interpretations until this point rather cautious, a new level of critique was then reached on 25 August. That day, an article's subheading stated quite straightforwardly, "China's dams pose a serious threat to Mekong river countries" (*Bangkok Post* 2008f).

In Laos, arguably affected worse by the flooding than Thailand, criticism of the Chinese dams was not as pronounced. Laos, though, does not have an active NGO environment or a developed civil society, which could act as a voice on behalf of affected villagers. The media, moreover, are state-controlled.[8] That locals in Laos nonetheless had similar suspicions about China's dams as their Thai neighbors was revealed by a report from the Bangkok-based Asia section of the *Inter Press Service*, a global news agency, from 9 September. The report cited a 38-year-old Vientiane resident with the words that "even though there was no concrete evidence to support the accusation, many people believe China was behind the severity of the recent floods" (*Inter Press Service* 2008). The resident went on,

> I disagree with the dam construction upstream as it will affect peoples downstream, but it is difficult to prohibit China to do so because China is not member of Mekong River Commission and we don't have the power to bargain with them. I am worried we might face even worse floods over the next years.
>
> (Ibid.)

Similar voices critical of Chinese dams were not heard from further downstream Cambodia and Vietnam at the time, perhaps primarily because the two countries were not affected by the flooding. Scattered pieces covering the flooding and mentioning Chinese dams could be found in news platforms with a wider regional outreach, though. Most notably among them, a report in the Hong Kong/Thailand-based *Asia Times Online*, published on 23 August, sought to uncover the hydro-politics behind the crisis. Headlined "China damned over floods," the piece first repeated the accusations on the part of Thai villagers and activists to be read in the *Bangkok Post*. In addition, the article criticized China's "lack of transparency" regarding its dam operation. At the end, the article arrived at the conclusion that "[w]hat is certain is that there have been ecological and hydrological changes in the Mekong River since the construction of the Chinese dams" (*Asia Times Online* 2008).

Meanwhile, the governments of the two countries affected, Thailand and Laos, as well as the MRC came to very different findings about the reasons for the flooding. The MRC rejected any correlation between the floods and the Chinese dams. A first statement issued on 15 August argued that

> [t]he current water levels are entirely the result of the meteorological and hydrological conditions and were not caused by water release from presently operating Chinese dams which have storage volumes far too small to affect the flood hydrology of the Mekong.
>
> (MRC 2008a)

An MRC Technical Paper on the flood situation published two weeks later, on 1 September, took the same line and emphasized that

> [t]he potential role of the three existing mainstream reservoir storages in Yunnan on the volume and peak discharge of major floods in the northern areas of the Lower Mekong Basin is insignificant. In other words, they do not have the capacity to materially modify natural flood conditions.
>
> (MRC 2008b: 8)

The Lao National Mekong Commission as well as several leading politicians in Thailand and Laos seconded the MRC assessment (LNMC 2008). For example, then Thai Prime Minister Samak Sundaravej was quoted as having said that "the water runoff was caused by an excessive amount of rainfall, not discharge from Chinese dams" (*Bangkok Post* 2008a). The Director General of Thailand's Water Resources Department followed suit and held that it was "not right to blame the dams in China for the flooding" (*Nation* 2008). And the Lao Deputy Chief of Water Resources said that "[b]laming China [for the flooding] without solid evidence would only hurt relations between the two countries" (RFA 2008).

That the MRC seemed to lean towards China earned the organization a real storm of criticism on the part of activist groups. A coordinator with the Chiang Mai-based local NGO Living River Siam said, "[w]e can't accept that the MRC, which is representative of the four countries, has given untrue information to help protect China" (*Bangkok Post* 2008b). Another activist, this time with the Thai Chiang Khong Conservation Group, was certain that the MRC had not "disclosed the whole truth about the flooding" (*Bangkok Post* 2008b). In another statement, the Thai People's Network on Mekong pointed to the "contradicting roles played by the MRC" during the flooding due to the release of "incomplete information" and "insist[ed]" that the MRC examine the reasons for the crisis more closely (TPNM 2008). More precisely, the statement posited that

> [w]e believe that the water in China has significant impact on the water flow and the hydrology of the lower Mekong, especially in the Chiang Rai province, Thailand. Nevertheless, cooperation and a flood alarm system among MRC, China, and the lower Mekong countries have completely failed to protect people living along the Mekong River.
>
> MRC's assertion that Chinese dams have storage volumes far too small to affect the Mekong hydrology is shameful, as it misses an issue central to the present disaster and suffering faced by people living in the lower Mekong countries, whom MRC is supposed to serve.
>
> (Ibid.)

At some point during the flooding, on 20 August, the *Bangkok Post* also mentioned that the MRC had actually turned to the Thai foreign ministry for help in its request for further information from China regarding its dam management – after China had apparently not responded satisfactorily to the MRC (*Bangkok Post* 2008d). The same day, it was additionally reported that MDRCs were contemplating asking China for warnings on water releases from its dams (TNA 2008). However, during all of this, China remained markedly silent. Publicly, no statements reacting to the accusations were to be heard or read. Cooperation behind the scenes was obviously meager as well; otherwise, the MRC would not have had a reason to ask for the help of the Thai foreign ministry. Apparently, China did not see the need to defend its activities or, at least, clarify its position by providing its own take on the reasons for the flooding. After only about 10 days, criticism of the Chinese dams, at least as far as publicly perceivable, receded – together with the floods.

While only a relatively short episode, the 2008 Mekong flooding nonetheless revealed a lot about Mekong hydro-politics in general as well as upstream-downstream interactions and China's behavior more specifically. On the one hand, the 2008 events re-emphasized the divisions and factions existent among the various downstream actors when it comes to (China's) dam building in the Mekong. Whereas the Thai and Lao governments as well as the MRC did, at least publicly, not leave room for any doubt that the Chinese dams had nothing to do with the flooding, activist groups and NGOs, frequently supported by the media, blamed the Chinese dams at least for not preventing the flooding, but rather aggravating it. On the other hand, the events likewise demonstrated the power constellations behind Mekong hydro-politics. As the most upstream and most powerful riparian country, China did what it also used to do before when cautious downstream mumblings about its dam building and possible adverse impacts could be heard, such as in 2004 (*Asia Times Online* 2008). China fully ignored both the blame and requests for more transparency, while waiting patiently until criticism petered out.

Nevertheless, the 2008 flooding was the first time that MDRC public concern over China's Mekong dams really entered the limelight in connection with extreme water levels on the river. In the next crisis not even two years later (see the two following chapters), Chinese dams were again in the spotlight of downstream criticism. This time, the scale and intensity of the accusations would be much higher and China had to think twice whether it could afford to continue following its preferred approach of sitting things out or whether it better make some modifications to its strategy.

China – the *potential* Mekong upstream hegemon

China's geographical upstream position and activities to date clearly demonstrate its role as the Mekong's single key riparian country. Possibly the most interesting fact in light of this constellation is that China's hydro-politics in the Mekong has witnessed both conflict *and* cooperation. On the one hand, the realist narrative of China as an upstream hegemon disinclined to cooperate (see Chapter 1) is certainly supported by a few empirical findings. First, China has displayed constant reluctance to join the Mekong's prime governance body, the MRC. Consequently, China has also not signed any agreement on water allocation or water quality protection with the MDRCs. The reason for China's aloof attitude towards the MRC, obviously, is that the organization, given its regulations, would quite likely constrain China's freedom of maneuver if it did join the body, and China does certainly not see why it should willingly let this happen. This is true in particular in view of a second aspect that backs the realist argument, namely, China's dam building. Driven largely by domestic motivations, China is not only the only riparian country to have completed mainstream dams in the Mekong to date, more critically, while building dams, China has continuously proceeded in a highly non-transparent and fully unilateral way, that is, without negotiation or at least consultation. Despite the potentially grave negative impacts of upstream dams for downstream countries, China has in fact never informed the MDRCs *ex ante* on its dam-building plans or, once online, on the operation schemes of the dams. Rather, China has solely, and steadfastly, pointed to what it considers to be the positive effects of its dams, especially the evening out of flood-drought patterns and, more broadly speaking, increased development opportunities. In this regard, it has moreover been very convenient for China that MDRC elites have increasingly revealed a similar take on large-scale dam building as China.

On the other hand, however, the realist perspective on China as an unrestrained upstream hegemon absolutely uncooperative remains incomplete and has to be supplemented. Indicative of this argument are instances where China has in fact cooperated irrespective of its advantageous geographical position and material superiority (see Chapter 3). For one thing, while China has rejected becoming a full member of the MRC, it has, from early on, agreed to be a dialogue partner. To be sure, being a dialogue partner implies a rather loose connection between China and the MRC, without any binding rules to abide by for the former. Nonetheless, accepting a dialogue partnership was a Chinese free decision and cooperative move which shows at least some interest on the part of China in having a channel for contact and for exchanging issues of concern with the MDRCs. What good such contact can bring for the MDRCs became obvious in 2002 when, for another thing, China approved the signing of an agreement for providing its downstream neighbors with hydrological flood season data. From a Chinese perspective, this cooperation move was certainly reactive in nature and only occurred after a disaster had inflicted human losses and the MDRCs had requested those data from China. Nevertheless, it was likewise a voluntary political gesture for which the Chinese have not sought compensation and which militates against the portrait of a relentless and across-the-board uncompromising Chinese upstream hegemon.

Meanwhile, it should also be clear that the cooperative side of Chinese behavior is unlikely to originate from altruistic feelings. As the episodes on China's rapid blasting and joint river patrols suggest, China certainly has its own national interests in mind as well when it comes to collaborating with the MDRCs. In fact, these two episodes also show that China has been relatively cooperative in areas where MDRC collaboration has essentially been indispensable for China. Notably, these areas actually go beyond narrow water resources management issues.

Sadoff and Grey (2002) have defined and distinguished between four different kinds of benefits of cooperation on international rivers. These are (1) benefits to the river, referring primarily to joint environmental management of the river; (2) benefits from the river, meaning the sharing of the economic productivity of river flows, for example in terms of hydropower generation or agricultural production; (3) benefits because of the river, when political tensions are reduced in light of international river cooperation; and (4) benefits beyond the river, describing regional integration through infrastructure, markets, and trade, with the river as catalyst. When judging China's Mekong hydro-politics against these four different kinds of benefits, it is striking that while China has neglected benefits *to* the river, it has all the more sought to generate benefits *from* the river. Further, as the previous chapter has illustrated, China has been highly interested in benefits *beyond* the river, for example through the Greater Mekong Sub-region. By pursuing the creation of benefits from and beyond the river, both for itself and the MDRCs, China has moreover aimed at producing benefits *because* of the river as well.

Altogether, then, China's hydro-political approach has not only been driven largely by domestic concerns, it has also been perfectly in line with its overarching foreign policy goals and their implementation when it comes to Southeast Asia (see Chapter 3). More precisely, China has, generally speaking, followed an economy-driven approach towards the MDRCs, putting a premium on markets and investment, and this approach has been reflected in China's Mekong hydro-politics as well. Moreover, China has cared about being perceived as a good and friendly neighbor by the MDRCs. As elaborations in the previous chapter have shown, in the period from the launch of China's Mekong dams in the 1990s to 2008, China's approach has largely been successful from an overall perspective on China–MDRC relations. China's uncooperative behavior in some hydro-political regards, most obviously its mainstream dam building, did not really mar this generally positive impression. For one thing, MDRC elites were, and continue to be, largely favorable of China's dams, in particular the resulting opportunities for energy trade. For another thing, local communities and activist groups opposing the Chinese dams, did not immediately have the means and clout to do so emphatically. In other words, at least until 2008, China's foreign policy vis-à-vis the MDRCs could easily afford to be uncooperative in certain hydro-political areas.

Conflicts alongside cooperation – this is the essential feature of China's Mekong hydro-politics as carved out by this chapter. In sum, it might therefore best be argued that China is a *potential* Mekong upstream hegemon in the realist sense. Most of the time, China has indeed pursued unilateral activities and uncooperative policies. Moreover, nobody has the means to stop China from taking any upstream actions it desires. However, time and again, China has also clearly deviated from this attitude. Even though these deviations have largely been reactive, that is, driven by the MDRCs, they yet indicate that China's Mekong hydro-politics is more complex than what the upstream hegemon narrative would have us believe. At the same time, China's hydro-political behavior has certainly been in sync with China's overarching foreign policy objectives as well as with its overall foreign relations vis-à-vis the MDRCs and Southeast Asia more broadly. The subsequent analysis of the relatively severe spring 2010 Mekong crisis will help paint a yet more detailed and comprehensive picture of China's hydro-political behavior in the Mekong.

Notes

1 Interestingly, as later chapters will show, China itself says it accounts for only 13 to 13.5 percent of the Mekong's entire flow.
2 It should be noted, though, that the MRC has been undergoing some restructuring lately. Details of this restructuring remain sketchy as of now, but obviously the MRC seeks to focus more on "riparianization" and "decentralization" (see Hunt 2016a). The reasons for this will be dealt with further below in this chapter.
3 For a valuable introduction on the concept of Integrated Water Resources Management, see Rahaman and Varis (2005).
4 To put this number in perspective, the hydropower potential of the Mekong basin is significantly lower than what is estimated for the Brahmaputra mainstream and its five main tributaries, whose 110,000 MW are the second highest in China following the Yangtze River Basin (Rahaman and Varis 2009: 70). Yet, the Mekong's potential is higher than, for example, the Salween's, which approximates 36,000 MW (Brown and Xu 2010: 785).
5 At the same time, plans exist for a second and less-known cascade, this one on the upper reaches of the Lancang (i.e., upstream of the first cascade) and probably comprising more than ten dams (Magee 2012: 177–17). One of them, the most downstream at Miaowei, was in May 2013 approved by China's National

Development and Reform Commission (Industrial Info Resources 2013). According to Fan et al. (2015), there are actually five dams of this upper cascade under construction now.
6 Notably, though, it has also been argued that large-scale dam building can contribute to the release of large amounts of methane, as organic material from formerly forested but now flooded land accumulates and decomposes in the dam reservoirs (Johnson-Reiser 2012).
7 This applies particularly to Thailand, where civil society is well developed and NGOs are very active as compared to Vietnam and Laos where such groups are highly constrained. Cambodia falls in between (Hirsch and Jensen 2006: 49–50).
8 Be reminded that Thailand around this time was still fairly democratic and had quite a free media system.

References

Adamson, P., and Bird, J. (2010) "The Mekong: A Drought-prone Tropical Environment?" *Water Resources Development*, 26(4), 579–594.
Asia Times Online (2008) "China Damned over Floods," 23 August, www.atimes.com/atimes/Southeast_Asia/JH23AeO2.html.
Babel, M., and Wahid, S. (2009) "Freshwater under Threat: Southeast Asia. Vulnerability Assessment of Freshwater Resources to Environmental Change (Mekong River Basin)," Bangkok: United Nations Environment Programme, Asian Institute of Technology, www.unep.org/pdf/SEA_Water_report.pdf.
Backer, E. (2006) "Paper Tiger Meets While Elephant. An Analysis of the Effectiveness of the Mekong River Regime," *Fridtjof Nansen Institute*, FNI Report 15, 2006.
Backer, E. (2007) "The Mekong River Commission: Does It Work, and How Does the Mekong Basin's Geography Influence Its Effectiveness," *Journal of Current Southeast Asian Affairs*, 26(4), 31–55.
Bangkok Post (2008a) "MRC Defends China over Thai Floods: Mekong Basin Flooding Worst in 100 Years," 16 August, www.livingriversiam.org/4river-tran/4mk/mek_ne93.html.
Bangkok Post (2008b) "Warnings on Floods Faulted: MRC Bulletins 'Not Reaching' Villagers," 17 August, www.livingriversiam.org/4river-tran/4mk/mek_ne95.html.
Bangkok Post (2008c) "Flood Warnings for Provinces in Isan," 18 August, www.livingriversiam.org/4river-tran/4mk/mek_ne96.html.
Bangkok Post (2008d) "Mekong Floods: China Asked for River Info," 20 August, www.livingriversiam.org/4river-tran/4mk/mek_ne99.html.
Bangkok Post (2008e) "Chinese Dams Still Blamed for Floods," 21 August, www.livingriversiam.org/4river-tran/4mk/mek_ne100.html.
Bangkok Post (2008f) "Mekong Shows Its New Face," 25 August, www.livingriversiam.org/4river-tran/4mk/mek_ne105.html.
Biba, S. (2012) "China's Continuous Dam-building on the Mekong," *Journal of Contemporary Asia*, 42(4), 603–628.
Biswas, A. (2012) "Impacts of Large Dams: Issues, Opportunities and Constraints," in C. Tortajada, D. Altinbilek, and A. Biswas (eds.), *Impacts of Large Dams: A Global Assessment*, Berlin and Heidelberg: Springer Verlag, 1–18.
Brown, P., and K. Xu (2010) "Hydropower Development and Resettlement Policy on China's Nu River," *Journal of Contemporary China*, 19(66), 777–797.

China Daily USA (2016) "China, Laos, Myanmar, Thailand Complete Joint Patrol on Mekong River," 24 July, http://usa.chinadaily.com.cn/world/2016-07/24/content_26201702.htm.

Dore, J., and K. Lazarus (2009) "De-marginalizing the Mekong River Commission," in F. Molle, T. Foran, and M. Kakonen (eds.), *Contested Waterscapes in the Mekong Region: Hydropower, Livelihoods and Governance*, London: Earthscan, 357–381.

Earth Rights International (2009) "I Want to Eat Fish. I Cannot Eat Electricity: Public Participation in Mekong Basin Development," http://d2zyt4oqqla0dw.cloudfront.net/sites/default/files/publications/I-Want-To-Eat-Fish.pdf.

Elhance, A. (1999) *Hydropolitics in the 3rd World: Conflict and Cooperation in International River Basins*, Washington DC: United States Institute of Peace Press.

Eyler, B. (2014) "The Coming Downturn of China-Vietnam Trade Relations," *East by Southeast*, 9 July, www.eastbysoutheast.com/fear-change-future-china-vietnam-trade-relations/.

Fan, H., D. He, and H. Wang (2015) "Environmental Consequences of Damming the Mainstream Lancang-Mekong River: A Review," *Earth Science Reviews*, 146, 77–91.

Freeman, J. (2009) "Taming the Mekong: The Possibilities and Pitfalls of a Mekong Basin Joint Energy Development Agreement," *Asian-Pacific Law & Policy Journal*, 10(2), 453–481.

Fox, C., and C. Sneddon (2007) "Transboundary River Basin Agreements in the Mekong and Zambezi Basins: Enhancing Environmental Security or Securitizing the Environment?" *International Environmental Agreements: Politics, Law and Economics*, 7(3), 237–261.

Goh, E. (2001) "The Hydro-politics of the Mekong River Basin: Regional Cooperation and Environmental Security," in T.H. Tan, and K. Boutin (eds.), *Non-traditional Security Issues in Southeast Asia*, Singapore: IDSS, 468–506.

Goh, E. (2004) "China in the Mekong River Basin: The Regional Security Implications of Resource Development on the Lancang Jiang," *Working Paper No. 69*, Singapore, Institute of Defence and Strategic Studies, www.rsis.edu.sg/publications/WorkingPapers/ WP69.pdf.

Grumbine, E., J. Dore, and J. Xu (2012) "Mekong Hydropower: Drivers of Change and Governance Challenges," *Frontiers in Ecology and the Environment*, 10(2), 91–98.

Ha, M. (2011) "The Role of Regional Institutions in Sustainable Development: A Review of the Mekong River Commission's First 15 Years," *Consilience: The Journal of Sustainable Development*, 5(1), 125–140.

Habich, S. (2016) *Dams, Migration, and Authoritarianism in China: The Local State in Yunnan*, London and New York: Routledge.

Hirsch, P. (2011) "China and the Cascading Geopolitics of Lower Mekong Dams," *The Asia-Pacific Journal*, 9(20), www.japanfocus.org/-Philip-Hirsch/3529.

Hirsch, P., and K. Jensen (2006) "National Interests and Transboundary Water Governance in the Mekong," Australian Mekong Research Centre, University of Sidney, in collaboration with Danish International Development Assistance (DANIDA), http://sydney.edu.au/mekong/documents/mekwatgov_mainreport.pdf.

Hunt, L. (2016a) "Mekong River Commission Faces Radical Change," *The Diplomat*, 22 January, http://thediplomat.com/2016/01/mekong-river-commission-faces-radical-change/.

Hunt, L. (2016b) "Drought Fans Tensions Along the Mekong," *The Diplomat*, 12 March, http://thediplomat.com/2016/03/drought-fans-tensions-along-the-mekong/.

Hunt, L. (2016c) "New Laos Dam Heightens Mekong Fears," *The Diplomat*, 11 November, http://thediplomat.com/2016/11/new-laos-dam-heightens-mekong-fears/.
Hunt, L. (2017) "Can ASEAN Save the Mekong River?," *The Diplomat*, 5 May, http://thediplomat.com/2017/05/can-asean-save-the-mekong-river/.
Industrial Info Resources (2013) "China Huaneng Group's Lancang River Miaowei Hydropower Station Receives Approval from NDRC," 12 June, www.industrialinfo.com/news/article.jsp?newsitemID=235880&qiSessionId=3523EA66E0707BF1C7AE37C81F31FB41.wolf.
International Centre for Environment Management (ICEM) (2010) "MRC Strategic Environmental Assessment of Hydropower on the Mekong Mainstream," www.mrcmekong.org/assets/Publications/Consultations/SEA-Hydropower/SEA-Main-Final-Report.pdf.
International Rivers (2014) "China's Overseas Dam List," www.internationalrivers.org/resources/china-overseas-dams-list-3611.
Inter Press Service (2008) "Laos: Questions Rise With Worst Floods in Decades," 9 September, www.livingriversiam.org/4river-tran/4mk/mek_ne106.html.
Jacobs, J. (2002) "The Mekong River Commission: Transboundary Water Resources Planning and Regional Security," *The Geographical Journal*, 168(4), 354–364.
Johnson-Reiser, S. (2012) "China's Hydropower Miscalculation," *China Brief* 12(11), www.jamestown.org/single/?tx_ttnews%5Btt_news%5d=39423&no_cache=1#.VRFIFlrgq2w.
Keskinen, M., K. Mehtonen, and O. Varis (2008) "Transboundary Cooperation vs. Internal Ambitions: The Role of China and Cambodia in the Mekong Region," in N. Pachova, M. Nakayama, and L. Jansky (eds.), *International Water Security: Domestic Threats and Opportunities*, Tokyo: UNU Press, 79–109.
Kuenzer, C., I. Campbell, M. Roch, P. Leinenkugel, V. Q. Tuan, and S. Dech (2013) "Understanding the Impact of Hydropower Developments in the Context of Upstream-Downstream Relations in the Mekong River Basin," *Sustainability Science*, 8(4), 565–584.
Laos National Mekong Committee (LNMC) (2008) "Lower Mekong Flood Update," 26 August, www.lnmc.gov.la/index.php?option=com_content&view=article&id=31:lower-mekong-basin-flood-update&catid=2:inter-news&Itemid=8.
Li, Z., D. He, and Y. Feng (2011) "Regional Hydropolitics of the Transboundary Impacts of the Lancang Cascade Dams," *Water International*, 36(3), 328–339.
Magee, D. (2012) "The Dragon Upstream: China's Role in Lancang-Mekong Development," in J. Öjendal, S. Hansson, and S. Hellberg (eds.), *Politics and Development in a Transboundary Watershed. The Case of the Lower Mekong Basin*, Heidelberg, London and New York: Springer, 171–193.
Matthews, N. (2012) "Water Grabbing in the Mekong Basin – An Analysis of the Winners and Losers of Thailand's Hydropower Development in Lao PDR," *Water Alternatives*, 5(2), 392–411.
McCartan, B. (2008) "China Damned over Floods," *Asia Times Online* 23 August, www.atimes.com/atimes/Southeast_Asia/JH23Ae02.html.
Mekong River Commission (MRC) (1995) "Agreement on the Cooperation for the Sustainable Development the Mekong River Basin," www.mrcmekong.org/assets/Publications/agreements/agreement-Apr95.pdf.

Mekong River Commission (MRC) (2008a) "Press Statement on Current Mekong Flood Situation," 15 August, www.mrcmekong.org/news-and-events/news/press-statement-on-current-mekong-flood-situation/.
Mekong River Commission (MRC) (2008b) "Flood Situation Report, August 2008," *Technical Paper* 21 (September), www.mrcmekong.org/assets/Publications/technical/tech-No21-flood-situation-report2008.pdf.
Mekong River Commission (MRC) (2009) "MRC Annual Flood Report 2008," September, www.mrcmekong.org/assets/Publications/basin-reports/Annual-Mekong-Flood-Report-2008.pdf.
Mekong River Commission (MRC) (2011) *Planning Atlas of the Lower Mekong River Basin*, Phnom Penh and Vientiane: Mekong River Commission.
Mekong River Commission (MRC) (2017a) "The Mekong Basin: Physiography," www.mrcmekong.org/the-mekong-basin/physiography/.
Mekong River Commission (MRC) (2017b) "The Mekong Basin: Hydrology," www.mrcmekong.org/the-mekong-basin/hydrology/.
Mekong River Commission (MRC) (2017c) "The Mekong Basin: Climate," www.mrcmekong.org/the-mekong-basin/climate/.
Mekong River Commission (MRC) (2017d) "The Mekong Basin: Natural Resources," www.mrcmekong.org/the-mekong-basin/natural-resources/.
Mekong River Commission (MRC) (2017e) "Topics: Agriculture & Irrigation," www.mrcmekong.org/topics/agriculture-and-irrigation/.
Mekong River Commission (MRC) (2017f) "Topics: Climate Change," www.mrcmekong.org/topics/climate-change/.
Mekong River Commission (MRC) (2017g) "Topics: Fisheries," www.mrcmekong.org/topics/fisheries/.
Mekong River Commission (MRC) (2017h) "Topics: Flood & Drought," www.mrcmekong.org/topics/flood-and-drought/.
Mekong River Commission (MRC) (2017i) "About the MRC: Governance and Organisational Structure," www.mrcmekong.org/about-mrc/governance-and-organisational-structure/.
Mekong River Commission (MRC) (2017j) "About the MRC: Upstream Partners," www.mrcmekong.org/about-the-mrc/upstream-partners/.
Menniken, T. (2007) "China's Performance in International Resource Politics: Lessons from the Mekong," *Contemporary Southeast Asia*, 29(1), 97–120.
Mehtonen, K. (2008) "Do the Downstream Countries Oppose the Upstream Dams?" in M. Kummu, M. Keskinen, and O. Varis (eds.), *Modern Myths of the Mekong. A Critical Review of Water and Development Concepts, Principles and Policies*, Helsinki: Helsinki University of Technology, 161–172.
Nation (2008) "Dams in China Not to Blame for Flooding," 16 August, www.nationmultimedia.com/national/Dams-in-China-not-to-blame-for-flooding-30080709.html.
Perlez, J. (2005) "In Life on the Mekong, China's Dams Dominate," *New York Times*, 19 March, www.nytimes.com/2005/03/19/international/asia/19mekong.html.
Radio Free Asia (RFA) (2008) "Laos Flood Kills 4, Recedes," 20 August, www.rfa.org/english/news/laos/flood-08202008203620.html?searchterm=mekong+flood.
Radio Free Asia (RFA) (2017) "The Mekong Part 4: Blasting the Rapids in Thailand," 27 January, www.rfa.org/english/thailand-mekong-01272017104723.html.
Rahaman, M., and O. Varis (2005) "Integrated Water Resources Management: Evolution, Prospects and Future Challenges," *Sustainability: Science, Practice, & Policy*, 1(1), 15–21.

Rahaman, M., and O. Varis (2009) "Integrated Water Management of the Brahmaputra Basin: Perspectives and Hope for Regional Development," *National Resources Forum*, 33(1), 60–75.

Sadoff, C., and D. Grey (2002) "Beyond the River: The Benefits of Cooperation on International Rivers," *Water Policy*, 4(5), 389–403.

Save the Mekong Coalition (SMC) (2010) "Drought Brings Severe Hardship to Riverside Communities, Demonstrates Need for Regional Cooperation to Protect Mekong River," *Statement*, 14 March, www.savethemekong.org/admin_controls/js/tiny_mce/plugins/imagemanager/files/StMStatement14.3.10.pdf.

Schmeier, S. (2009) "Regional Cooperation Efforts in the Mekong River Basin: Mitigating River-related Security Threats and Promoting Regional Development," *Austrian Journal of Southeast Asian Studies*, 2(2), 28–52.

Song, T. (2010) "Remarks at the First MRC Summit," 5 April, Thailand, Hua Hin, www.mrcmekong.org/news-and-events/speeches/first-mrc-summit-5/.

Suhardiman, D., M. Giordano, and F. Molle (2012) "Scalar Disconnect: The Logic of Transboundary Water Governance in the Mekong," *Society & Natural Resources: An International Journal*, 25(6), 572–586.

Thai News Agency (TNA) (2008) "Mekong Countries May Ask China for Warning on Water Release," 20 August, http://mathaba.net/news/?x=603223.

Thai People's Network on Mekong (TPNM) (2008) "Mekong Flood, MRC's Roles, Dams in China, and a Failed Alarm System," *Statement*, 16 August, www.livingriversiam.org/4river-tran/4mk/mek_ne94.html.

Xinhua (2008) "China Completes New Hydropower Station," 19 June, www.livingriversiam.org/4river-tran/4mk/mek_ne70.html.

Yoffe, S., A. Wolf, and M. Giordano (2003) "Conflict and Cooperation over International Freshwater Resources: Indicators of Basins at Risk," *Journal of the American Water Resources Association*, 39(5), 1109–1126.

5 The spring 2010 Mekong crisis, part one
China faces criticism

Introduction

The previous two chapters have discussed China's relations with the Mekong downstream riparian countries (MDRCs, i.e., Laos, Thailand, Cambodia, and Vietnam), thereby moving from more general aspects of the relationship to those more specifically concerned with hydro-politics. In doing so, the two chapters have shown that on the one hand, the MDRCs – together with the broader Southeast Asian sub-region to which they belong – are fairly relevant for the pursuit of China's overall foreign policy objectives, while on the other hand cooperation and conflict have co-existed when it comes to China's hydro-political approach towards the MDRCs. This chapter now is the first of two to present, in a very detailed way and embedded in the larger regional international relations context, a crucial case study of China's Mekong hydro-politics through the prism of securitization theory. This case study is the spring 2010 Mekong crisis, during which the water levels in wide stretches of the lower river sank to a record low and the Chinese dams on the upper reaches of the Mekong mainstream received much of the blame for this situation.

While the next chapter will comprehensively dissect the Chinese reactions to the spring 2010 Mekong crisis and in particular to the blame put on its dams, the task of this chapter is to introduce this crisis in the first place, thus laying the focus on the MDRCs. The chapter not only discusses the magnitude of the crisis, its possible reasons, and the impacts on the people dependent on the river's resources. It also, and in fact primarily, outlines and subsequently analyzes the harsh criticism of the Chinese dams which were considered to be a potential cause for the low water levels. This criticism, in theoretical terms understood and analyzed as attempts at securitizing China's dam building, mainly came from activist groups and NGOs across the MDRCs and was echoed – if not often also supported – by several media inside and outside the Mekong basin. In other words, the criticism of the Chinese dams was put forth by non-state actors. But what did state actors in the MDRCs think of the criticism? Their view on the crisis was likewise important and cannot thus be neglected. Consequently, the chapter also looks at the MDRC governments' and the Mekong River Commission's (MRC) takes on the spring 2010 situation and how these state actors responded to the accusations of the Chinese dams. The primary goal of this chapter as a whole is to depict the spring 2010 Mekong crisis as an unprecedented challenge to China's Mekong hydro-politics, evoking a set of sensitive security concerns on the part of MDRC actors and putting China's positive image in the Mekong and beyond at risk. The chapter therefore also sets the scene for China's response to be discussed in the next chapter.

Finally, it is noteworthy that this chapter makes use of a wide set of primary sources, mostly English news articles from various Mekong regional and US outlets as well as public documents issued by activist groups and the MRC, in order to trace the process of events. This use of English sources – in contrast to sources using the respective national languages – might be seen as controversial at first sight. However, it makes sense because those involved in, or intended to be drawn into, the crisis came from different countries. Through the use of English, it could be ensured that everybody would get the messages directed at each other. Moreover, the chapter benefits from a number of interviews the author held with local activists and NGO employees, journalists, university professors, experts from think-tanks, as well as MRC and government officials in the MDRCs during the fall of 2012.

The spring 2010 record-low water levels in the lower Mekong and their impacts

From January to April 2010, water levels in the lower Mekong, that is, downstream of China and Myanmar, shrank dramatically. According to the MRC, water levels in the Mekong widely sank even below those of the previous 1993 record low. More precisely, an MRC news release from 26 February 2010 concerning the situation read,

> [t]he current water level on the mainstream Mekong River is significantly below average in Northern Lao PDR and Thailand. Levels at mainstream measuring stations [...] are below those that occurred in the low flow season of 1993 [...] All mainstream water levels measured north of Stung Treng [Cambodia] are significantly below the average for this time of year and are expected to decrease further for another month.
> (MRC 2010a)

This situation brought along various negative consequences for the MDRCs and, more specifically, the people living in the Lower Mekong Basin. Broadly speaking, the impacts included fewer fish catches, less water for irrigated agriculture, livestock, and drinking, and suspended river transportation affecting trade and tourism (Middleton 2011: 17). More than 20 million people were reportedly facing water shortages (*Voice of America* 2010d).

A more precise look at each of the four MDRCs separately reveals the following picture. In Thailand, the low Mekong water levels affected at least

14,000 villages (*New York Times* 2010). In early March, 18 districts in Chiang Rai Province in northern Thailand and bordering the Mekong were declared disaster zones, with damages caused to farm crops worth Bt19.3 million (around US $0.6 million) (*Nation* 2010a). Water trucks had to be dispatched to Thailand's four northeastern provinces in order to help local authorities provide assistance (*Nation* 2010c). Moreover, boat and ferry services around Chiang Rai, both cargo and tourist, had to be suspended. This led to a 20-percent decline in tourists (*Nation* 2010b) as well as to the fact that cargo worth an estimated US $4.6 million was left stranded on Thai stretches of the river (*Asia Times Online* 2010a).

In Laos, whose northern provinces belong to the country's poorest and were hit particularly hard, the low Mekong water levels resulted in a 50 percent reduction in the water supplied to the Lao capital Vientiane (*Voice of America* 2010a). This was because water shortages were so severe that the situation exceeded the capacity to pump up enough water for treatment to supply the city (*Voice of America* 2010b). In Luang Prabang, a popular tourist destination in northern Laos, there were also reports of drinking water shortages, with only the tourist areas in the city center receiving 24-hour service. However, not only drinking water was affected. Several irrigation projects encountered insufficient water inflow because the river level was falling too rapidly, with 10 cm per day. As a result, some 3,680 hectares of rice fields were affected in the districts of Hadxaifong and Pakngum (close to Vientiane) alone (*Vientiane Times* 2010a). What is more, the boat association in Luang Prabang Province had to announce that cargo boats and slow boats for tourism had to stop running (*Vientiane Times* 2010b). This put local boat owners out of business, as the association lost around US $2,000 a day according to their own estimations (*Vientiane Times* 2010c).

In Cambodia, media coverage of the situation was scarce. However, a senior representative of the Cambodian National Mekong Committee (NMC) remembered that in early 2010, there were impacts in terms of water shortages as well as on rice crops. According to him, the Cambodian Ministry of Water Resources and Meteorology had to intervene and have water pumped onto the rice fields. Moreover, the International Red Cross provided additional rice to the people affected (Interview 4 November 2012).

All the way downstream in Vietnam, finally, the low water levels caused the Mekong delta coast to dry up (*Thanh Nien News* 2010a). According to the Vietnamese Institute of Irrigation, there was saltwater in areas situated from 50 to 70 km off the sea as early as late January. This worsened the serious salinization of the soil and threatened 620,000 hectares of winter-spring crops – an area accounting for 40 percent of the delta's total rice growing area (*Inter Press Service* 2010b). Besides, one-third of the population in the delta's countryside was in dire need of fresh water for consumption, and locals had to buy fresh water at extremely overrated prices (*Thanh Nien News* 2010b).

Blaming the Chinese dams

The extremely low water levels and its corollaries gradually turned into a regional crisis. However, while it was unambiguous that the Mekong carried far too little water in the spring of 2010, the cause of this situation was up to heated debate. This was still the case when the author toured China and the MDRCs in summer and fall 2012, that is, more than two years after the crisis. Some observers, both in China (also see Chapter 6) and the MDRCs, attributed the low water levels solely to mother nature, that is, to the after-effects of a severe drought aggravated by very little rainfall and, possibly, climate change. For example, a scholar at the Yunnan Academy of Social Sciences explicitly highlighted that any accusations of the Chinese dams playing a role in the 2010 low water levels could "not be sustained by the facts" (Interview 27 August 2012). This view was generally backed by (semi-)officials in the MDRCs. A Thai former ambassador in the region underlined that it was very difficult to prove whether Chinese dams played a part in the sinking water levels or whether it was actually water from Mekong downstream tributaries getting less. He also mentioned deforestation in northern Thailand as a possible contributing factor (Interview 8 October 2012). A senior representative of the Thai NMC emphasized that Thailand had *de facto* received more water during the dry season since the Chinese dams had been operating (Interview 10 October 2012). A senior representative of the Cambodian NMC concurred, arguing that "the 2010 situation was not caused by Chinese dams" and referring to the fact that China contributes only 16 percent to the Mekong's runoff (Interview 4 November 2012). Notably, though, it was not only MDRC officials that could identify with this standpoint. One professor at the University of Chiang Mai, a city in northern Thailand, for instance, stressed that drought issues in northern Thailand happened every year and that this was simply part of the normal seasonality (Interview 11 October 2012).

Meanwhile, others – not necessarily rejecting the drought explanation entirely – held that China's mainstream dams on the upper reaches, particularly the dry season filling of the Xiaowan Dam, were at least a contributing factor. Two local activists with Living River Siam, a Chiang Mai-based NGO, for example, presented data of Mekong water levels measured by the grouping around the time of the crisis. These data indicated a temporary 40-cm increase of water levels in the weeks following the lowest point on 24/25 February. The problem with these rising water levels, however, was that there was no rainfall at all during the time. Also, in its news release from 26 February 2010 mentioned before, the MRC (2010a) had stated that water levels were "expected to decrease further for another month." For the two activists, it was therefore clear that the Chinese dams must have released water. Who released water, however, might also have impounded it in the first place, so the two activists' thinking (Interview 12 October 2012). While both the exactness and correctness of their data should be treated with some caution, it is yet quite noteworthy that the MRC apparently – but not officially – observed a similar phenomenon of fluctuating water levels at the time. As an MRC hydrologist conceded, from February to April 2010 there first was a huge drop and then a slight increase in water levels. This pattern, according to the hydrologist, was likely triggered by dam activities of water storage and water releases (Interview 6 November 2012). An MRC donor representative, moreover, was likewise suspicious of the Chinese dams. As he described,

> [t]here is some incoherence involved in Chinese statements about their upstream dams: On the one hand, the Chinese say, "we are not affecting you with our dams; our dams don't have an impact." On the other hand, however, they also say, "our dams affect you in a positive way by releasing water in the dry season."
>
> (Interview 16 October 2012)

As a matter of fact, the actual role the Chinese dams played in the spring 2010 situation has remained somewhat inconclusive until today. Nonetheless, local communities directly affected by the low water levels, regional and international activist and NGO groups committed to sustainable development, and the media inside and outside the Mekong region certainly did at the time launch a week-long series of harsh criticism of China's dams. One important reason was the high degree of mistrust of China prevalent among many in the MDRCs, caused in part by China's continuous non-transparency about its dam-building activities (Interview 16 October 2012). However, ultimately, it was not even decisive whether or not the Chinese dams on the Mekong mainstream actually aggravated – or even triggered – the 2010 conditions. What did matter, though, were perceptions. As a senior riparian MRC staff member aptly explained, "How many people know about the hundreds of tributaries along the Mekong and their role for hydrology? Not many. But everybody knows about the Chinese dams" (Interview 24 October 2012). Consequently, the following sections outline the blame the Chinese dams received. They do not ask in how far this blame was justified.

Blame coming directly from activist groups and NGOs across the MDRCs

During the spring 2010 Mekong crisis, various activist groups and NGOs across the MDRCs were at the forefront of advocating local communities' concerns and criticizing the Chinese dams. Above all, it was the Save the Mekong Coalition (SMC) that took on the leading role. The SMC itself is a network of NGOs, community groups, academics, journalists, artists, fishers, farmers, and ordinary people both from within the Mekong countries and internationally. It can be seen as the Mekong activists' "umbrella mechanism." While the views of many activists were repeatedly cited in a large number of news articles during the crisis (see below), the SMC also issued its own public statements that blamed the Chinese dams for the low water levels at the time.

The first of these statements came out on 14 March 2010 when the crisis was already going on for some time. It first stated that "[t]he Mekong River is facing an increasingly severe drought that holds serious implications for riverside communities and the wider population of the Mekong region" (SMC 2010a: 1). Importantly, however, a connection was also drawn between the drought and China's mainstream dams, particularly the filling of the then recently finished Xiaowan Dam. In this regard, the statement read,

> China began filling the reservoir of the Xiaowan Dam [...] in October 2009. This timing, and the subsequent drop in downstream flows, coincides with the MRC's identified onset of the drought [...] It is not surprising that communities in downstream countries are suspicious of the Lancang dams' contribution to the current drought. Changes to the Mekong River's daily hydrology and sediment load since the early 1990s have already been linked to the operation of the Lancang dam cascade by academics [...] These dams in China have been built without consultation, apology, disclosure of data, compensation or restitution, all of which are now long overdue. The first turbine of the Manwan dam – the first dam built on the Lancang – came online in 1992, coinciding with the 1992–1993 Mekong drought. Construction of the second Lancang dam was completed in October 2003, coinciding with the 2003–2004 drought. Construction of the third dam, Jinghong, was completed in late 2008. The Xiaowan Dam, presently filling its reservoir, has a reservoir capacity approximately five times larger than that of the combined storage of these three earlier dams. The role that these dams played in earlier droughts has never been clarified or communicated; instead the facts have often been muddied.
>
> (SMC 2010a: 2)

The statement therefore made it very clear that, in view of the SMC, there was a conspicuous temporal coincidence between the spring 2010 low water levels in the Mekong and China's dam-building activities on the upper reaches of the river, with the latter very likely aggravating the former. What was more, even, the SMC also claimed that such a coincidence did not occur for the first time, but had in fact happened before when China engaged in similar activities (also see the 2008 flooding discussed in Chapter 4). The SMC did not leave it at that, though. Rather, in the following weeks, the SMC stepped up its efforts to raise more awareness of the situation and its possible causes. On 1 April, 190 representatives from civil society, academia, media, and government agencies met at Chulalongkorn University in Bangkok for the SMC "Public Forum on Sharing the Mekong Basin." On the agenda were, among other things, the drought and the potential role of the Chinese dams (SMC 2010b, 2010c). The forum report later revealed that many participants again blamed China's dam building. As an illustrative example, the report referred to a Thai activist working with International Rivers, a US-based

NGO struggling to protect rivers, who had opined that "dams in the Mekong basin had greatly disturbed the river ecosystem, resulting in a loss of fisheries, aquatic life, as well as flood and drought. [Especially,] the river had behaved unnaturally since dams were built upstream in China" (SMC 2010c: 3).

Two days later, on 3 April, a public protest in front of the Chinese embassy in Bangkok was organized under the SMC roof and a letter of complaint, open and available online, for the attention of the Chinese premier and government was handed over. The introduction letter to the letter of complaint highlighted that

> [s]ince the People's Republic of China built four dams on the upper Mekong River, the people in downstream countries, namely Burma, Laos, Thailand, Cambodia and Vietnam, have suffered impacts on their ecosystems, food security, culture, economy, and society. The People's Republic of China has constantly ignored the petition letters from affected downstream communities.
>
> (SMC 2010d)

The actual letter of complaint, headlined "Stop Mekong mainstream dams: Let the Mekong flow freely," was then once again very straightforward in making the causal link between China's Mekong dams and the spring 2010 low water levels, this time also directly accusing the dams of having quite severe security impacts (SMC 2010e). This letter of complaint must be seen as the climax of SMC criticism of China's dams during the Spring 2010 crisis. Therefore, several parts of the letter deserve to be quoted in some length. At the beginning, the letter emphasized that

> these dams have spurred a drought crisis on the mainstream Mekong River in 2010, such that even the assumption that *"dams assist to prevent dry rivers in dry season and control flooding"* is not true anymore. Actually *"[d]ams can't control flooding and dams cause rivers to become dry."* It is these dams that have caused the water level to rise and fall rapidly and abnormally both during the flood and dry seasons. The dams have caused huge impacts on ecosystems, natural resources, food security, cultures, social well-being, local economies, trade and tourism in the lower Mekong countries.
>
> (SMC 2010e: 1; emphases in original)

As in the earlier statement published on 14 March, the letter also made a concrete reference to previous crisis situations in the Mekong, especially the 2008 flooding. For that event, the authors of the letter likewise saw a connection between China's dams and the extreme water levels. The letter thus stressed that

> [f]or over a decade, [the Chinese] Government's development plan for the upper Mekong River (Lancang Jiang) has had many impacts on the

people who live downstream along the river. Specifically 4 dams, the Manwan (1996), Dachaoshan (2003), Jinghong (2008), and Xiaowan (started storing water and the first turbine's operation in September 2009) caused the largest flood disaster in the past 40 years in August of 2008.
(Ibid.)

The letter then continued on a more general note, pointing at the assumed unnecessity and unfairness of the Chinese Mekong dam-building projects, benefiting the few and adversely affecting the many. Precisely, the letter read,

[a]ll of us who live downstream have suffered the disaster caused by your dam development project, whilst the electricity generated by these dams is sent to China's Eastern Industrial Area and the profit gained by Huaneng Company. [...] This demonstrates that the Chinese Government is willing to seize a common property resource shared by all the people who live along the Mekong River and allot it for the benefit of a few people.
(Ibid.)

At the end of the letter, the SMC finally directed its concern into the future, for which it saw even greater potential disasters on the horizon:

Finally, we raise our concern over a potentially devastating consequence of building dams on the upper Mekong River in China, which may cause the end of Mekong civilization itself. The large amount of water stored in the reservoirs of Dachaoshan, Manwan and Xiaowan is located on a powerful fault-line called the "Dragon's Teeth Fault" [...] If there is an earthquake, [...] it could also destroy one of these dams. Our fear here is that the massive amount of water unleashed from one dam will flow rapidly downstream breaking the dams downstream in a domino effect.
(Ibid. 2)

Apart from these self-issued statements, the views of the SMC, in the form of numerous individual voices contributing to the SMC cause, were also reported in various media outlets inside and outside the Mekong region.

Echoes of the blame in the MDRC media

Criticism of the Chinese dams was echoed in the regional media at the time. As a matter of fact, for local communities and the SMC the media therefore functioned as an important multiplier of their concerns. This was particularly the case in Thailand, where coverage from several media outlets led to a real flood of criticism, and, to a somewhat lesser degree, also in Vietnam. In Cambodia, meanwhile, criticism of China's dams was infrequent and much more cautious, while no accusations of China's dam-building activities could be found in Lao media outlets.

Thailand

In Thailand, the *Bangkok Post*, the country's most widely circulated English-language newspaper, was leading the criticism of the Chinese dams. On 25 February 2010, that is, weeks before the first official SMC statement, the *Bangkok Post* published a first editorial concerning the situation. The editorial's headline could have hardly been more outspoken, as it stated: "China's dams killing Mekong" (*Bangkok Post* 2010a). After delineating the impacts of the low water levels, the editorial first acknowledged that less rainfall might have been one of the reasons. Yet, importantly, it was also reported that

> non-governmental organisations which have been closely monitoring ecological changes in the Mekong River have been quick to point accusatory fingers at China. They blame China for storing up water, especially at the newly-completed Xiaowan hydro-electric dam, to generate electricity.
> (Ibid.)

The editorial also referred to the MRC which had "voiced serious concern about the adverse impact caused by the [Chinese] dams to the ecological system of the river basin and to the millions of people living downstream." Not hiding behind NGOs or the MRC any more, the editorial then went on and criticized China's dam-building directly and explicitly: "Beijing built the dams to harness the Mekong for its own benefit, with complete disregard for the potential adversity rendered to the river's ecological system and the livelihoods of the peoples [...] along the lower reaches of the river" (ibid.).

At the end, the editorial concluded with the bigger picture in mind, namely, that

> China has established itself as an economic behemoth. But the way it has treated its small neighbours to the south, especially regarding the use of the Mekong River, leaves much to be desired. To earn the genuine respect and recognition of these countries, China must not only act responsibly but also accountably, befitting its status as an emerging super power.
> (Ibid.)

One week later, on 4 March, the *Nation*, another widely read English-language Thai newspaper, released its first noteworthy report on the Mekong situation, in which a lecturer at Ubon Ratchathani University (near the Thai-Lao border and close to the Mekong) was referred to as having said that "[m]any people suspect that China-based dams are the main reasons the Mekong's water level has been getting so low this year." Further, "[w]hen farmers cannot rely on water from the Mekong, many of them will have to seek new jobs and change their way of life." Therefore, "China should think about the peoples of down-river countries too" (*Nation* 2010b). On 8 March, another piece published by the *Nation* stressed that "[f]armers in Laos and Thailand accuse China of saving water for local use. Civil society is greatly concerned about the impact of the three dams in China on the water level." After all, the low level made it "impossible for villagers to pump water from the canal to their farms" which entailed that they might have to "look for a job in a big city, if the water does not rise in the near future" (*Nation* 2010d).

Then, on 10 March, the *Bangkok Post* put out a second editorial. The opening paragraph of this second editorial directly came to the point and accused China of not contributing to a solution to the "current emergency," instead putting "millions of lives" in need (*Bangkok Post* 2010b). Precisely, it was argued that China was

> fast failing the good-neighbour test in the current Mekong River crisis. [...] officials in [China] are not participating in the search for solutions to this problem. It is not a new phenomenon. For close to a decade, there has been widespread criticism of China's actions along the Mekong.
>
> (Ibid.)

Since "[f]armers, fishermen and tradesmen literally depend on the river for their lives," the editorial continued that the

> trouble is China's unilateral decision to harness the Mekong with eight hydro-electric dams. [...] Since the first dams were built, the Mekong's ebbs and flows have changed. [...] What is extremely troubling and frustrating, however, is the lackadaisical and repetitious denials by Chinese officials.
>
> (Ibid.)

Another week later, on 17 March, the *Inter Press Service* also published a first relevant online article. The *Inter Press Service* is a global news agency focusing on issues such as poverty, civil society, and sustainable development and its Asia-Pacific section is based in Bangkok. Its article, which also cited parts of the second *Bangkok Post* editorial, read that

> [e]nvironmentalists and sections of the regional media are blaming the Chinese dams being built or operating on the upper reaches of the Mekong for contributing to the dramatic drop in water levels that are affecting communities [...] in the lower Mekong countries.
>
> (*Inter Press Service* 2010a)

Quoting an activist working with a Thai NGO, the same article more specifically highlighted that "[t]he local communities along the river banks in northern Thailand believe that the change in the water levels began after the Chinese dams," as the dam-building had "impacted their fisheries activity" (ibid.). On 18 March, *Inter Press Service* then shifted the focus from Thailand to the Mekong Delta and underlined in another article that

> [m]any Mekong Delta farmers [...] say that Mother Nature is not solely to blame for their predicament. They say dams – especially those built by China – [...] have caused lower water levels downstream, along with reduced river running speeds and altered ecosystems.
>
> (*Inter Press Service* 2010b)

Moreover, this second article also referred to the chairman of Vietnam's Institute for Southeast Asian Water Resources and Environment's Scientific Council as saying that

> the first impact [of Chinese dams built for the production of electricity] would be a remarkable reduction of aquatic resources and the volume of alluvium in the delta, resulting in landslides to balance the alluvial volume. It would be very dangerous for people who live in the lower section.
>
> (Ibid.)

This was followed by a third piece from the *Inter Press Service*, reporting on 24 March on the situation in Laos and quoting a farmer with the following words:

> The low rainfall last year might be a small part of the drought, but too many dams [being built] up in China should be the main cause. They need to stock up water in their reservoirs to produce electricity so they block the water.
>
> (*Inter Press Service* 2010c)

Subsequently, on 31 March, it was again the *Nation* to release another relevant piece in which previous charges were repeated and which was written by a non-staff Thai expert. This expert held that

> people have pointed the finger at China – which has already constructed several dams along the upper mainstream reaches of the Mekong, known as the Lancang – for causing the low levels of water in the downstream sections of the river. This is becoming a hot issue.
>
> (*Nation* 2010g)

The final related article in this cycle of criticizing Chinese dams from Thailand-based sources then came out on 8 April and was released by *Asia Times Online*, a popular Hong Kong/Thailand-based bilingual English–Chinese online newspaper. It stressed that "downstream Mekong communities angrily blame [China] for pushing the river to record low levels and exacerbating the worst drought they have seen in decades." Moreover, it was found that "[i]ndeed, the Mekong's erratic behavior is an emotional issue for the 65 million people who depend on it for survival" (*Asia Times Online* 2010b).

Vietnam

In contrast to Thailand, in Vietnam it was primarily one English-language media outlet that was clearly at the forefront of criticizing the Chinese dams, and this outlet was *Thanh Nien News*, one of the most important newspapers in Vietnam and based in Ho Chi Minh City, the largest city in Vietnam, situated close to the Mekong Delta. *Than Nien News* released its first piece blaming the Chinese dams in connection with the extremely low water levels in the Mekong around the time on 13 March. Bearing on a 2008 Chinese documentary about how residents in all Mekong riparian countries were "nourished by the same river," the article underscored that "the film doesn't tell you about how the dozens of dams being built upstream and how the lack of cooperation among regional nations is killing the mighty river" (*Thanh Nien News* 2010c). Another article, published on 15 March and including the subheading "Damn those dams," read, "scientists said the biggest threat to the stretch of water [i.e., the Mekong] that supplies life and sustenance to millions was the collection of upstream hydropower dams slowly sucking it dry" (*Thanh Nien News* 2010d). Moreover, the same article cited a senior research fellow with the Institute of Southeast Asian Studies in Singapore, maintaining in connection with the ongoing crisis that "the sheer scale of China's engineering to harness the power of the Mekong and change its natural flow was setting off alarm bells" (ibid.). After that, there was a two-weeks' silence.

On 29 March, the accusations resumed by asserting that it was time for China "to take responsibility for the drought and floods that they have caused, hurting people living downstream" (*Thanh Nien News* 2010e). On 4 April, Le Duc Trung, director general of the Vietnamese NMC, was quoted as saying that "any operation in the river will leave an impact. Power dams that hold water will cause certain effects" (*Thanh Nien News* 2010f). While he did not mention China explicitly, his remarks nevertheless were a rather thinly veiled criticism of the Chinese dams. Subsequently, on 5 April, another article referred to a Thai fisherman claiming that "[i]n the past few years it's been hard to catch a lot of fish because of China's dams" and demanding that "the government needs to talk to the Chinese and tell them to release the water." The article further stated that as a result of the reduced fish catch, the fisherman's income had decreased from Bt10,000 per month in previous years to about Bt3,000 (*Thanh Nien News* 2010g).

The culmination point, however, at least as far as Vietnam was concerned, was eventually reached on 9 April, when *Than Nien News* put out a final harsh piece in which it connected the assumed dots between China's dams and the crisis. The article opened by stating that "[u]pstream [...] dams could render the Mekong Delta unviable, and China's intransigence in building them and refusing to share information about their operations will negatively impact the lives of more than 60 million people" (*Thanh Nien News* 2010h).

Later in the article, two Western experts were repeatedly quoted. Under the subheading "Critics slam China's hegemonic behavior in the Greater Mekong

Sub-region," one of the experts said that it was "clear already that Chinese dam construction is having a negative impact on downstream states." However, he added, "[u]p to now China has asserted its rights but not undertaken its obligations. China must be more transparent about technical data collection." This made him conclude that "China condemns great power bullying of smaller countries, but a close look at China's behavior in the Greater Mekong Sub-region indicates that it is Beijing acting like a hegemon" (ibid.). This geopolitical note was echoed by the second expert who was quoted that "China is determined to incorporate the natural resources of the Mekong Basin into its manufacturing supply chain, expanding its political and economic influence" (ibid.).

Cambodia

In Cambodia, it was only on 6 April that the *Phnom Penh Post*, the country's oldest and a widely circulated English-language newspaper, published an article on the crisis that also brought the Chinese dams into play. Interestingly, however, this article mainly told the story of how the situation was perceived in upstream Laos and Thailand. The article first stated that "[t]he cause of the dwindling waterway is a matter of fierce debate, with activists pointing the finger upstream to China's hydroelectric dams, which they believe channel water away from the upper reaches of the Mekong" (*Phnom Penh Post* 2010b).

After that, a Lao fisherman was quoted that he and his fellow fishermen "can't even catch enough to feed ourselves." Next, referring to an activist, the article went on that "[w]ith a dozen dams proposed downstream as well as in China, […] locals were 'worrying about the threats to the ecosystem, the livelihoods and food security'." Finally, the article concluded that "[o]ver the past five years, significant changes have taken place in water-related resources, and this is likely to continue, which may put livelihoods under threat" (ibid.). That "changes" actually referred to Chinese dams remained open for interpretation, though.

On 12 April, the *Phnom Penh Post* released a second report, whose headline ran "Coalition weighs in on China's dam plans." This article opened that the Rivers Coalition in Cambodia, an alliance of local environmental groupings, had "added its voice to a chorus of regional concerns about the likely downstream impact of eight hydropower dam projects planned in China, saying they will have negative effects on Cambodian fisheries" (*Phnom Penh Post* 2010d).

Moreover, the executive director of the NGO Forum on Cambodia was referred to as having said that

> previous knowledge about the development of dams in Cambodia and other countries suggested that the series along the Mekong would severely affect the livelihoods of people living in communities along the river. […]

When a dam is built it affects the fish and so the people who rely on the fish are also affected.

(Ibid.)

Echoes of the blame in the US media

Due likely to the severity and duration of the spring 2010 Mekong crisis, media coverage went even beyond the MDRCs. In particular, many US media picked up on the topic and thus carried the criticism of the Chinese dams far beyond the Mekong region. The *Wall Street Journal* and the *New York Times*, that is, two of the most widely circulated US newspapers, as well as the *Voice of America*, the official external broadcast institution of the US government all reported on the low Mekong water levels in spring 2010 and echoed the blame put on the Chinese dams.

An online piece published by *Voice of America* on 4 March marked the beginning of US coverage on the crisis. The piece described the situation focusing on Laos, an interesting note given that from Lao media themselves no accusation of the Chinese dams could be heard. At the beginning, the article stressed that water levels were "at a record low in 6 decades" and that this situation "not only threatens the irrigation system that supplies water to dry-season rice crop [...], but also renders it impossible for [...] boats to make their routine runs on the Mekong." Notably, the report then depicted debates about the possible reasons for the low water levels as follows:

> Despite the gravity of the situation, Lao media have made no mention of the cause attributing to the drying up of the Mekong River. But environmentalists believe the major cause to be the construction of big dams in China's Yun[n]an province.
>
> (*Voice of America* 2010a)

More precisely, it was maintained in the report that "[t]hese dams allow China to regulate the flows of water downstream of the Mekong, contributing to water level fluctuation, and causing the river to dry up whenever China closes the gates of its dams" (ibid.).

Almost two weeks later, on 18 March, the *Wall Street Journal* released an opinion piece on the crisis, headlined "Frustration on the Mekong: Falling water levels reveal the hidden shoals of mistrust" (*Wall Street Journal* 2010). In the first paragraph, talking about the "worst drought in half a century," the article found that "[i]n the past such a disaster would be cause to blame heaven. This time a lot of the anger, rightly or wrongly, is directed at China." The piece then went on explaining the situation as it read,

> [t]he suspicion is that four large hydroelectric dams built along the Mekong in [China] are holding back water to benefit Chinese users at the cost of people downstream. [MDRCs] have all expressed some level of

concern to China, but their citizens, especially in Thailand, have been more forthright in pointing the finger.

(Ibid.)

The article also explicitly mentioned the *Bangkok Post* editorial headlined "China's dams killing Mekong" (see above). While the article tried not to leave neutral ground, stating the possibility that China was getting a "bum rap," it nevertheless reached the conclusion that "Beijing has only itself to blame, since its lack of transparency and cooperation has sown mistrust. China has steadfastly refused to reveal its dam-building plans until they are already underway, and ignored the expressions of concern of its neighbors" (ibid.).

This was followed by a second report by *Voice of America*, put out on 24 March and this time laying the focus on Thailand. In an interesting exception from the more frequent quotes from activists and experts, this piece stated that

[h]igh ranking officials of Thailand's Water Resources Department insist that data collected over the past five years show that the major cause of the severe drought in the Mekong River is the construction of huge dams along the river in China's Yunnan province.

(*Voice of America* 2010b)

Subsequently, the report then also referred to the activists' attitude and emphasized that

[e]nvironmentalists [...] echo Thai officials' opinion that the drought in the Mekong basin is definitely linked to Chinese dams because [...] most of the water feeding the Mekong River comes from the snow melt-down in the Tibetan region of China and, with massive dams blocking the river, that water cannot flow down[stream].

(Ibid.)

Only one day later, on 25 March, *Voice of America* upped the ante, when another article looked at the regional picture. The article referred to an SMC spokesperson saying that this was "not a natural drought," but that it rather was

the impact from the large scale infrastructure which is the dam upstream and the fishermen and farmers have been suffering from the change of the eco-system of the Mekong River very much. And they suspect that this is because of the way the damming upstream controls the water flow.

(*Voice of America* 2010c)

Another week later, the *New York Times* then also published an article covering the crisis. On 1 April, the newspaper circulated a piece with a headline that read: "Countries blame China, not nature, for water shortage" (*New York Times* 2010). The opening statement said that a "drought is causing shortages across Southeast Asia, but China is being forced to counter the perception that its dams are hijacking resources." The article continued that "despite what appears to be firm scientific evidence that low rainfall is responsible for the plunging levels of the river, not China's hydroelectric power stations," "[f]armers and fishermen in countries that share the Mekong River with China [...] have lashed out at China over four dams that span the Chinese portion of the 3,000-mile river" (ibid.). Towards the end, the article found very strong words to describe the situation in Thailand, where "water wars between farmers" were going on in order "to keep their crops alive" (ibid.).

Finally, the last US media piece on the spring 2010 Mekong crisis was again published by *Voice of America*, came out on 5 April, and put emphasis on the situation in Cambodia. This last piece first quoted a Cambodian fisherman arguing that the "river becomes lower and lower, so the fish cannot come up here." More generally speaking, the piece then read that "[v]illagers have surely noticed the lower levels, but they don't agree on how it has happened. Many blamed deforestation, or changes in nature. But environmentalists say dams on the upper Mekong, especially in China, are the cause" (*Voice of America* 2010d).

Analysis: the blame as attempts to securitize China's Mekong dam building

It is one of the central arguments of this book that China's international hydro-politics can be explained fittingly by the use of securitization theory. Therefore, how can the criticism of the Chinese dams described extensively above be understood in terms of this very theory? As outlined in Chapter 2, for individuals it is usually deemed hard to, in securitization theory jargon, "speak security" and be heard without assistance. This is even more the case in non-democratic settings like the MDRCs (with the notable exception of Thailand, at least in early 2010). Yet, advocacy for individuals feeling threatened may come in the form of activist groups and lobbying NGOs committed to effective action on environmental issues and taking on the role of what has previously been introduced as lead actors. Moreover, the media may play an important facilitative role in that it is able to multiply certain viewpoints, thereby supporting, not necessarily in an explicit way, lead actors as well as the communities and individuals behind them (also see Buzan et al. 1998: 77–79). This is exactly what happened in the spring 2010 Mekong crisis. Through their harsh criticism of the Chinese dams, actors such as the SMC and several media outlets from inside and outside the region produced quite a high number of security speech acts that as a matter of fact often followed quite a specific three-tier pattern.

First, the speech acts frequently referred to the extraordinarily low water levels in the Mekong around the time. Concrete examples mentioned above include that water levels were "at the lowest point in a generation" (*Bangkok Post* 2010a) and "at a record low in 6 decades" (*Voice of America* 2010a). This linguistic usage of superlatives was significant in that it made the situation special and gave it the feature of being something unprecedented. Being something unprecedented, however, also implied that the situation was likely to have consequences more severe than ever before, and therefore also had to be dealt with in new ways. Additional strength for this argumentation was drawn from the fact that the record-low water levels had a scientific character because they were something that could actually be measured.

Second, the speech acts linked the extremely low water levels, in part or in full, to the Chinese upstream dams. Among the most straightforward examples blaming the Chinese dams were forceful expressions such as "China's dams killing Mekong" (*Bangkok Post* 2010a) and "Damn those dams" (*Thanh Nien News* 2010d). Usually, the link between China's dams and the Mekong water levels was established by means of emphasizing a time component, that is, the concurrence of Chinese dam building and water level fluctuations. Precisely, it could oftentimes be read that water levels in the Mekong fluctuated so extremely *since* the Chinese dams had been built and begun operating. Before China had built dams, so the argument, there were no (extreme and unpredictable) fluctuations in the water levels of the Mekong. While it was hard – as stated before – to prove the exact role of the Chinese dams in the 2010 crisis, fluctuation levels can generally be shown through scientific data. Given China's non-transparency about its dam-building plans and operation schemes in addition to the water level fluctuations, it seemed almost natural for many to blame the Chinese dams.

Third, the speech acts highlighted that because of the low water levels (supposedly) caused by the Chinese dams people's livelihoods in the Mekong were being threatened. This message becomes very apparent when reiterating that the situation was seen as a "threat" for "farmers, fishermen and tradesmen [who] literally depend on the river for their lives" as well as for the "65 million people who depend on [the Mekong] for survival" and whose "livelihoods, food security and economies" have been "struck" by the "loss of fisheries, crops, livestock and drinking water," with only "few alternative means to see them through this disaster" (see above). The use of such wording without doubt conveyed a very strong message. As a matter of fact, it not only invoked security concerns, but also underlined the high degree of urgency and existentiality to find solutions to the problem. For the SMC, those solutions, most clearly framed as "demands" in its letter to the Chinese government mentioned above, were that the Chinese: (1) "stop building all dams" on the upper Mekong mainstream; (2) release data detailing the dam operation schemes as well as past hydrological records before dam building started; (3) ratify the UN Watercourse Convention (UNWC) regulating non-navigational uses of international watercourses; and (4) establish a joint committee (together with the MDRCs but also representing the affected people) whose mission it should be to manage the river in a "just and sustainable way," also revising the management of the completed dams (SMC 2010b: 2). In other words, for the SMC the solution to the problem lay in taking risk management measures today in order to avoid disaster in the future.

In sum, then, this three-tier pattern clearly identifiable in most of the speech acts launched by the SMC and echoed by the media during the spring 2010 Mekong crisis can be viewed as attempts to securitize Chinese dam building on the upper Mekong mainstream, as this activity was seen as a direct threat to downstream people's livelihoods and thus both to their food security and economic base as well as to certain traits of their culture and identity.[1] Moreover, however, it is not only noticeable *that* securitization moves directed at China's dam building were launched, but also *how intense* these moves were in their entirety. Compared to similar previous crisis situations, for example the 2008 Mekong flooding (see Chapter 4), the 2010 securitization moves by far exceeded earlier blame of the Chinese dams in terms of the number of both actors involved in making securitization moves and securitization moves themselves; the length of the time period over which such moves repeatedly occurred; the variety of sources as well as the strong and unequivocal wording the various actors made use of; and the scope of the moves, referring to past, present, and possible future scenarios.

However, in addition to treating and analyzing the accusations of China's dam building as a "united front," it is also interesting and necessary to say at least a few words on the country-specific differences with regard to such accusations. After all, it has become quite obvious that the quality of the blame put on the Chinese dams has varied across the four MDRCs. Against the backdrop that Thailand in 2010 was the only country among the four MDRCs with fairly democratic features, it did not surprise that the majority of activist groups and NGOs involved in blaming China was based in Thailand. Neither was it surprising that the Thai media landscape was most active in criticizing China. A Chinese scholar further underlined this fact by holding that Thai television stations had an enormous influence on opinion making in Thailand's rural areas around the time of the crisis and that the Thai media were also successful at instigating the Thai civil society against China's dams (Interview 22 August 2012).

Outside Thailand in the other MDRCs, criticism of the Chinese Mekong dams was generally not as intense and frequent. Importantly, however, it must be kept in mind that in a domestic environment like in Vietnam, where there is no freedom of the press, but all media are state-owned, coverage blaming China's dam building for their negative downstream impacts was almost certainly previously endorsed by the government. While Vietnam's government was much more cautious in its official statements around the time (see below), as both Vietnamese and Chinese experts concurred, it used the media to vent its displeasure with the Chinese neighbor (Interviews 19 August and 15 November 2012). In contrast, the governments of Laos and Cambodia did apparently not follow the Vietnamese example and endorse critical coverage of the role of Chinese dams in the spring 2010 Mekong crisis (again, see below; also for the respective reasons). As a result, media-released accusations of the Chinese dams generally kept within very narrow bounds in these two countries. Nevertheless, in comparison with Laos, Cambodia has an active NGO sector that also managed to get its voice heard in the Cambodian media at least occasionally. Besides, as several sources cited above have revealed, the fact that the Lao and Cambodian media largely refrained from echoing the blame of the Chinese dams did not mean that Lao and Cambodian individuals affected by the low water levels were necessarily thinking the Chinese dams had no role in the situation.

In any case, however, what ultimately mattered for China and its relevant foreign policy objectives (see Chapter 3), such as its image abroad, was the overall intensity of criticism Beijing saw itself confronted with, not so much the country-specific nuances. Consequently, what additionally increased the pressure on China certainly was the fact that critical voices of its dam building were spread beyond the Mekong and even reached the US. Country-specific differences, in turn, were more relevant for the respective reactions of the four MDRC governments, to which we will turn now.

Reactions from the MDRC governments and the MRC

The SMC not only targeted the Chinese government and its dam-building activities. The activist network also sought to draw the MDRC governments and the MRC into the situation. In particular, when the SMC protested in front of the Chinese embassy in Bangkok on 3 April and handed over its letter of complaint to the Chinese, it also presented a second letter, this one addressed to the Thai government and the MRC. This letter, among other things, pressed the Thai government and the MRC (and thus also the other three MDRC governments) to (1) "revise their stance towards the Chinese government regarding dam building on the upper Mekong River"; (2) "cooperate with other Mekong governments to urge the Chinese government to review their operation of the upper Mekong dams"; and (3) "to release the past records of the river conditions before the dams were built" (SMC 2010f).

In a similar vein, the Thai media also sought to involve the MDRC governments and the MRC and have them play a more active role in confronting China over its dam-building activities. The *Bangkok Post*'s first editorial on the crisis published on 25 February, for example, tried to provoke some government reaction, as it stressed that the

> most disturbing [aspect] about the whole tragic saga of this crucial water lifeline [i.e., the Mekong] appears to be the quiet submission to Beijing's blatant abuse of the river by governments in the region and their seeming acceptance of the consequences as a fait accompli.
>
> (*Bangkok Post* 2010a)

The editorial thus reached the conclusion that

> [u]nless the governments of the Mekong riparian countries act collectively as a single entity, there is little chance that Beijing will come to the negotiating table or be willing to part with crucial information about the dam projects and, more importantly, water management.
>
> (Ibid.)

Therefore, before turning to China's reaction to the criticism it received (see Chapter 6), the question first is what stance the MDRC governments and the MRC took on the blame coming from various non-state downstream actors and directed at the Chinese dams. This stance became obvious in numerous MDRC/MRC reactions that were similar to the criticism of the Chinese dams often transmitted via the media and overlapped with this criticism in the time period mostly from late February to late March 2010.

Reactions from the MDRC governments

The first public government reaction of any of the MDRCs came from Thailand on 7 March 2010, when several Thai media reported on then Thai Prime Minister Abhisit Vejjajiva's views on the situation, which he had voiced in his weekly television program. For one thing, the prime minister was quoted as saying that "[w]e will ask the [Thai] foreign ministry to talk with a representative from China in terms of co-operation and in terms of management systems in the region" (*Terra Daily* 2010). For another thing, he reportedly also said that he did "not think China had intentionally brought suffering to downstream countries" (*Nation* 2010c). Rather,

> [t]he cause of the current water shortage must be investigated first and Thai authorities will look up the agreements on international water management to see what they could do next [...]. It is still too early to conclude that China should be blamed for not releasing water retained upstream.
>
> (*Nation* 2010c)

Also on 7 March, a secretary to the Thai foreign ministry was quoted that Thailand was "not accusing anyone" and "blamed the drought on low rainfall across the region." Besides, the secretary stated that "[t]he help that we want to get from China is that we want to talk with them" so that Thailand can "solve the problem with them" (*Terra Daily* 2010).

The next day, on 8 March, the Thai prime minister held a meeting with China's Assistant Foreign Minister Hu Zhengyue, who was visiting Bangkok. According to the Nation (2010e), during this meeting, Abhisit told Hu that "people in [the] lower part of the river [were] worried about the drought as they have no clear information about the dams in China." Further, he said that "[i]t would be useful if there was a forum for experts to share information." After all, "China plays a significant role in the region development and I believe China does not want to see people in the lower Mekong basin are in difficulties." In addition, Thailand's Foreign Minister Kasit Piromya, who met Hu separately, argued that "countries in the lower Mekong should not blame China for the drought since 35 per cent of the river's water supply came from rain in Laos" and the "dams in China held only 4 per cent of total water in the Mekong." As a result, Kasit told reporters after his meeting with Hu that "[w]e should not blame each other but should find ways to cooperate with China for water management of the Mekong" (*Nation* 2010f).

Finally, Thailand's Natural Resources and Environment Minister Suwit Khunkitti separately largely echoed his colleagues' stance, as he said, "Chinese dams were not a big contributing factor to the drought in the Mekong basin. There are many other factors in the region that could have caused the river's low water level." Moreover, he found it "difficult to blame China, as it shares only some 15 per cent of the water flow" while "[w]ater supply to the river from Thailand and Laos is more than half of the total." At the same time, however, Suwit conceded that "[t]he problem is that we don't have sufficient information about water in Chinese dams and we also have a problem of water management." Therefore, "better solutions for water management" had to be found, "otherwise we will face drought in the dry season and flood in the wet season" (*Nation* 2010f). A few weeks later, a Thai government spokesman was quoted as once again emphasizing that "Thailand will be requesting more information, more cooperation and more coordination from China" (*New York Times* 2010).

In the other three MDRCs, public reactions from the governments were relatively sparse. But this was unsurprising given that, as illustrated above, Thailand also was the base for the most vocal activism against the Chinese dams, due to Thailand's relatively open political system. In Vietnam, in contrast, the only related statement could be read in *Thanh Nien News* on 29 March. Briefly, it informed that Vietnam's Prime Minister Nguyen Tan Dung had the intention "to talk to Chinese officials about the Mekong River and current problems with water resources on the sidelines of the [MRC] summit next month" (*Thanh Nien News* 2010e). In Cambodia, meanwhile, the *Phnom Penh Post* reported, also on 29 March, that "government officials did not believe the falling water level of the Mekong River had been caused by the construction of Chinese dams, arguing that climate change was instead to blame." More precisely, a foreign ministry spokesman was quoted as saying that "[s]ome countries say falling water levels in the Mekong River are caused by China's damming practices, but Cambodia sees it is as a result of climate change" (*Phnom Penh Post* 2010a). Besides, Cambodia's Minister of Water Resources and Meteorology Lim Kean Hor opined on 6 April that "some parts of China, Thailand and Laos are currently facing drought," adding that "the cause was low rainfall and climate change." As far as the Chinese dams were concerned, he underscored that the

The spring 2010 Mekong crisis, part one 117

"current drought situation on the upper stream is not caused by the hydropower dam projects" since "the dam projects have been studied and found not to cause any significant environmental impact" (*Phnom Penh Post* 2010c). Last but not least, no public reactions whatsoever could be heard from the Lao government. But as previously shown, there was also no blame on the Chinese dams coming from Lao-based activists or media in the first place.

Reactions from the MRC

As a matter of fact, the first official MRC reaction could be heard well before the first MDRC government responses. Only one day after the *Bangkok Post* had on 25 February released its first editorial, which can be seen as marking the beginning of publicly blaming the Chinese dams for the low Mekong water levels around the time, the MRC published a news release headlined "Drought conditions cause low Mekong water flow" (MRC 2010a). The press release first highlighted that "the river levels in Southwestern China have [just like in the MDRCs] been at their lowest in 50 years, with water flowing at only half the level that would be considered normal for February." Subsequently, the focus was turned to discussing the causes of the low water levels. Here, the news release left no doubt that

> [s]uch low water levels on the mainstream Mekong are the result of drought conditions in Northern Thailand and Lao PDR and are part of a wider regional drought being experienced upstream in Yunnan Province in China. The 2009 flood season was drier than normal with wet season river levels in Vientiane for example being among the 5th lowest levels on record in the last 98 years.
>
> (Ibid.)

Moreover, the press release brought in the aspect of equally low water levels on the Mekong's tributaries. Exactly, it stated that

> [s]tarting from that low base, analysis of the rainfall at selected hydrological stations in Yunnan, Chiang Saen and Luang Prabang has shown a consistent pattern of monthly precipitation significantly below average amounts since September 2009. [...] The very low water levels recorded at monitoring stations in the mainstream between Chiang Saen and Nong Khai show that tributaries in Laos and Thailand are not feeding as much water into the mainstream as would be expected.
>
> (Ibid.)

Following this news release was a technical report made publicly available online on 5 March. Ten pages long, the "Preliminary report on low water level conditions in the Mekong mainstream" in its first section analyzed rainfall patterns in southern China and the northern parts of Laos and Thailand. The section summed up that

> [f]rom these preliminary rainfall data, the indications are that the 2009 SW monsoon ended early. [...] The early withdrawal of the monsoon in 2009 meant that the discharges on the Mekong and its northern tributaries started to recede early in the season, drawing on what natural catchment and groundwater resources there were. Natural and groundwater storage in the northern parts of the basin are not large so a deficit situation would have arisen relatively quickly, particularly on the large tributaries in northern Lao PDR, leading to considerably reduced flow contributions to the mainstream.
>
> (MRC 2010b: 4)

After delineating rainfall patterns, the report then went on discussing water levels. Precisely, the report read,

> [a]t Chiang Saen water levels up to the end of January 2010 were above those of January 1993 [i.e., the date of the previously lowest water levels in the Mekong]. These higher levels appear to be a result of releases from dam operations upstream. Between 24 January and 23 February 2010, the levels then fell by 1 metre [...]. This reduction over a period of 3 to 4 weeks is steeper than in previous years and may be explained by drought conditions upstream, meaning that flow releases through the hydropower operations that had been evident earlier in January could no longer be sustained. Very low levels of reservoir storage have also been reported by Chinese news agencies.
>
> (Ibid.: 5–6)

Finally, the report reached the "preliminary conclusions" that

> [t]he main causes of low water levels being experienced in the 2010 dry season in the Mekong mainstream are a combination of an early end to the 2009 wet season, low monsoon rainfall and very low rainfall in the dry season which together have led to regional drought conditions.
>
> (Ibid.: 10)

In addition to the press release and the technical report, then Chief Executive Officer (CEO) of the MRC Secretariat Jeremy Bird wrote a comprehensive op-ed article published in the *Bangkok Post* on 16 March, thus following the newspaper's second editorial on the crisis. The op-ed was headlined "Low river levels caused by extreme low rainfall" (Bird 2010). It was a piece very rich in relevant information, restating and re-emphasizing the MRC position very clearly. Therefore, several passages deserve to be quoted in full length. At first, Bird once again underlined that drought, and therefore natural, conditions led to the low water levels. As he put it,

[a]nalysis of the Mekong River Commission's data reveals that the low water levels in the Mekong and its tributaries are the result of extreme natural conditions. Very low rainfall this dry season, following a particularly early end to the wet season in 2009, has led to river levels below those seen in at least 50 years. For example, at Chiang Saen in northern Thailand close to the Chinese border, the 2009 wet season ended about one and a half months early and rainfall in both September and October 2009 was more than 30 percent less than average. Rainfall in Yun[n]an province has also been low, with amounts consistently below average since August 2009.

(Ibid.)

After making this point about the causes of the low water levels, Bird turned to the supposedly negative role of Chinese Mekong dams, trying to reverse this claim. Precisely, he remarked that

[w]here hydroelectric dams have been constructed, such as on the Nam Ngum, flows downstream tend to be higher as water stored in the wet season is released for hydroelectricity production in the dry season. In Thailand, many media reports place the blame for low Mekong levels on the mainstream Chinese hydropower schemes and yet they operate in the same way, to store water during the wet season that can be used during the dry season. In the next few years, the completed storage capacity of the Chinese dams will lead to increased dry season flows downstream, perhaps as much as 40 percent more in Vientiane. At the moment however those projects that have been completed are not sufficiently large to consistently deliver such benefits.

(Ibid.)

As a result of this general assessment of the role of dams in the Mekong basin, Bird came up with two questions in relation to the Chinese upstream dams, only to answer them himself:

First, did they [i.e., the Chinese dams] in anyway reduce levels below natural conditions? The underlying trend of flow recorded at Chiang Saen for the period from the end of the wet season 2009 indicates a similar pattern to previous dry years although with a more extreme slope due to the very low rainfall conditions. [...] limited storage upstream appears to have been a constraint to further supplementing low river flows. Secondly, [is there] any scope for release of water stored upstream from last year's wet season to raise the historically low water levels? This is where further information and discussion is required, but it is important to note that China also has a common interest in raising water levels if it can to alleviate the problems being faced on its river trade route through to northern Thailand. Low volumes of reservoir storage may currently provide little opportunity to act in this way.

(Ibid.)

In light of the need for further information from China, Bird lastly sought to reassure readers that the MRC would be in touch with Beijing and that both sides would cooperate closely. As he said,

[t]he Mekong River Commission is engaging with China to better understand how dams and other human activities on the river impact on those downstream, as well as to model future changes, including the potential impact of climate change. A team of MRC modellers will be working with Chinese counterparts over the next weeks to exchange information and better analyze and understand both the current situation and longer term changes. These include increased dry season flow due to dam operation and the prospects for more extremes of flood and drought.

(Ibid.)

All in all, Bird's op-ed in the *Bangkok Post* therefore primarily echoed, but also strengthened, previous MRC arguments in other statements. In addition, however, it was striking that Bird deemed the role of Chinese dams mainly positive, particularly for the future when all dams would have reached their full operating capacities.

Last but not least, the MRC reactions were seconded by remarks coming from officials with the NMCs that coordinate the MRC's work at the national level. The most prominent example was Pich Dun, then secretary general of Cambodia's NMC, who claimed that only "[p]eople who don't know the facts put the blame on China's dams." Rather, "the falling water levels in the Mekong are caused by drought in China, Laos and Thailand" (*Phnom Penh Post* 2010a).

Analysis: rejecting the attempts at securitizing China's dam building

According to what has been delineated in Chapter 2, the MDRC governments and the MRC functioned as elite and scientific audiences respectively to the various non-state actors' attempts at securitizing China's Mekong dam building outlined and dissected above. Looking, first, at the MDRC governments, there were certainly some minor differences in their respective responses. The Thai government, to be sure, was by far the most vocal. The Vietnamese government had already used its state-owned media to vent criticism of the Chinese dams and now acted much more cautiously in terms of immediate government statements. Meanwhile, Cambodia's government representatives were the most active in defending China. And from the Lao side – no longer unanticipated – all was silent. More striking than their differences, however, was the accordance with which all four MDRC governments ultimately performed. This accordance was mainly established through the fact that MDRC governments did not (publicly) contradict each other over the crisis as well as through the way the MRC, after all a joint intergovernmental organization between the four MDRCs, responded to the blame on the Chinese dams.

Therefore, when summarizing the reactions from the MDRC governments as a whole, the picture is unequivocal. While there might have been a few private doubts about the Chinese dams, none of the four governments officially echoed, and thus accepted, the blame on Chinese dam building for the spring 2010 low water levels in the Mekong as it was expressed by local communities, activist and NGO groups, and the media. Even less so did any of the MDRC governments mention the Chinese dams in connection with a threat to people's livelihoods so that they clearly rejected the securitization attempts. Instead, the MDRC governments' official reactions generally comprised the two following aspects. First, it was frequently highlighted that the Chinese dams were explicitly *not* to blame for the low water levels. Rather, the situation was deemed to be caused by a severe drought that might have been aggravated by creeping climate change. At the same time, second, it was occasionally conceded, however, that the MDRCs did not actually have sufficient information on the Chinese dams and their operating schemes in order to be perfectly sure about the impacts of the Chinese dams on the lower basin. As a result, the MDRC governments announced the intention of asking the Chinese for help and cooperation on the matter.

The first part of this reaction from the MDRC governments, that is, the rejection of the securitization attempts, was not really unexpected. As a matter of fact, that the MDRC governments did not officially approve of and repeat the blame on the Chinese dams can be explained quite well by taking into consideration the MDRCs' bilateral relationships with China (see Chapter 3) as well as their respective elites' interests in harnessing the Mekong's resources (see Chapter 4). Briefly recollecting the key facts outlined earlier, the following must be stated about MDRC-China relations around early 2010: (1) With the notable exception of Vietnam which has long been embroiled with China in the South China Sea disputes, all MDRC governments held a rather positive view of China; (2) China had already emerged as one of the MDRCs' top traders, investors, and donors, thus becoming a crucial partner for MDRC future economic development; (3) relations between both sides were asymmetric, with much more leverage and material resources on the part of China; and (4) due to rising energy demand in their countries, MDRC governments were all involved in the plans for regional hydropower trade, in which China's Yunnan province and Chinese state-owned river developers would play critical roles.

In sum, hence, the non-state actors' interest in securitizing China's dam building – and in doing so likely antagonizing China (see Chapter 2) – was almost diametrically opposed to the governments' interest in maintaining good relations with China and reaping material benefits from this relationship. Against this backdrop, it was certainly reasonable that the MDRC governments did not easily go out on a limb and risk their relations with Beijing over dam-building issues, which were not even exactly against their own interests. As a Thai professor from Chiang Mai University summarized pithily for the Thai case, "the Thai government does not usually see a problem with China over the Mekong. It only wants to make money with China. Investment from and trade with China are more important than the river" (Interview 12 October 2012).

Against this background, what was clearly more remarkable, and therefore also more interesting, was the second part of the reaction, which – despite existing MDRC dependencies on China – in particular included cautious complaints about China's information policy on its dam-building activities as well as circumspect hopes for more future cooperation with China on hydropolitical issues. These points were certainly not made in an equally pronounced way across the four MDRC governments. Additionally, in Thailand at least, they were to some extent also caused by domestic circumstances, that is, the fact that the Thai media was "extremely influential so that there was the need for a government response" in order to calm the waves and reassure the Thai population affected by the spring 2010 conditions (Interview 3 October 2012). Nonetheless, there obviously was a widespread desire to have more coordination with China on Mekong-related water issues. This, again, was effectively proven by the MRC response.

In essence, the MRC completely followed the two-pronged MDRC governments' approach of rejecting the blame on the Chinese dams on the one hand, while simultaneously pursuing the goal of enhanced future cooperation with China on the other. How can this reaction be explained? As described earlier (see Chapter 4), the MRC is the Mekong's prime governance body and therefore has the tools and resources to gain enormous technical and scientific knowledge on the river. In a sense, it is nothing else but one of the MRC's main tasks to gather data on the river and circulate its findings, particularly during crisis situations. During the spring 2010 Mekong crisis, the MDRC governments were in dire need of more information and more data on the situation and thus put enormous pressure on the MRC so as to find out what the reasons for the low water levels were (Interview 5 November 2012). Interviews have exposed that the time pressure for the MRC was so huge that not enough data for conclusive findings could be collected (Interview 6 November 2012) because it was vital for the MDRC governments and their NMCs that the MRC quickly delivered (the right) results behind which the former could then hide (Interview 17 October 2012). The decisive factor for understanding the MRC response therefore was that the organizational set-up of the MRC prevented the body to make decisions against the will of its member states, that is, the four MDRCs, in the first place. More precisely, the MRC is an inter-governmental organization without any supranational characteristics. The MRC Secretariat, which issued the various reports on the crisis, was therefore subject to directives coming from its member countries that usually make their decisions in consensus. As a result, the MRC reaction showed that all MDRC governments championed the dual approach of not provoking China while rather seeking further engagement with the upstream neighbor. In this context, it was also significant that the MRC actually stressed the positive role of the Chinese dams in terms of the evening out of floods and droughts.

The reasons of the MDRC governments (and the MRC) for seeking more cooperation with China on Mekong-related issues, finally, were understandable, too. China is the most upstream country in the Mekong and it has been somewhat opaque about its dam-building activities, even though these activities bear potential to negatively affect the MDRCs (see Chapter 4). While, as has been elucidated, the MDRC governments have not really been opponents of the Chinese Mekong dams, even for those elites it could only be beneficial to have more information on the dams in hand – be that, for instance, to be better able to implement their own future Mekong development plans, to reassure anti-dam activists in their countries, or out of real concern. The following remarks of a Vietnamese professor from the Diplomatic Academy of Vietnam in Hanoi serve as an illustrative example of at least the Vietnamese governments' rationale at the time. As he expounded, the Mekong had become the most important issue in his country's relations with China, second only to the South China Sea dispute. In the future, it might even become the single most important issue between the two countries, as it was a "real threat" whereas the South China Sea was only a "perceived threat." Therefore, and despite the economic dependencies on China, the Vietnamese government was "quite happy" to see that the Mekong turned into a big issue in regional affairs in spring 2010, thereby raising more awareness of the problems in the basin and thus hopefully making the Chinese more cooperative in the future (Interview 15 November 2012). Meanwhile, the MRC, or at least its secretariat, has been highly interested in implementing Integrated Water Resources Management (see, for example, Rahaman and Varis 2005) of the river, which, however, is only possible when all riparian countries are members of the organization. In the past, China has several times been invited to join the MRC as a full member, but has always declined (see Chapter 4). The spring 2010 crisis was seen as a chance to use the widespread criticism of China as a chance to eventually bring Beijing closer to the MRC.

Synopsis: setting the scene for China's response

The spring 2010 Mekong crisis was unique in at least two regards. First, the degree of the low water levels in wide stretches of the river around the time was unprecedented. Therefore, the negative impacts on the people living in the basin and being dependent on the river's resources also were relatively severe as compared to similar situations in the past. Second, while there occasionally was rather cautious criticism of the Chinese dam-building activities in the Mekong prior to spring 2010, never before – or after – was the blame activist groups and NGOs as well as the media put on the Chinese dams for causing extreme water levels in the Mekong as harsh and sustained as during the spring 2010 crisis. As a matter of fact, the criticism of the Chinese dams was tantamount to attempts at securitizing China's dam building because these dams were seen as a direct threat to people's livelihoods in the MDRCs, and thus also to their food security, economic base as well as certain aspects of their culture and identity.

Additionally, the two unique features of the spring 2010 Mekong crisis were flanked by at least two other noteworthy, and even more remarkable, circumstances, namely, some ambiguities about the actual role of the Chinese dams as well as what could be seen as diplomatically smart behavior of the MDRC governments. For one thing, the actual role the Chinese dams really played in the low water levels – if they caused or aggravated the situation or if they did not contribute to it at all – could not be answered for sure during the crisis, or even until today. This is simply because the relevant data, if existent at all, have never been made public. In other words, it is still possible that the Chinese dams were criticized wrongly. The fact, however, that accusations of the Chinese dams were nevertheless as strong as they were therefore was indicative of two things: first, of the large extent to which various non-state actors in the MDRCs distrusted China and the alleged benefits of its dam building; and second, of how perceptions mattered enormously, especially in light of previous Chinese non-transparency about the operating schemes of its dams. All of this should give China pause.

For another thing, the behavior of the MDRC governments, always in combination with the MRC, showed a fair degree of diplomatic cleverness – even though this cleverness might have been somewhat unwitting because ultimately there were no real alternatives. Confronted by various MDRC-based actors with the forceful criticism of the Chinese dams and requested to support this criticism, the MDRC governments could not help but take a stand. But how to maneuver between Scylla, that is, the NGOs and activist groups as well as the media, and Charybdis, that is, China? On the one hand, the priority clearly was not to antagonize China, as this would have most likely been detrimental to the MDRC governments' own (economic) interests. Therefore, the MDRC governments refused to join in the accusations of the Chinese dams. On the other hand, however, and this was the more outstanding part of their reaction, the MDRC governments also took the crisis and the blame on the Chinese dams as an opportunity to ask, not press, the Chinese for more future cooperation. In following this dual approach, the MDRC governments were able to convey to China the message that they were intent on being, and remaining, loyal partners to Beijing, but that it would also be appreciated if this loyalty were somehow rewarded, in hydro-political terms. In other words, the MDRC governments tried to open a door for China. The question – to be answered in the next chapter – still was whether the Chinese would go through that door.

All in all, the spring 2010 Mekong crisis represented a huge challenge for China and its hydro-political approach in this important international river basin. Could Beijing still allow itself to continue with following the old approach of sitting those situations out as it had done during earlier Mekong crises such as the 2008 flooding (see Chapter 4)? Or did Beijing eventually have to change its course, at least to some extent, in order to allow for more cooperation so as to avoid more conflict? These questions certainly gained even further in importance for Beijing because the spring 2010 Mekong crisis was in fact the fourth major foreign policy problem China had to face in its relations with its Southeast Asian neighbors at the time. The other three, as previously mentioned, were the renewed flaring up of tensions in the South China Sea, Southeast Asian concerns about the imminent coming into force of the China-ASEAN Free Trade Area, and the returning focus of US foreign policy on Southeast Asia in general and the Mekong in particular.

Interviews cited

Activist, 3 October 2012, Bangkok, Thailand.
Chinese expert I, 19 August 2012, Beijing, China.
Chinese expert II, 22 August 2012, Kunming, China.
Chinese expert III, 27 August 2012, Kunming, China.
CWPF representative, 17 October 2012, Vientiane, Laos.
MRC donor representative, 16 October 2012, Vientiane, Laos.
MRC official I, 24 October 2012, Vientiane, Laos.
MRC official II, 5 November 2012, Phnom Penh, Cambodia.
MRC official III, 6 November 2012, Phnom Penh, Cambodia.
NMC Cambodia official, 4 November 2012, Phnom Penh, Cambodia.
NMC Thailand official, 10 October 2012, Bangkok, Thailand.
Thai former ambassador, 8 October 2012, Bangkok, Thailand.
Thai expert, 12 October 2012, Chiang Mai, Thailand.
Two activists, 13 October 2012, Chiang Mai, Thailand.
Vietnamese scholar, 15 November 2012, Hanoi, Vietnam.
Western expert, 11 October 2012, Chiang Mai, Thailand.

Note

1 Note that the demands made by the SMC did not (clearly) indicate actions outside the normal bounds of politics, which the Copenhagen School has championed as a condition for successful securitization under securitization theory. However, as outlined in Chapter 2, it should be kept in mind that the distinction between "normal politics" and "emergency politics" is a difficult one and that it has therefore been argued compellingly that risk management to prevent future disaster should be seen as a sufficient, and in fact more realistic, criterion (Abrahamsen 2005: 59 and Jutila 2006: 172). Further, in

this case, we are not talking about successful securitization, but, at least for now, about securitization attempts only.

References

Abrahamsen, R. (2005) "Blair's Africa: The Politics of Securitization and Fear," *Alternatives: Global, Local, Political*, 30(55), 55–80.

Asia Times Online (2010a) "When the Mekong Runs Dry," 13 March, www.atimes.com/atimes/Southeast_Asia/LC13Ae01.html.

Asia Times Online (2010b) "Mistrust Lingers Over Dams," 8 April, www.atimes.com/atimes/China/LD08Ad03.html.

Bangkok Post (2010a) "China's Dams Killing Mekong," Editorial, 25 February, www.savethemekong.org/news_detail.php?nid=93.

Bangkok Post (2010b) "Response from Beijing Needed," Editorial, 10 March, http://savethemekong.org/ news_detail.php?nid=102.

Bird, J. (2010) "Low River Levels Caused by Extreme Low Rainfall," Op-ed in the *Bangkok Post*, 16 March, www.mrcmekong.org/news-and-events/news/op-ed-low-river-levels-caused-by-extreme-low-rainfall/.

Buzan, B., O. Wæver, and J. de Wilde (1998) *Security: A New Framework for Analysis*, London: Lynne Rienner.

Inter Press Service (2010a) "Chinese Dams Blamed As Mekong Level Falls," 17 March, http://proquest.umi.com.ezproxy.lib.nccu.edu.tw:8090/pqdweb?did=1985250511&sid=2&Fmt=3&clientId=23855&RQT=309&VName=PQD.

Inter Press Service (2010b) "Salinisation, Drought Bring Worries to Mekong Delta," 18 March, www.ipsnews.net/2010/03/vietnam-salinisation-drought-bring-worries-to-mekong-delta/.

Inter Press Service (2010c) "Laos: Residents Fret Over Parched Mekong River," 24 March, www.ipsnews.net/2010/03/laos-residents-fret-over-parched-mekong-river/.

Jutila, M. (2006) "Desecuritizing Minority Rights: Against Determinism," *Security Dialogue*, 37(2), 167–185.

Mekong River Commission (MRC) (2010a) "Drought Conditions Cause Low Mekong Water Flow," 26 February, www.mrcmekong.org/news-and-events/news/drought-conditions-cause-low-mekong-water-flow/.

Mekong River Commission (MRC) (2010b) "Preliminary Report on Low Water Level Conditions in the Mekong Mainstream," 5 March, www.mrcmekong.org/assets/Publications/governance/REVISED-Report-on-low-Mekong-Flows-5mar10.pdf.

Middleton, C. (2011) "Conflict, Cooperation and the Trans-border Commons: The Controversy of Mainstream Dams on the Mekong River," Conference Paper for the 3rd International Winter Symposium of the Global COE Program "Reshaping Japan's Border Studies" "Weaving the Borders Together – Network between Japan and the World," Slavic Research Center, Hokkaido University, Sapporo, Japan, 25–27 November.

Nation (2010a) "Chiang Rai's 18 Districts Declared Drought-hit Disaster Zones," 2 March, www.nationmultimedia.com/breakingnews/Chiang-Rai-s-18-districts-declared-drought-hit-dis-30123774.html.

Nation (2010b) "Boat Services Suspended As Level of Mekong Plunges," 4 March, www.nationmultimedia.com/national/Boat-services-suspended-as-level-of-Mekong-plunges-30123903.html.

Nation (2010c) "Lower Mekong Level Endangers Giant Catfish," 7 March, www.nationmultimedia.com/national/Lower-Mekong-level-endangers-giant-catfish-30124089.html.

Nation (2010d) "Hua Hin Summit to Discuss Crisis," 8 March, www.nationmultimedia.com/national/Hua-Hin-summit-to-discuss-crisis-30124149.html.

Nation (2010e) "China's Dams Make No Impact to Upstream," 8 March, www.nationmultimedia.com/national/China-s-dams-make-no-impact-to-upstream-30124199.html.

Nation (2010f) "China Brushes Off Accusation on Dams' Effect," 9 March, www.nationmultimedia.com/business/China-brushes-off-accusation-on-dams-effect-30124233.html.

Nation (2010g) "The Lancang-Mekong: An ASEAN-China-MRC Shared Challenge," 31 March, www.nationmultimedia.com/others/The-Lancang-Mekong-An-Asean-China-MRC-Shared-Chall-30126042.html.

New York Times (2010) "Countries Blame China, Not Nature, for Water Shortage," 1 April, www.nytimes.com/2010/04/02/world/asia/02drought.html?_r=0.

Phnom Penh Post (2010a) "Low Mekong Isn't Caused by Dams: Govt," 29 March, www.phnompenhpost.com/national/low-mekong-isn't-caused-dams-govt.

Phnom Penh Post (2010b) "Fishermen Fear Financial Ruin As Mekong Continues to Ebb," 6 April, www.phnompenhpost.com/national/fishermen-fear-financial-ruin-mekong-continues-ebb.

Phnom Penh Post (2010c) "Summit Sets Mekong Agenda," 6 April, www.phnompenhpost.com/national/summit-sets-mekong-agenda.

Phnom Penh Post (2010d) "Coalition Weighs In on China's Dam Plans," 12 April, www.phnompenhpost.com/national/coalition-weighs-china's-dam-plans.

Rahaman, M., and O. Varis (2005) "Integrated Water Resources Management: Evolution, Prospects and Future Challenges," *Sustainability: Science, Practice, & Policy*, 1(1), 15–21.

Save the Mekong Coalition (SMC) (2010a) "Drought Brings Severe Hardship to Riverside Communities, Demonstrates Need for Regional Cooperation to Protect Mekong River," Statement, 14 March, www.savethemekong.org/admin_controls/js/tiny_mce/plugins/imagemanager/files/StMStatement14.3.10.pdf.

Save the Mekong Coalition (SMC) (2010b) "Agenda: Public Forum on Sharing the Mekong," 1 April, www.savethemekong.org/admin_controls/js/tiny_mce/plugins/imagemanager/files/AgendaEng.pdf.

Save the Mekong Coalition (SMC) (2010c) "Public Forum on Sharing the Mekong," Forum Report, 1 April, www.savethemekong.org/news_detail.php?nid=97.

Save the Mekong Coalition (SMC) (2010d) "Complaint on Impacts and Proposal about Dams on the Upper Mekong River in China," Introduction Letter, 3 April, www.savethemekong.org/admin_controls/js/tiny_mce/plugins/imagemanager/files/LetterToChina3.4.10.pdf.

Save the Mekong Coalition (SMC) (2010e) "Stop Mekong Mainstream Dams: Let the Mekong River Flow Freely," Third Complaint to the Chinese Government, 3 April, www.savethemekong.org/admin_controls/js/tiny_mce/plugins/imagemanager/files/StattoChina3.4.10.pdf.

Save the Mekong Coalition (SMC) (2010f) "Let the Mekong Flow Freely," Statement to the Thai Government and the MRC, 3 April, www.savethemekong.org/admin_controls/js/tiny_mce/plugins/imagemanager/files/StattoThaiMRC3.4.10.pdf.

Terra Daily (2010) "Thailand Wants China's Help with Mekong Drought: PM," 7 March, www.terradaily.com/reports/Thailand_wants_Chinas_help_with_Mekong_drought_PM_999.html.

Thanh Nien News (2010a) "Vietnam Delta Coast Drying Up," 25 February, www.thanhniennews.com/2010/Pages/20102259287055261.aspx.

Thanh Nien News (2010b) "Mekong Delta Faces Severe Drought, Salinity Worsens," 13 March, www.thanhniennews.com/2010/Pages/Mekong-Delta-faces-severe-drought.aspx.

Thanh Nien News (2010c) "If You Keep Adding Stones the Water Will Be Lost in the Well," 13 March, www.thanhniennews.com/index/pages/if-you-keep-adding-stones-the-water-will-be-lost-in-the-well.aspx.

Thanh Nien News (2010d) "Record-low Rivers Strand Farmers," 15 March, www.thanhniennews.com/2010/Pages/Record-low-rivers-strand-farmers.aspx.

Thanh Nien News (2010e) "China To Be Asked Mekong Questions at Regional Summit," 29 March, www.thanhniennews.com/index/pages/20100329142253.aspx.

Thanh Nien News (2010f) "China Blamed for Holding Back Important Mekong Info," 4 April, www.thanhniennews.com/index/pages/20100405102959.aspx.

Thanh Nien News (2010g) "Mekong Nations Call for China Assistance amid Drought," 5 April, www.thanhniennews.com/index/pages/20100405230431.aspx.

Thanh Nien News (2010h) "Dams Portend Grim Future for Mekong Delta: Experts," 9 April, www.thanhniennews.com/2010/Pages/20100410165640.aspx.

Vientiane Times (2010a) "Farmers Need Emergency Aid As Mekong Falls," 23 February, www.livingriversiam.org/4river-tran/4mk/mek_ne180.html.

Vientiane Times (2010b) "Shallow Mekong Stops Northern Tourist, Cargo Boats," 2 March, www.livingriversiam.org/4river-tran/4mk/mek_ne183.html.

Vientiane Times (2010c) "Slow Boat Owners Lose Millions As Mekong Drops," 4 March, www.livingriversiam.org/4river-tran/4mk/mek_ne188.html.

Voice of America (2010a) "Mekong Water Levels At Six-Decade Record Low," 4 March, www.savethemekong.org/news_detail.php?nid=99.

Voice of America (2010b) "Thai Officials Insist Chinese Dams Cause Mekong Drought," 24 March, www.savethemekong.org/news_detail.php?nid=117.

Voice of America (2010c) "Southeast Asia Drought Triggers Debate Over Region's Water Resources," 25 March, www.savethemekong.org/news_detail.php?nid=114.

Voice of America (2010d) "River Residents Watch as Mekong Shrinks," 5 April, www.savethemekong.org/news_detail.php?nid=130.

Wall Street Journal (2010) "Frustration on the Mekong: Falling Water Levels Reveal the Hidden Shoals of Mistrust," 18 March, http://www.savethemekong.org/news_detail.php?nid=111.

6 The spring 2010 Mekong crisis, part two
China responds

Introduction

The previous chapter has introduced the spring 2010 Mekong crisis. As shown, this crisis, lasting from February to April, saw extremely low water levels in wide stretches of the river, impacting on the lives of millions of people in the Mekong downstream riparian countries (MDRCs, i.e., Laos, Thailand, Cambodia, and Vietnam). In this situation, many in the MDRCs started to blame the Chinese dams on the upper reaches of the Mekong mainstream for storing water and thus causing, or at least contributing to, the low water levels. More precisely, local communities directly affected by the low water levels, regional and international activist groups and NGOs committed to sustainable development, and the media inside and outside the region launched a week-long series of statements and articles that were harshly critical of China's dam building – even though its precise role in the crisis has remained somewhat inconclusive to this day. In theoretical terms, this criticism of the Chinese dams was presented as attempts by the various non-state actors mentioned to securitize Chinese dam building, as this activity was seen as a direct threat to people's livelihoods and thus to their food security, economic base, and aspects of their culture and identity. At the same time, though, the previous chapter has also highlighted that the MDRC governments and the Mekong River Commission (MRC) did not join in the blame on the Chinese dams, but nevertheless tried to use the situation to ask China for more cooperation and coordination on Mekong-related water issues.

This chapter now turns the spotlight back on China and its Mekong hydropolitics, which was extremely challenged by the spring 2010 events. The chapter does so by focusing on China's response to the criticism it had to face during the spring 2010 Mekong crisis. In other words, the chapter portrays China as what securitization theory calls an audience to the attempts at securitizing China's dam building – similar to the role also played by the MDRC governments and the MRC (see Chapter 5). As will be exposed, China – similar, again, to the MDRC governments and the MRC – rejected the securitization moves, thereby precipitating securitization failure. However, China's response also represents a highly illustrative case study bringing out the nuances of China's hydro-political behavior and thus going much deeper than the overview as outlined in Chapter 4. Notably, China's response came in four different phases that were partly overlapping, but yet had distinctive characteristics each. Besides, these four phases covered all of the three previously identified behavioral strategies for audiences to reject securitization moves (see Chapter 2). This complexity in China's response was, *per se*, quite remarkable given China's reactions to earlier criticism of its Mekong dam building when it tended to ignore the blame until it petered out (also see Mekong 2008 flooding in Chapter 4). For each of the four phases, this chapter in a first step delineates China's exact response and then in a second step analyzes the respective response, explaining in particular the what and why. In doing so, the chapter aims not only at re-emphasizing the parallel existence of conflict and cooperation in China's Mekong hydro-politics but also at showing under what conditions and for what reasons and purposes China is willing to cooperate. Methodologically, this chapter proceeds similarly as the previous one. That is to say, it makes use of various primary sources, primarily online newspaper articles and public statements, in order to trace the process of events. Again, it also draws on a number of expert interviews to help analyze the events.

Phase One: China faces a severe drought

Chinese media coverage of what was going on in the Lancang, the Chinese stretch of the Mekong, began in early February 2010. On 4 February, the *China Daily* released a first piece describing vividly the severity of the situation in China's southwest. Precisely, the piece read, "[t]he worst drought in 50 years is leaving millions of people and animals without drinking water in Yunnan province and the Guangxi Zhuang autonomous region," and further emphasized, "[t]he drought relief department in Yunnan has declared a red alert drought emergency for the area." Moreover, the news article highlighted that "3.39 million people are short of drinking water" and that "[t]he drought has affected 1.14 million hectares of crops, resulting in direct economic losses of more than 3.6 billion yuan ($527 million) in the agriculture sector in Yunnan and Guangxi" (*China Daily* 2010a).

This article also set the tone for the following weeks. On 9 February, for example, it could be read that "[t]he worst drought in 60 years [...] has left millions of people in Yunnan province lacking drinking water [and] has also fueled forest fires and threatened local energy supplies." Getting more precise, the article went on stating that

> [t]he drought, which began in July [2009], has left 4.9 million residents and 3.34 million livestock with a shortage of drinking water. More than 2 million hectares of crops, 81.7 percent of the total, have been [a]ffected. About 534,600 hectares have been destroyed.
>
> (*China Daily* 2010b)

As a result of this situation, Yunnan

> will suffer a drop of more than 40 percent in its summer grain output. [...] It also caused six times more forest fires and a 50 percent drop in the generation of hydropower. Yunnan's rainfall since last July was 29 percent [of the average].
>
> (Ibid.)

This brief reference to a drop in hydropower generation was further underlined by quoting an official with China's Huaneng Lancang River Hydropower Company (Lancang Hydro), the developer of China's Mekong power stations, who held that "[t]he long-term drought had caused the water level [in the Mekong] to drop, which might [a]ffect the electronic plant" (ibid.).

In mid-March, the drought narrative intensified even further. On 15 March, another *China Daily* report, headlined "No end in sight to prolonged drought in south," noted that

> [s]ince last September, rainfall in Guangxi, as well as neighboring Yunnan and Guizhou provinces, has fallen to the lowest levels since 1952, said the China Meteorological Administration. Coupled with persistent high temperatures, the lack of rain has resulted in a severe drought that is affecting about 11 million people.
>
> (*China Daily* 2010c)

This was followed by yet another detailed article running the headline "Waiting for a miracle called rain" released on 18 March. This article stated that "[t]he local government has been rationing water to each household in the village since January, but just a meager amount, enough to keep everyone alive. Bathing, or for that matter even washing their faces, is out of the question" (*China Daily* 2010d).

The article then went on stressing that, according to the provincial climate center in Yunnan, the drought was "the worst in any living person's memory" and added the latest statistics from the provincial agriculture bureau, saying that the dry spell had "affected about 2 million hectares of farmland, about 86 percent of the total in Yunnan, causing more than 13 billion yuan ($2 billion) in direct economic losses." Further, it was mentioned that the bureau predicted that "[g]rain output will drop by over 50 percent and sugarcane output will be reduced by 20 percent" (ibid.).

A new aspect then gained center stage on 24 March, as another report ran the headline "Drought paralyzes power supply." While already anticipated in early February, the article declared that the "severe drought in Southwest China has [indeed] caused a drop in Yunnan province's electricity supply, as about 70 percent of the power in the province is from hydropower stations." Additionally, the article attached another series of numbers, showing that the drought had in the meantime "affected 51 million Chinese," "left more than 16 million people and 11 million livestock with water shortages," and "incurred 19.02 billion yuan ($2.79 billion) in direct economic losses" (*China Daily* 2010e).

On 28 March, finally, the drought was related to yet another issue. That is to say, several Chinese experts were referred to as making the connection to climate change. For example, one of them was quoted to "believe that the drought was a result of anomalous atmospheric currents," while another one claimed that "the year has seen anomalous climate conditions globally" and that "the drought in China is part of the phenomenon" (*China Daily* 2010f). With these statements, the first phase of China's response came to an end.

Analysis: China as a passive recipient of criticism

The first phase of China's response to downstream criticism was clearly characterized by ignoring the blame. The Chinese state-owned media did just not pick up on the blame Chinese dams received by various voices coming from out of the MDRCs and solely covered the situation from a domestic drought perspective. This attitude of ignoring criticism corresponded to Chinese behavior in previous Mekong crises, such as the summer 2008 flooding introduced in Chapter 4. Moreover, this attitude reflects what has previously been described in theoretical terms as a passive recipient audience to incoming securitization moves, which refers to the rejection of those moves by seeking to just wait criticism out (see Chapter 2).

Digging deeper into what China did during this first phase, and linking it to why China acted the way it did, a few more things are noticeable. The first aspect is about timing. China's media coverage on what it described as a very bad drought in its southwestern areas began in early February 2010, that is, around the same time when similar reports about low Mekong water levels came out in the MDRC media. There, the crucial starting point for media-circulated criticism of the Chinese dams was marked by the first *Bangkok Post* editorial released on 25 February, which accused the Chinese dams of "killing [the] Mekong" (*Bangkok Post* 2010a; also see Chapter 5). In the following weeks, China's decision makers must have been aware of the mounting criticism in the MDRCs. One piece of striking evidence in this regard is that China's Assistant Foreign Minister Hu Zhengyue visited Bangkok on 8 March and held a meeting with Thai Prime Minister Abhisit Vejjajiva, in which the situation in the Mekong was at least one of the topics, as the Thai media cited both politicians remarking on the crisis (*Nation* 2010). Yet, apart from Hu's statement (see below), which by the way did not enter the Chinese press, China's decision makers would not make or launch any public official statements about downstream criticism for roughly another four weeks until the end of March.

While it cannot be said with certainty, one possible reason for the Chinese silence on the accusations might have been the scale of the domestic drought problem that made China initially neglect the international dimension of the situation. Another possible reason might actually have been unrelated to events in the Mekong and be found in China's National People's Congress, which is annually convened in early March and upstages everything else. After all, there was not much press coverage on China's domestic drought situation during the first two weeks of March, either. Yet, neither the Congress, which ended on 14 March already, nor the domestic scale can fully explain why the downstream blame of the Chinese dams was not countered at all by the Chinese media for such a long time. Much more likely, therefore, is that China's reaction was at least partly based on a conscious call by China's government which must have known about the criticism launched downstream.

Second, apart from what China did not say, it is also quite interesting to examine what open messages China actually did send during phase one. In this regard, one thing that was particularly prominent were the numbers of, for instance, people and land affected, which were included in the majority of news articles. Those numbers, which spoke to the domestic scale of the situation, were going up steeply throughout the crisis and were thus a helpful means for China to underline the severity of what Chinese media vividly depicted as an extreme domestic drought on China's own territory as well as to highlight the enormous sufferings of China's own people. Also adding a scientific note to what was going on, for the Chinese side, it was simply clear that those numbers proved the point that the situation was caused by natural phenomena that had also taken a very high toll on China itself (Interviews 27 August and 29 August 2012).

All in all, China's silence regarding a potential negative role of its dams in the situation was not surprising. China had followed the exact same strategy in similar previous situations such as the summer 2008 flooding and, from the Chinese perspective, this strategy also seemed to have worked rather well for China in the past. Besides, as a Beijing-based Chinese scholar remarked after the crisis, given its advantageous upstream location and material superiority in the Mekong, China has not generally felt the need to discuss and justify its hydro-political strategies, including its dam building, in front of its neighbors (Interview 15 August 2012). In other words, China's early response was rooted in the image of an upstream hegemon who believed that it could sit blame out.

Phase Two: China rejects the blame on its dams

Only two days after the article bringing in climate change considerations as a reason for the severity of the drought situation in China's southwest, on 30 March, a sudden and overall shift in China's response occurred. This shift became most pronounced through the fact that the Chinese media no longer solely focused on its domestic drought conditions, but significantly, also included the foreign blame on the Chinese dams in its coverage. In fact, the Chinese media turned to countering the criticism and to denying vigorously any negative impacts of the Chinese dams on the MDRCs.

The first sign of this new strategy came out in a brief article running the headline "China taps upper Mekong water resources reasonably" (*China Daily* 2010g). In the article, it was stated that China "refut[ed] reports that construction of a dam on the Lancang River, the upper Mekong River, has caused a drop in water levels and brought drought to countries downstream." In addition, a spokesman of the foreign ministry commented that "[w]e take a responsible attitude in water resources exploration, maintaining rational and sustainable development and utilization of water resources and fully considering the concerns of countries downriver" (ibid.).

The following day, on 31 March, this stance was repeated and reinforced in another *China Daily* piece. Headlined "China denies dams worsen drought in Mekong basin," the piece first referred broadly to "[w]ater resources authorities in southwest China" who had "denied reports that China's dams on the Lancang River have exacerbated the drought in the Mekong River basin." Turning against "[s]ome conservationists in the lower-reach countries in Southeast Asia" who "had accused China of failing to release enough water in the dams, worsening drought with low river water levels downstream," the piece subsequently quoted an official with Lancang Hydro as saying that in contrast to allegations, "[s]ome dams even helped to manage water flow by storing water in the rainy season and releasing water in the dry season." Additionally, the same official emphasized that China did not "divert river water" and the dams would "not affect the total amount of water flow in the river as most hydropower stations had no reservoirs." Therefore, "[t]he amount of water flowing into and out of the hydropower stations was basically the same." In particularly mentioning the Xiaowan Dam (i.e., the dam especially blamed for storing water at the time), the official moreover highlighted that the water level in the dam's reservoir

> had fallen by 7.12 meters from the pre-dry-season level with the release of 560 million cubic meters of water to the lower reaches. [...] This could only help adjust river water flows in border areas because the Chinese section accounted for only a small amount of water flow on the whole Mekong River.
>
> (*China Daily* 2010h)

Another day later, on 1 April, *China Daily* published a report that had several experts express their opinion on the role of the Chinese dams. The first expert was the President of the International Commission of Large Dams Jia Jinsheng who at the time happened to be Chinese and found that "[t]he water reservoirs and hydropower stations on the upper reaches of the Mekong River should not be blamed for the drought in Southeast Asia." For in fact, he said, "[d]ams have been built since a century ago; in the dry season, they release water to add to the supply, while in the rainy season, they hold back water to help reduce the damage." In China, "[d]ams built on the Yangtze and Yellow rivers, two of China's longest, have been proven effective in doing both."

Moreover, he argued that "China does not channel water away from the Lancang River, and [...] all hydropower stations in Yunnan have undergone strict environmental and ecological evaluations." The article then went on to quote Liu Ning, then China's Vice-Minister of Water Resources, who held that it was "not right to say reservoirs have 'hijacked' water resources." This view was seconded by Zhou Xuewen, then head of the same ministry's planning department, stressing that "the water blocked by China's dams on the Lancang River accounts for only 3 percent of the total flow in the river, which is too little to influence the lower-reach countries in Southeast Asia." Finally, the article also brought in a foreign voice, namely, Pich Dun, then Secretary General of Cambodia's National Mekong Commission, who basically repeated what he had already told his home press (see Chapter 5). Precisely, he was referred to as having said that the "drop in the Mekong water level was caused by poor rainfall and climate change rather than dams on the Lancang River." In particular, "[t]he Mekong River Commission (MRC) has found no evidence that the dams on the upper reaches have an impact on the water flow downstream." Rather, "the water flow in lower parts of the Mekong River in the dry season was much higher after the dams were built, thanks to hydropower stations releasing water to generate power" (*China Daily* 2010i).

The same principal thrust continued in yet another article issued by *China Daily* on 3 April. Once again, the article cited domestic and international experts. This time, the first expert was Chen Mingzhong, then Director General of the Department of International Cooperation, Science and Technology with China's Ministry of Water Resources. According to him, "[t]he extremely dry weather in the lower Mekong river basin is the root cause of the reduced run-off water and declining water levels in the Mekong." By contrast, the "hydropower stations built on the Lancang River will not increase the chances of floods and drought disasters downstream, instead, [they] will considerably enhance the capacity of flood controls, drought relief, irrigation and the overall water supply for downstream countries" (*China Daily* 2010j).

Next, Ma Chaode, then Director of the Freshwater Program with the World Wide Fund for Nature in China (WWF China), was quoted as saying that "[t]he drought is a natural phenomenon in the ecosystem process and, with the climate change in recent years, and [thus speaks to] an increase in extreme weather." Therefore, it was "unfair to say this is China's responsibility." From the international expert circles, this view was echoed by a senior environmentalist with the MRC who apparently was formerly quoted by *Asia Times Online* and whose quote was now reprinted by *China Daily* with the following words: "[t]he wet season started late and ended early last year. This is why rivers such as the Mekong are experiencing low water levels" (ibid.).

With the article on 3 April, this short, but very intense second phase of China's response to downstream criticism ended. On 4–5 April, the MRC was to convene its first-ever summit meeting in Hua Hin, Thailand. China, as an MRC dialogue partner, was invited to join. However, China's second phase of response would be incomplete without mentioning another very interesting episode. It has been stated in the previous chapter that the first official Thai government reaction to activist blame of the Chinese dams for the spring 2010 low Mekong water levels occurred on 7 March, about two weeks after the release of the first *Bangkok Post* editorial on the issue. As a matter of fact, the first official Chinese statement countering the accusations could actually be heard around the same time already, that is to say, three weeks before the first related *China Daily* piece and directly after the 8 March meeting between Thai Prime Minister Abhisit Vejjajiva and Chinese Assistant Foreign Minister Hu Zhengyue (see above and also Chapter 5). In this meeting, Hu held the opinion that the Chinese Mekong dams "made no significant impact on the water flow in the lower part of the river." Besides, Hu was quoted as maintaining that "Beijing and local administration[s] paid a lot of attention to the drought in the region" and that "China would not do anything to damage mutual interest with neighbouring countries in the Mekong" (*Nation* 2010).

Shortly afterwards, Hu's statement was backed by remarks from Chen Dehai, a counselor with the Chinese embassy in Bangkok, on a specially convened press conference on 11 March. During the press conference, Chen made it clear that the Chinese dams built on the Mekong mainstream had "not affected river flows downstream." He further claimed that "[c]hanges in the Mekong River have nothing to do with our activities" since "[o]nly [...] about 13% of the water that feeds the Mekong comes from China." Referring to an MRC news release from 26 February blaming a drought for the low Mekong water levels (see Chapter 5), Chen underlined that "statistics" showed the low rainfall volume and added that this drought had "not only wreaked havoc in the lower Mekong countries but also [in] many regions of China such as Yunnan and Sichuan." Finally, Chen also stressed that his country was "standing firm in its desire to develop the Mekong River" as it was "for the mutual benefit of countries along the river." After all, China had "good relations with the lower Mekong countries" and there was "no reason to create problems for our friends" since they all were "facing the problem of water shortages together" (*Bangkok Post* 2010c).

The absolutely remarkable thing about these two early official rejections of a negative role of the Chinese dams in the situation was that they did not make their way into the Chinese media, but were only reported in the downstream press. Obviously, China's leadership wanted this event to remain low-key.

Analysis: China as a blocker of criticism

Whereas China during the first phase of response to downstream criticism of its dams ignored the accusations, in the second phase, China now turned to forcefully rejecting the blame. In securitization theory terminology, China became a blocker audience that no longer remains silent, but becomes vocal in order to turn down securitization moves. This shift in China's behavior certainly was, in itself, quite dramatic. What is more, however, it was also rather unexpected because it was unprecedented that China actually *reacted* to downstream criticism of its dams. This was also reflected in the non-Chinese press. A piece from the *Inter Press Service* noted that "[s]tung by this latest barrage of criticism, China has taken the unusual step of breaking its silence to mount its own defence" (*Inter Press Service* 2010a). In the *New York Times*, it could be read that "Chinese officials, normally media shy, recently held a news conference [...] to make their case that the drought is purely a natural phenomenon (*New York Times* 2010).

Apart from this astonishing general shift, not less interesting is a closer look at how exactly China staged its defense. Contents-wise, a few aspects were constantly repeated. First (and like all the MDRC governments; see previous chapter), China kept attributing the low Mekong water levels to be the result of a severe drought in the aftermath of extremely low rainfall. Second, China was adamant to highlight that the country only contributed a meager 13-ish percent to the Mekong's entire flow – a number far too little to have a noticeable effect on Mekong water levels at all. Third, China put forth a noteworthy – for, in fact, somewhat contradictory – assessment of the effects of its dams. On the one hand, it was stated that the dams had not impacted on water levels at all. On the other hand, the view was advanced that the dams had actually had a positive impact on the water levels, namely, by means of releasing water in the early stages of the drought. These ambivalent comments were later criticized by an MRC donor representative, too (Interview 16 October 2012). Fourth, China stressed that it was a responsible neighbor who attached great importance to its friendly cooperation with the MDRCs.

While contents were one thing, frequency was another. While this second phase (leaving out the rejections in early March which were only circulated in the MDRCs) only lasted a few days, from 30 March to 3 April, *China Daily* really launched a dense series of almost daily coverage, basically repeating nearly the same arguments over and over. However, while the arguments remained very similar, the high number of different sources (i.e., experts from different backgrounds and even including foreigners) these articles quoted to substantiate the Chinese argumentation was quite exceptional.

All in all, then, it can be maintained that China did not only dramatically alter its response to downstream criticism when transitioning from phase one into phase two, China also went to great lengths to convince downstream actors of its new narrative that the Chinese dams played no negative role in the low water levels. In doing so, notably, China tried to persuade the minds of the people downstream, rather than win their hearts. Once again, China paid more attention to arguing in a fairly sober scientific and rational way, mostly along the lines of China's share of Mekong water simply not being sufficient to make an impact. Although references about China being a responsible and friendly neighbor were also part of the second phase, attempts at making emotional connections with the MDRCs were overall not very pronounced.

But why did China, for the first time ever, change its strategy on treating criticism of its dams in the first place? The answer lay in the coincidence of two aspects. For one thing, when China chose to start rejecting the blame on its dams, criticism had already continued unabatedly for more than a month and therefore much longer than in the past. In addition, criticism was also more intense than ever before. As a matter of fact, Chinese experts have argued that the unparalleled intensity of the downstream accusations caught China off guard and left its decision makers impressed (Interviews 19 August and 27 August 2012). Consequently, China decided to counter an unprecedented extent of criticism with equally unprecedented measures. For another thing, and further aggravating the situation from the Chinese perspective, the first-ever MRC summit was just around the corner and China could certainly tell – also from the media coverage in the MDRCs – that its dams would be high on the agenda. In that sense, as an MRC donor representative highlighted, China sought to prepare for its summit attendance by defining loud and clear its position (Interview 16 October 2012). As a result, however, this second phase also gave an indication that China, the "potential upstream hegemon," as I called it in Chapter 4, has in fact been not fully immune to downstream criticism.

Phase Three: China turns to damage control

While China's open rejection of the downstream criticism of its dams was already a new feature of its Mekong hydro-politics, the Chinese side would not stop there. As a matter of fact, China indicated rather early in the crisis – that is to say, when phases one and two were still ongoing – that it was willing to cooperate much more on water-related issues in the Mekong than in the past. Storey (2010: 8) found correctly that China had turned on its "damage control mode." The first signal in this direction was already reported in MDRC media on 10 March, namely, that "China has invited countries from the lower Mekong subregion to visit its Jinghong dam in a bid to counter claims that its poor water management is causing drought in downstream countries" (*Bangkok Post* 2010b).

On 15 March, *Asia Times Online* (2010) repeated that "in response to the criticism, China extended invitations […] for Mekong country representatives to visit its Jinghong dam later this month [i.e., March]" which was "viewed as an encouraging step towards more transparency and multilateral cooperation."

Such an invitation to MRC representatives was special in that it was unequalled. Never before had MRC representatives been allowed to visit any of the Chinese dams on the Mekong mainstream. While the visit did – for unknown reasons – not materialize in March as announced, it finally did happen in early June 2010. More precisely, from 7–9 June, an MRC delegation for which each member state sent three senior representatives could complete a technical visit of both the Xiaowan and the Jinghong Dams on the Mekong mainstream. An MRC report should later outline that

> [d]uring the visit, Chinese experts gave a brief introduction on the engineering characteristics and operating rules of the two dams. The

participants have seen and learnt the Chinese experience in trying not only to optimize their overall development performance but also their aim to advance sustainable forms of hydropower through mitigation measures gradually incorporated into the operation of their dams, including several measures aimed to reduce any negative impacts to the lower part of the Mekong Basin.

(MRC 2010e: 6, 8)

Earlier, an MRC news release from 7 June had already referred to then Chief Executive Officer (CEO) of the MRC Secretariat, Jeremy Bird, as having noted that during the visit of the dams

Chinese officials have provided the MRC with information on the planning and design of upstream hydropower projects and confirmed that the natural minimum flow downstream will not be reduced and that adequate standards of water quality will be maintained.

(MRC 2010d)

A second signal was China's decision to provide the MDRCs with hydrological data from two of its upstream stations for the time of the crisis. More precisely, on 25 March, the *Bangkok Post* stated that according to then Thai Natural Resources and Environment Minister Suwit Khunkitti, China had "agreed to provide water level data from two dams in Yunnan province until the end of this year's drought in the lower Mekong River basin." Suwit said that "China recently sent a letter to the Mekong River Commission saying it was willing to provide it with hydrological data from Jinghong and Manwan dams." As for details, the data would be delivered every Monday at 9 a.m. starting immediately and would end at "the end of drought." The data were supposed to "include information on water levels, flow and rainfall at 8 a.m. on each day" (*Bangkok Post* 2010d).

The following day, on 26 March, the MRC issued a news release that confirmed the *Bangkok Post* report. The release, which was less informative and detailed than the *Bangkok Post* article, quoted CEO Bird stating "China has indicated that it is prepared to begin providing the MRC Secretariat with data during this dry season from the hydro-meteorological stations at Jinghong and Man[w]an, starting this week" (MRC 2010a).

The data were then actually shared once a week during a period from 22 March to 17 May 2010 (MRC 2011: 29). What was so noticeable about this provision of data is that it had never happened before that China had shared dry season data on Mekong water levels and rainfall. Under the "Agreement on the Provision of Hydrological Information on the Lancang/Mekong River" signed between China and the MRC in 2002, Beijing has only shared water level data from two stations on its territory during the flood season, from 15 June to 15 October, annually and once per day (MRC 2017). That China in the course of the spring 2010 Mekong crisis decided to provide dry season data thus was a unilateral move that was not enforced by any agreement.

Together with the vigorous rejection of the downstream claim that China's dams played a negative role in the low Mekong water levels which was prevalent during China's second response phase, these two signals were, in the words of an MRC donor representative, meant to set the scene for the upcoming MRC summit, during which China sought to ease downstream criticism and present itself as a benevolent upstream neighbor (Interview 16 October 2012). In fact, on the eve of the summit, the Chinese Embassy in Bangkok issued an official statement, headlined "Information about the Severe Drought in Southwest China and the Hydropower Development in Lancang River" and setting the tone for what was to come. The last paragraph of the statement read as follows:

> China and the countries along the Mekong River are good neighbors. Rational[ly] harnessing the water resources of the Mekong River is in the interests of all countries in the Great Mekong Sub-region. While harnessing the water resources of Lancang River, China takes seriously into consideration the impact on the environment, ecology and natural resources and takes care of the concerns of the lower-reach countries in an active manner and keeps smooth communication with them. As a responsible upper-reach country, China will never do things that harm the interests of the lower-reach countries. *China stands ready to strengthen communication and coordination with the parties concerned on the basis of equal consultation and mutual benefit and [to] jointly promote the social and economic development of this region.*
>
> (CEB 2010; emphasis by author)

This narrative, in contrast to before expanded by a new focus on increased future cooperation, was then echoed, and in fact amplified, by Chinese rhetoric during the summit itself. Notably, China had sent a big and high-ranking delegation, led by then Vice-Foreign Minister Song Tao, and also including then Director General of the Department of International Cooperation, Science and Technology with China's Ministry of Water Resources Chen Mingzhong. Song gave a speech in which he comprehensively outlined China's viewpoints regarding the situation. Apart from emphasizing the "good-neighborly and cooperative relations" as well as highlighting common achievements in terms of "economic and social development" between China and the MDRCs both in the bigger frame of China's interactions with the Association of Southeast Asian Nations (ASEAN) as well as in the other Mekong sub-region organization, the Greater Mekong Subregion, Song also covered the Mekong and hydropower issues explicitly. More precisely, he held that the

> Chinese Government has been developing and making use of the water resources of the Lancang River in a scientific and reasonable manner.

This is not only what's needed to help people in the region emerge from poverty, build a better life and promote social and economic development, but also an important step taken by the Chinese Government to vigorously develop renewable and clean energy and contribute to the global endeavor to counter climate change. [...] We lay equal emphasis on development and conservation and seek to serve the common interests of China and downstream countries.

(Song 2010)

While this passage focused on rather general remarks on China's Mekong approach, it was apparent that Song's speech was supposed to go in the direction of reassuring the Chinese Mekong neighbors. In the following, Song became more specific and stressed some concrete efforts made by China to accommodate the MDRCs' interests. Here, it is worthy to quote one paragraph more fully:

[in] response to the concerns of some downstream countries, we took many steps on our own initiative to protect the environment. Some actions even came at the expense of hydropower development. [...] To avoid impact on fish migration, we cancelled the Mengsong hydropower plant project on the Lancang River; to prevent abnormal downstream water level fluctuations caused by power plant operation, we plan to build the Ganlanba counter-regulation reservoir; and in order not to affect the water temperature of the Lancang River, we set aside RMB200 million yuan for the stratified water intake project in the Nuozhadu hydropower plant construction plan. Substantial scientific survey and research has suggested that China's ongoing hydropower development of the Lancang River has little impact on the water amount and environment of the Lancang River and the lower reaches. Quite the contrary, by way of the regulating effect of the water dams, hydropower development of the Lancang River can improve navigation conditions and help with flood prevention, drought relief and farmland irrigation of the lower reaches.

(Ibid.)

Obviously, China meant to cast a more positive light upon its Mekong hydropolitics. In doing so, Song's news about the cancellation of the Mengsong Dam and plans to build the Ganlanba Dam as a counter-regulation reservoir were particularly interesting. Moreover, however, Song not only looked back into the past, highlighting what China had already done to avoid, or at least lessen, negative impacts on the Mekong through its dam-building. Importantly, he also looked ahead into the future and promised to enhance cooperation: "[t]he Chinese side will strengthen dialogue and cooperation with the MRC and jointly contribute to the economic and social development of this region, guided by the principle of 'equal consultation, stronger cooperation, mutual benefit and common development'" (ibid.).

More specifically, Song announced that China would "increase communication and strengthen mutual trust," "expand the cooperation platform," "advance cooperation in disaster reduction," "actively carry out cooperation in hydropower development and promote sustainable development," as well as "strengthen technical exchanges and personnel interflow to jointly improve development capacity" (ibid.).

This new tone from the Chinese government side also accompanied by similar statements in the Chinese press. A *China Daily* article published on 4 April ran the headline "China to boost co-op with downstream Mekong countries" (*China Daily* 2010k). The article referred to Song and emphasized that China was "ready to strengthen the cooperation with the downstream Mekong countries in drought-and-flood relief, hydrological information and technique sharing, as well as mutual hydrographic experts visit[s]" (ibid.).

The article then listed "six dimensions in which China is willing to push forward the collaboration with MRC and the lower Mekong countries" (ibid.). These dimensions – very similar to what Song outlined in his speech at the summit – were making full use of the existing annual MRC–China dialogue mechanism; widening the cooperation platform under the framework of the ASEAN-China Free Trade Area to include areas such as waterway transportation, tourism, agriculture, fishery, environment protection, irrigation, forest management, environment assessment; advancing the joint work on disaster relief, including flood reporting and flood/drought relief training; collaborating on hydropower development; and organizing more technique sharing and mutual visits of the related officials and experts (ibid.).

Two days later, on 6 April, *China Daily* repeated its supportive coverage, re-stating that "China would cooperate with other Mekong-bordering countries in drought-and-flood relief, cooperation on hydropower development, and sharing information." This was because "[i]n the fight against a regional calamity, it's only natural that China and its Southeast Asian neighbors unite in their fight against the disaster" (*China Daily* 2010l). In the aftermath of the MRC summit, the immediate crisis came to a close, amid slowly increasing Mekong water levels and decreasing criticism of the Chinese dams.

Analysis: China as a cautious re-shaper of criticism

The key features of China's third response phase were that it made a few unprecedented cooperation moves and put forward proposals for enhanced future cooperation. In that sense, and viewed through the prism of securitization theory, China shifted from being a blocker audience to incoming securitization moves to becoming an at least cautious re-shaper of these moves. That is to say, China's third phase was by no means tantamount to any backpedaling from previous positions held during the first two phases. In other words, China still rejected the securitization moves and continued (1) to maintain that the crisis was triggered by natural drought conditions and (2) to deny that its dams had aggravated the situation. At the same time, however, China also sought to meet its critics halfway in order to suppress further criticism.

Altogether, China's two previously unheard-of cooperative measures, that is, the sharing of dry season data as well as the visit of Chinese dams made possible for MDRC officials, were clearly aimed at increasing transparency. As such, these measures were particularly important because they could produce immediate and tangible results. As a Chinese scholar noted, "the transparency measures were critical to put the facts on the table and to clarify the situation" (Interview 27 August 2012). Put differently, these measures were meant to resolve all doubt that the Chinese dams did not aggravated the crisis. Consequently, they also constituted the continuation of China's more scientifically driven rationale to reassure its neighbors. At the same time, however, it cannot go unmentioned that these two measures were one-time events. Especially the sharing of dry season data would not be repeated in the following years. Therefore, these two measures were not continuing, but in fact lacked a more long-term time horizon.

Yet, China did not stop at seeking to increase transparency. The venue for rolling out its new strategy was the first-ever MRC summit meeting. The Chinese attached utmost attention to this summit: never before had a Chinese official in the rank of a vice-foreign minister attended a Mekong meeting; never before had the Chinese government expressed itself publicly on Mekong water issues. According to a Chinese expert, these gestures were meant to convey the message that China took MDRC concerns seriously – or, at least, more seriously than in the past – and that Beijing could be reasoned with (Interview 19 August 2012). Meanwhile, as the MRC donor representative argued, the MRC summit was the perfect opportunity for China to take up the reins (Interview 16 October 2012).

Consequently, during the summit, China did two more things. On the one hand, China now put much more emphasis than before on also playing the emotional card, thereby also trying to re-channel the prevailing discourse away from more sensitive security connotations towards less controversial issues of joint development and towards creating a we-feeling between China and the MDRCs. China's Vice-Foreign Minister Song Tao's speech at the summit reflected this rationale very well. Throughout his speech, Song intended to highlight commonalities over possible points of contention. In particular, Song emphasized the goal of "common social and economic development" and stressed the importance of China for the MDRCs to reach this goal. Further, although China was by far the most powerful actor involved in the spring 2010 Mekong crisis, Song repeatedly used words that were meant to conjure up a common spirit between China and the MDRCs (e.g., "good-neighborly," "partners," "common," "equal," and "mutual") and should thus counter the activists' hopes of driving a wedge between China and the MDRCs.

On the other hand, the summit also served China to promise more future cooperation on water-related aspects. In his speech, Song also underlined that even though China had already taken several measures on its "own initiative" to protect the environment and MDRC interests (such as the cancellation of the Mengsong Dam), it was still willing to deepen cooperation in several specifically mentioned areas in the future. This would moreover not just be done somehow, but based on "equal consultation" and to the "mutual benefit" of all parties. In order to pave the way for enhanced future cooperation, it was furthermore important for China to emphasize the beneficial character of its dams. This became apparent when Song held that the dams would "improve navigation conditions and help with flood prevention, drought relief and farmland irrigation of the lower reaches," once the entire cascade was completed and operating normally.

That China engaged in those cooperative measures was certainly not really expectable from a pre-crisis point of view. The reasons why China moved into this third phase, however, were, partly at least, not very different from those why China had launched its second phase. That is to say, as Chinese experts confirmed, China was simply surprised, but also increasingly alarmed, by the duration and intensity with which downstream actors blamed the Chinese dams for at least aggravating the crisis (Interviews 19 August and 21 August 2012). According to one Chinese expert, this was because for China (and in contrast to the MDRCs), water resources had never been a big issue in China-MDRC relations before (Interview 27 August 2012).

However, this was not the only reason. An important step for the Chinese announcement during the MRC summit to deepen cooperation in the future had to be seen in the fact that there were forces in some of the MDRC governments as well as the MRC which seemed to be not averse to keeping Mekong water issues on the regional political agenda and to also seeking more cooperation with China on these matters. As described in the previous chapter, the Thai government, for instance, was interested in passing part of the pressure it received from Thailand-based activists on to China by promising to consult with Beijing over the Mekong. In other words, China could reciprocate such promises and knew it would charge open doors.

How about the transparency measures, though? After all, these were launched even before the Chinese media started to vigorously reject the blame put on its dams. Given this timing, it stands to reason that the transparency measures – albeit included in China's third response phase – were actually meant to be part of China's initial intention to keep a lid on downstream criticism from early on and consequently have much less of a crisis and a much quieter MRC summit than it turned out to be. It is also possible that those measures were already agreed upon in the Abhisit-Hu meeting on 8 March, in which case they would have been an early indicator that China was willing to secure MDRC government support in what was to come. Remember that information about China's invitation for Mekong country representatives to visit its Jinghong Dam was leaked only two days after the meeting. Be that as it may, though, while China's transparency measures were, of course, unparalleled and thus likely to make a good impression on the MDRCs, they were likewise comparatively low-hanging fruit that China could give away relatively easily. As a result, China's strategy did not work out. Rather, the events in the pre-summit period showed that China had to keep reacting to downstream criticism instead of being able to prevent it. Only during the MRC summit turned China into a more active player.

Ambiguous downstream reactions to China's Phase Three

China's "damage control mode" was something entirely new, at least as far as its Mekong hydro-politics was concerned. Naturally, the various downstream actors who were responsible for bringing China in this position in the first place had their own view on China's cooperation signals so far. At this point, it is therefore expedient to insert a closer look at their reactions to China's cooperation offers. This will also help to better understand China's subsequent fourth phase of response to criticism of its dams.

Overall, the MDRC reactions to China's cooperation signals were quite ambiguous. While the various non-state actors, that is, the activist groups and NGOs that were the ones initiating the criticism of the Chinese dams in the first place, remained skeptical, the MDRC governments and the MRC received China's cooperative measures rather warmly. This could no longer surprise, however, given their respective roles in the crisis as outlined in the previous chapter. More precisely, then, the MDRC governments as well as the MRC showed themselves very open to Beijing's reassuring attitude and praised China's cooperation during the crisis as being very positive. This became apparent in various statements made already during the Hua Hin Summit. To begin with, in his opening address to the meeting, then Thai Prime Minister Abhisit Vejjajiva stated that "[o]n behalf of the Member Countries, I would like to thank the Chinese Government for this valuable cooperation [i.e., the provision of dry season data], which provides us with a good opportunity to engage in truly region-wide cooperative efforts" (Vejjajiva 2010).

The Thai premier's view was echoed by then Lao Prime Minister Bouasone Bouphavanh who in his address to the meeting highlighted, "I wish to commend [...] the People's Republic of China [...] for [the] cooperation and willingness to further intensify [...] collaboration with the MRC, in particular in meteorological and hydrological information sharing" (Bouphavanh 2010).

In the words of the Vietnamese Prime Minister Nguyen Tan Dung, the positive feedback read as follows: "Viet Nam appreciates China's recent provision of hydrological data during this dry season which enable lower-Mekong countries to better assess the current flow of the Mekong River" (Nguyen 2010).

Only consequently, the Hua Hin Summit Declaration which ended the meeting "acknowledg[ed] the progress made to extend cooperation between the MRC and [...] China" and emphasized that "[t]he sharing of hydro-meteorological data by [the] People's Republic of China in the current drought situation is highly appreciated" (MRC 2010b).

In an MRC news release issued the same day of the Declaration, that is, 5 April, then CEO Bird, referring to China's increased data sharing, additionally emphasized that

> [t]his is a significant step forwards in engagement between China and the countries of the Lower Mekong Basin as it improves transparency. It is the first time that China has shared this dry season data with downstream countries […] and [it] is a significant increase in the level of cooperation also seen by the participation of a high level delegation from China at the summit.
>
> (MRC 2010c)

All in all, this kind of reaction on the part of the MDRC governments and the MRC might be best interpreted as a continuation of their strategy as outlined in the previous chapter. That is to say, while there was no intention of confronting China over its Mekong dam building and related issues, there yet *was* a growing interest in deepening the cooperation with the upstream neighbor. Interestingly, the Lao government, which had not earlier made its mark as publicly taking position, now officially joined in to support this approach as well, as made evident by the summit remarks of the Lao prime minister.

On the part of the non-state actors based in the MDRCs, in contrast, the reactions were much more reserved. Criticism of the Chinese dams could still be heard in many places across the MDRCs the days following the summit. Interestingly, as has been shown, this was also, and in particular, true for Vietnam's media. Given what Chapter 5 unveiled also in terms of how the Vietnamese government used its state-owned media to vent criticism of the Chinese dams, the Vietnamese media reports issued after the summit are indicative that the Vietnamese government, nice words at the summit aside, was unofficially interested in keeping some pressure on the Chinese side to follow through with the latter's cooperation promises. Even months later, in early July 2010, the Vietnamese press reported on a letter sent from the Save the Mekong Coalition, the umbrella mechanism under whose roof the criticism of China's dam building was largely organized in the spring 2010 crisis (see Chapter 5), to the MRC on 15 June. The letter read, "[w]hile less rainfall was undoubtedly a key factor in the 2010 drought, a question that remains urgent and unanswered is whether the Xiaowan dam's reservoir filling compounded the drought's severity" (*Talk Vietnam* 2010).

In a similar vein, but this time totally unrelated to possible hidden intentions of the Vietnamese government, the *Inter Press Service* published a piece on 27 August in which it quoted one of the leading activists during the crisis with the following words:

> [m]any people living in the lower Mekong region will still believe that the filling of the Xiaowan dam reservoir contributes to a drop in the water

level during the dry season [...] It will remain so until the Chinese make public all the information related to its dam operations.

(*Inter Press Service* 2010b)

The activist went on saying that "China has been taking positive steps to be cooperative by releasing some details. But it still needs to be willing to be more accountable and transparent, since local communities have not seen the information given to the MRC" (ibid.).

Personal interviews conducted with some of the formerly leading activists more than two years after the crisis furthermore underlined the common thinking after the 2010 MRC summit. One activist contended that China's data sharing was "significant but certainly not enough" (Interview 9 October 2012). Another activist elaborated a bit more on the limits of the Chinese provision of dry season data. For this second activist, the data were ultimately "useless" for two reasons. First, the data were only transmitted once a week and not on a daily basis, which would not have been a technical problem for the Chinese. Thus, however, nobody could tell what happened with the water levels within those respective seven days from one to the next dataset. Second, the data shared came from stations downstream of the Xiaowan Dam, that is, the dam accused of holding back water. With no comparative data, the activist maintained, on how much water actually entered Xiaowan, data on how much water was released further downstream was not meaningful. Therefore, the activist reached the conclusion that China's data sharing was ultimately meant to primarily propitiate the media (Interview 3 October 2012). Apart from the data sharing, China's vice-foreign minister's remark that China had cancelled the Mengsong Dam "to avoid impact on fish migration" could not arouse any storm of enthusiasm, either. No activist believed that the main reason for the cancellation was to protect fish migration. Even a Chinese scholar conceded that the prime reason likely was that the dam would have been "economically not viable" (Interview 22 August 2012).

As a result, China's damage control mode was only partly successful. While the MDRC governments and the MRC seemed to (officially) be satisfied with China's degree of cooperation during the crisis and were looking forward to what China had promised for the future, the activists based in the MDRCs were not really convinced of the genuine character of the Chinese cooperation measures. Above all, though, as the newspaper quotations from after the crisis suggest, China had not yet done anything that would refrain the activists from launching another round of criticism in the next possible crisis.

Phase Four: China works to prevent future blame

After the MRC summit, the media, generally speaking, soon lost interest in the topic and water levels in the Mekong began to rise again. Under these circumstances, and a few solitary exceptions aside, local communities and activists in the MDRCs lacked the resources to effectively resume their forceful criticism of the Chinese dams for much longer. While China had therefore eventually achieved its primary objective for the time being, it was yet striking that the Chinese side did, again, not stop here, but indeed sought to establish and strengthen a few more areas of cooperation with its downstream neighbors that outlasted the immediate crisis for quite some time and might help prevent, or at least defuse, possible future blame over similar crisis situations. In doing so, China followed two parallel tracks; one was more official and intended to enhance China-MRC cooperation; the other was rather low-key and mainly involved exchange between Chinese river developers and downstream-based NGOs and expert networks.

Regarding the official track, China-MRC cooperation temporarily increased in a few areas in the months following the crisis. One of the areas where cooperation was strengthened most evidently was in terms of personnel interflow. As a matter of fact, China dispatched several staff to the MRC Secretariat under the Integrated Capacity Building Program through the Junior Riparian Professional (JRP) Project. The first JRP from China joined the Secretariat in early March 2011 to work with the MRC Information and Knowledge Management Program focusing on flood management until June 2011 and then with the MRC Initiative on Sustainable Hydropower (ISH) Program for two more months from July to August 2011 (MRC 2011: 7). Later, from February through August 2012, two more Chinese JRPs (one from the Chinese Ministry of Water Resources) also worked with the ISH Program, each focusing on projects concerning the lower basin and sharing Chinese experience (Interview 12 November 2012).

Another area of cooperation in which China was actually active already before the crisis but which the Chinese side sought to deepen after the crisis was disaster management. This included hands-on workshops and trainings as well as the provision of further hydrological data. As regards the former, China attended the MRC 8th Annual Mekong Flood Forum convened on 26–27 May 2010 in Vientiane, Laos (MRC 2010e: 5); co-sponsored the International Training Program on Management of Flood Control and Disaster Mitigation on 16–30 June 2010, aimed at providing a better understanding of flood and drought hazards as well as knowledge on flood control and disaster relief (MRC 2010e: 10); and invited experts on flood forecasting from the MRDCs to join an international training project on flood forecasting technologies in Wuhan, located at China's Yangtze River, for November 2011. The training courses would be on technical aspects of flood management such as data acquisition, information management, and flood forecasting (MRC 2011: 6–7, 10).

In terms of data sharing, the following headway was made. For one thing, a joint visit to upgrade the two hydrological stations at Jinghong and Manwan was conducted by MRC staff and officers of the Yunnan Hydrology and Water Resources Bureau during 26 July to 1 August 2010. The two stations were upgraded with new standard equipment so that data were then automatically sent to the MRC via the Kunming data terminal with a 15-minutes' interval of data transfer using advanced technology provided by mobile phone services (MRC 2010e: 51 and 2011: 29). For another thing, China agreed to the provision of automatic water level equipment and related installation, telecommunication and data management systems, the delivery of a discharge measurement motor boat and a set of electronic discharge measurement as well as the provision of technical training for operators at the data terminal and at both hydrological stations in using the new hydrological equipment (MRC 2011: 29).

These kinds of more practical cooperation were embedded in what could be termed attempts at enhancing "strategic cooperation." Such attempts primarily included meetings of senior management staff on both sides in an effort to explore options for future cooperation trajectories. For example, following their dam visits on 7–9 June mentioned above, staff of the MRC Secretariat met on 10 June 2010 in Beijing with relevant agencies in China, including the Chinese National Energy Administration, its Ministry of Foreign Affairs, and the Ministry of Water Resources in order to discuss future cooperation (MRC 2010e: 98). Similarly, on 4 November 2010, officials of the Chinese Ministry of Water Resources once again received then MRC Secretariat CEO Jeremy Bird in Beijing to exchange ideas on hydrological information provision by the Chinese side and on other issues for cooperation going forward. Issues discussed included Chinese regular sharing of dry season data, the deputation of Chinese officials to the MRC, and joint studies on sediment management (MRC 2011: 27–28, 35). China at least reassured the MRC that it was willing to provide hydrological data to the MDRCs in case of a recurrence of a "drought situation" similar to 2010 and moreover confirmed to further study the technical requirements and the necessity of the sharing of dry season data once the upstream hydropower station operated normally (MRC 2011: 4).

The MRC was also interested in strengthening its cooperation with China on sustainable hydropower development. However, while the Chinese side loosely acknowledged opportunities to promote the "mutual understanding of the laws and regulations, evaluation standards, technical methods, environmental management and monitoring between upstream and downstream countries" (MRC 2011: 5), in this specific area, the Chinese side obviously preferred to follow a rather low-key track of cooperation.

Three actors were key in promoting this second track. First, there was World Wide Fund for Nature (WWF), an international NGO and the first international conservation organization invited to work in China in 1980. Next, there was M-POWER (standing for "Mekong Program on Water, Environment and Resilience"), a network of collaborators engaged in action-based research, dialogues, and knowledge brokering to improve water governance in the Mekong in ways beneficial to sustainable livelihoods and healthy communities and ecosystems. Partners came from the MDRCs, China, and beyond. Most members were from academic and non-government organizations but also belonged to international organizations and government agencies (M-POWER 2017). Finally, there was the Challenge Program on Water and Food (CPWF) in the Mekong, a program of the Consultative

Group on International Agricultural Research (CGIAR, a global partnership committed to research on food security and unaffiliated to an international institution) and a network operating at the global and river basin levels. CPWF's global objectives included promoting the resilience of social and ecological systems through better water management for food production. In the Mekong, CPWF pursued poverty reduction and development through optimizing the use of water (CPWF Mekong 2013).[1]

Back in December 2009, WWF China had gathered Chinese research institutes, river developers, government agencies, and the Chinese NGO The Nature Conservancy in Kunming to have a first consultation on promoting the Hydropower Sustainability Assessment Protocol (HSAP). HSAP is a universal tool developed by the international Hydropower Sustainability Assessment Forum and used to measure and guide performance in the hydropower sector through assessing the four main stages of hydropower development (early stage, preparation, implementation, and operation) by covering different aspects of sustainability (i.e., technical, environmental, social, economic and financial, and integrative) (IHA 2013 and M-POWER 2013).

Around the same time, M-POWER, actively supporting more sustainable hydropower governance, also considered HSAP an important tool it hoped to utilize in the Mekong. Therefore, when the spring 2010 crisis witnessed harsh criticism of the Chinese dams, M-POWER saw a chance to reach out to WWF China in order to explore options for collaboration and draw in Chinese hydropower stakeholders. WWF China reacted positively, agreed to collaborate, and to convince Chinese hydropower stakeholders to focus more specifically on the Mekong. As a result, and after some preparatory steps, several Chinese hydropower stakeholders involved in the Mekong indeed got engaged in various forms of joint meetings, workshops, and trials on sustainable hydropower development with downstream actors (Interview 23 October 2012).

On 27 September 2011, M-POWER, CPWF Mekong, and WWF China co-organized a one-day "Roundtable on Sustainable Hydropower Development in the Mekong" in Vientiane in an effort to identify ways of improving hydropower development by bringing together relevant upstream and downstream stakeholders. Altogether, there were 65 participants. Significantly, from the Chinese side, participants included those from Hydro Lancang, the developer of the Chinese Mekong dams (M-POWER 2011).

Three months later, on 14–18 December 2011, CPWF Mekong co-organized a study tour to Laos, aiming at the study of hydropower development in the Lower Mekong Basin (along Mekong tributaries) and the potential for sustainable projects. A Chinese delegation also joined the tour. Delegation members encompassed, among others, representatives from the National Development and Reform Commission, the Chinese Ministry of Commerce, the China Exim Bank, the Chinese Academy of Social Sciences, Peking University, and the Chinese NGO Green Watershed (Interview 23 October 2012).

This study tour was then followed by a four-day workshop providing training on HSAP, which took place in Vientiane on 18–21 February 2012.

The workshop was co-hosted by the International Hydropower Association (i.e., the developer of HSAP), M-POWER, and CPWF Mekong. The workshop was meant to be an opportunity to demonstrate the value and applicability of HSAP to a wide group of hydropower stakeholders and receive their feedback. This time, Chinese stakeholders participating included representatives from the Yunnan Provincial Energy Bureau, the Foreign Affairs Office of the People's Government of Yunnan Province, the Assessment Center for Environmental Engineering with the Ministry of Environment Protection as well as Hohai University and Yunnan University (M-POWER 2012a).

Following up on the December 2011 study tour to Laos, on 26–30 August 2012, a second visit by a delegation of energy planners and hydropower developers from China to an MDRC (this time Cambodia) took place upon organization by M-POWER, CPWF Mekong, and WWF China. Objectives of the exchange visit were to promote communication and discussion between hydropower development stakeholders; to facilitate a better understanding of best practices for environmental and social considerations in hydropower development; to enhance chances to share experiences in sustainable hydropower development and explore possible opportunities for cooperation between China and the MDRCs; and to further the overall improvement of water and hydropower governance in the Mekong. Main activities included a visit to the Tonle Sap Lake to discuss the impact of upstream dams on Mekong fisheries and a roundtable dialogue bringing together the relevant Cambodian ministries and agencies, energy developers, researchers, and civil society organizations in Cambodia with the Chinese visitors. These included representatives from Hydro Lancang and the Yunnan Energy Bureau (M-POWER 2012b).

As a concrete result of all these meetings, workshops, and study tours, Hydro Lancang eventually agreed to HSAP trial assessments. In June 2011, the HSAP was first launched on the Jinghong Dam. In July 2012, the Nuozhadu Dam was then also put under HSAP assessment (Interview 14 November 2012). In other words, HSAP trials were implemented on two of China's recently before completed Mekong mainstream dams. Unfortunately, however, results of the assessments have not been made publicly available.

After mid-2012, it could then be observed that water-related cooperation between China and the MDRCs, generally speaking, decreased again. This was partly related to red lines that the Chinese side did not want to cross at the time. It was, however, also related to a gradual, but overarching shift in MDRC attention away from China's dams and towards the first Mekong mainstream dam in an MDRC, namely, the Xayaburi Dam in Laos (more details in the following chapter). Only on 30 August 2013, was there a solitary sign of continued cooperation intentions, as the MRC published a news release stating that China had not only agreed to extend the 2002 Agreement to provide hydrological data to the MDRCs, but had in fact also

> agreed to extend the period of hydrological data sharing and increase the frequency of the information exchange. Under the previous agreement,

China had shared its hydrological data from June 15th to October 15th every year. From now on, China will extend the hydrological data provision by 30 days, starting on June 1st until October 31st, every year. China also agrees to increase the frequency of the data sharing from once a day to twice a day.

(MRC 2013)

As a result, data sharing during the critical flood season would become a bit more comprehensive in the future.

Analysis: China as a re-shaper of criticism

While China's cooperation moves during the crisis had mainly aimed at one-time transparency measures as well as assuaging rhetoric about increased future cooperation, its efforts after the crisis sought to turn its rhetoric crisis into action. While China's collaboration during the crisis was geared towards ending the crisis, its measures after the crisis were meant to prevent similar criticism in the future. Consequently, from a theoretical point of view, China finally became a full re-shaper of securitization moves, meaning to ease (some of) the MDRC concerns and bring in a few own ideas on how to move ahead with water-related cooperation in the Mekong.

In his address at the MRC summit, China's then Vice-Foreign Minister Song Tao had announced to strengthen cooperation with MDRC actors in the areas of strategic cooperation, sustainable hydropower development, disaster management, technical exchanges, and personnel interflow. As the previous descriptions have demonstrated, Beijing largely kept its word and markedly increased its interactions with MDRC(-based) actors on water-related issues in the roughly two years following the spring 2010 crisis. Particularly interesting was that China built this increased cooperation upon two different pillars independent from each other, namely, the more official MRC track and the more low-key track involving non-state actors.

Regarding the MRC track, it was conspicuous to see that – apart from a few specially convened encounters between leading officials from both sides which did not bring about any major breakthroughs – increased cooperation mainly included conference meetings and workshops, study tours, and training programs. In other words, the new cooperation efforts usually remained limited to the technical and working levels. This caused varying assessments on the part of MRC officials involved. One leading staff member of the Thai National Mekong Committee complained that the Chinese only sent junior delegates who only engaged in technical, but not political talks, since they did not have any authority or decision-making power (Interview 10 October 2012). In contrast, a senior riparian MRC staff member underlined that China after the crisis sent bigger delegations to the various meetings and requested to make presentations, whose quality had improved enormously (Interview 24 October 2012). Obviously, the increased number of meetings on the technical and working levels did not revolutionize the overall framework of China-MRC relations, especially not in a time period of just two years. From the Chinese point of view, however, the rationale certainly was to gradually get to know each other better, build inter-personal relationships, and thus, over time, create more mutual understanding and trust. Once created, mutual understanding and trust could have served as a springboard for more strategic cooperation. That this trust was not there after the 2010 crisis, though, was, for example, indicated by the fact that China continued to shy away from a regular sharing of more dry season data while at the same time enhancing cooperation on flood management which China regards as far less sensitive.

China's second track differed from the MRC track in some important ways. It not only involved different types of actors, it also produced a different depth of cooperation and was meant to address a different audience. More precisely, in contrast to the MRC track, the second track involved both state and *non-state* actors. This entailed that this track was far less official – something the Chinese side welcomed very much (Interview 17 October 2012). Together with the fact that this track had a sole focus on improvements in the area of sustainable hydropower cooperation, this unofficial character also helped explain why – temporarily at least – the second track actually moved further and produced more palpable results than the MRC track, particularly when taking the HSAP assessments on two of China's mainstream dams into consideration. An MRC staff member working on ISH with the Chinese side also explained the difference between the two tracks regarding interaction on hydropower issues. As he stated, MRC interactions with Chinese officials were "dialogue-focused" whereas river developers such as Hydro Lancang came with "hierarchy" and vested with "decision-making powers." This, however, likewise meant that they would not engage with more official channels such as the MRC (Interview 12 November 2012).

In sum, for China, both tracks were important in that they complemented each other exactly *because* they involved different players. The more official MRC track was pivotal for Beijing to keep reassuring MDRC political elites that China was a benevolent neighbor following up on its promises and increasingly willing to discuss Mekong water issues. The less official track was significant for Beijing to gradually reach out to the activists and NGOs so critical of China's dams.

These findings directly lead over to China's reasons for initiating this fourth phase of response to MDRC criticism of its dams. In other words, why did China enhance cooperation when the immediate crisis was already over? Surely, one rather obvious reason was that China had promised to do so. Another was that China hoped to prevent similar blame in the future. But what exactly made the Chinese side change its mind so much as compared to previous crises? On the one hand, it certainly played a role that the 2010 crisis was the second time in less than two years that China was put on the spot and its Mekong dam building heavily and openly criticized (Interview 24 October 2012). Since the Mekong features an erratic behavior in terms of extreme water levels even as far as purely natural phenomena are concerned (see Chapter 4), more crises going forward could not be ruled out. This, however, also implied that if China made no changes to its Mekong strategy, if it did not start to re-shape the securitization moves it had already received repeatedly, it would likely have to face storms of criticism over Mekong water issues again and again. As even a Chinese expert had to admit, this was clearly not in China's interest, not least because it tarnished China's image abroad at a time when China has grown increasingly fond of having a positive reputation (Interview 22 August 2012).

On the other hand, it was not just the fact that future crises were expectable which made the Chinese side quite nervous at the time. What was more was the trend of what seemed to be a rapidly increasing intensity of criticism from one past crisis to the next, which must have raised red flags in Beijing. During extreme water levels before 2008, only scattered mumblings, if at all, could be heard from within the MDRCs. But this had also to do with the fact that China had only completed two mainstream dams at the time and knowledge of the dams was still rudimentary and not widely spread. In summer 2008, then, the situation had already changed and China for the first time received a series of negative headlines for its Mekong dam building in the media of various countries. Not even two years later, in spring 2010, criticism finally turned into week-long sustained and substantial securitization moves. As a result, and using the words of a Chinese expert, "in 2010 had the pressure on China become so huge that it had to do something about it" (Interview 22 August 2012).

This assessment was likely correct in view of the facts that (1) the NGO and activist sectors blaming the Chinese dams during the spring 2010 events had not left much doubt that they were not really satisfied with China's cooperative measures before and during the MRC summit as well as that (2) the media had demonstrated quite clearly that they could pick up on such a topic very quickly and extensively. The Chinese side therefore did well to work on longer-lasting strategies to convince these actors about Chinese intentions to cooperate more in the future. For as an MDRC-based researcher watching regional water issues for years remarked, already the 2010 crisis had shown that even though China was the most powerful actor in the regional water game, this did not mean that other players could not contest China and its policies (Interview 25 October 2012).

Synopsis: China's spring 2010 Mekong crisis behavior *in toto*

Bringing together the findings on China's various response phases to the blame put on its dam building during the spring 2010 Mekong crisis, a few things should be (re-)emphasized. Above all, it is noteworthy that parts of China's strategy remained constant throughout the crisis, whereas others showed evolutionary elements. The key constants certainly were that China remained adamant about two related things: first, the low Mekong water levels were caused by natural drought conditions; and, second, China's dams played no role in aggravating the crisis. In these regards, by the way, China's argumentation regarding the reasons for the crisis resembled what the previous chapter found out about the position of the MDRC governments and the MRC. Moreover, in theoretical terms, China left no doubt that it rejected the attempts at securitizing its dam building. This is fully in line with what Chapter 2 has elaborated on China's "securitization preferences." That is to say, China has in general not been interested in making, or in letting others make, its Mekong hydro-political behavior a matter of security. This is because full securitization tends to produce categories of "us" versus "them" (Aradau 2004) that could inflame or increase tensions between China and its neighbors – something which is against China's economic and image interests.

More striking than what remained constant in China's approach, however, clearly was in how far China's behavior also evolved and changed during the crisis. As could be shown, China went through four partly overlapping, yet distinct, phases of responding to the criticism of its dams. More precisely, China went from ignoring the blame, through openly rejecting it, to making one-time offers on increased transparency, to pursuing more long-term and enhanced cooperation measures on water-related issues with the MDRCs. This evolutionary behavior was so remarkable because it was unprecedented. To be sure, on the one hand, the basic underlying pattern that China reacted to criticism and certain events with somewhat increased cooperation was not an entirely new feature to the country's Mekong hydro-politics (see Chapter 4). On the other hand, though, the 2010 crisis was different in that it was the first time that China could not sit out the blame put on its dams until some time after the crisis, wait for MDRC requests on enhanced cooperation, and then decide, with time on its side, how far Chinese "benevolence" should go. Rather, during the 2010 crisis, criticism of China's dams was so intense that the Chinese – whether they liked it or not – were essentially pressured to react much more immediately and comprehensively. This was certainly not expectable from a pre-crisis point of view and it also hit China's decision makers quite unprepared. Therefore, China first had to learn how to adapt, step-by-step, to the unending and unprecedentedly forceful criticism. In doing so, China from a theoretical perspective gradually moved from a passive recipient to a blocker to a re-shaper of the downstream securitization moves directed at its dam building. Significantly, only when China reached the stage of re-shaping, which seeks to accommodate at least some of the securitizing actors' concerns, was it able to better control the situation. This, again, is not only in sync with what has been outlined on possible audience strategies to incoming securitization attempts in Chapter 2, it also produced a degree of water-related cooperation between China and the MDRCs previously unmatched, albeit fragile.

All in all, the spring 2010 Mekong crisis then once again revealed, and in fact highlighted, the parallel existence of conflict and cooperation in China's Mekong hydro-politics. In particular, however, the spring 2010 events also exposed under what conditions and for what reasons and purposes China has been willing to enhance cooperation. Regarding the conditions, it has become apparent that it takes crises and a certain extent of pressure in order to make China react and increase hydro-political cooperation. As concerns the reasons, it has turned out that China is clearly not keen on standing in the pillory lest this could tarnish its image and reputation abroad and thus ultimately run counter its overarching foreign policy objectives such as having a friendly and stable neighborhood conducive to continued economic development at home. Therefore, China's purpose has increasingly been to work on trying to prevent similar situations in the future.

Bringing the larger context back in

It has been said before in this book that China's Mekong hydro-politics constitutes only one issue-area in China's foreign relations with the MDRCs and the wider Southeast Asian region. At the same time, we have also seen earlier that the general characteristics of China's Mekong hydro-politics certainly feed into China's overall foreign policy goals vis-à-vis its neighboring countries. To repeat briefly previous elaborations, first, China's overarching foreign policy objectives primarily consist of sovereignty and territorial integrity, economic development, and international status. Second, Southeast Asia, including the Mekong sub-region, has generally featured prominently when it comes to achieving these objectives – look, for example, at the protracted territorial disputes in the South China Sea, the important markets for Chinese import, export, and investment, as well as the more or less open, but certainly intensifying, contest with the United States (US) about the status as the number one power in the region. Third, China's Mekong hydro-politics, especially its dam building, has above all been meant to serve the economic development rationale, primarily for China itself, but also, so at least Chinese official rhetoric, for the entire Mekong sub-region, for example, through energy trade. Through framing its dam building at home as well as its investment in dam building and related infrastructure projects in the MDRCs as parts of a joint development agenda, China has also hoped to foster its reputation amongst its Mekong neighbors.

What now happened in 2010, however, was that not only China's hydro-politics in the Mekong was dealt a blow. As Chapter 3 has already discussed in some detail, China's foreign relations with its Southeast Asian neighbors had also entered into a general rough patch in the months preceding the spring 2010 Mekong crisis. This was because of three other challenges China's foreign policy had to face around the time: first, risen concerns among some ASEAN states about the coming into force of the China-ASEAN Free Trade Agreement (CAFTA) in January 2010; second, heightened tensions over the maritime territorial disputes in the South China Sea ever since summer 2009; and, third, increasing re-engagement of the US ever since the Obama Administration had taken office, resulting in greater US attention to the South China Sea dispute as well as to the Mekong sub-region through its newly established Lower Mekong Initiative (LMI). In other words, all of China's major foreign policy objectives were suddenly put at risk in Southeast Asia.

Under these circumstances, how was China's hydro-politics and, more precisely, its ultimately comparatively forthcoming behavior in the spring 2010 crisis linked to the country's other foreign policy hot spots in Southeast Asia at the time? On the one hand, as should have become clear throughout this and the previous chapter, pressure on China's hydro-politics during the spring 2010 Mekong crisis was quite high. Therefore, even without the other regional foreign policy issues, China might have reacted the way it eventually did. Remember the remarks from Chinese experts that have indicated this point of view above. Nonetheless, on the other hand, the other three regional challenges China was confronted with should not be totally neglected in the Mekong narrative and may well have played a contributing role to China's behavior in the Mekong crisis as well.

First of all, it is crucial to realize that the South China Sea issue has certainly been the single most important foreign policy topic for China in its relations with Southeast Asia for many years. Tellingly, in March 2010, it was reported that China had elevated the South China Sea to representing a "core interest" (see Wong 2010) of its foreign policy – a designation that was previously given to Taiwan, for instance. As a result, when tensions in the South China Sea built up during the second half of 2009 and when, in addition, the US was seeking to once again play a much more active role in the region, including as a potential protector of ASEAN states' claims in the South China Sea,[2] China would benefit from having partners in the region. Laos, Cambodia, and Thailand, that is, three of the four MDRCs, were clearly qualified. None of them was directly embroiled in the South China Sea disputes; for Laos and Cambodia, being two of ASEAN's least developed countries, CAFTA would not take effect until five years later, while Thailand was one of the ASEAN countries that ran a positive trade balance with China; and, as shown in Chapter 3, the three countries' governments held largely positive views of China.

Therefore, what seemed more natural for China than reaching out to some of its closest partners in Southeast Asia in an effort to win their support, or at least their neutrality, regarding the South China Sea?[3] The only problem, of course, was that exactly with these partners, China now also had some trouble over the Mekong. Yet, in contrast to the South China Sea territorial disputes, hydro-politics has not, at least not until 2010, constituted an area of high politics for Beijing (Interviews 19 August and 27 August 2012). As a result, it was clearly easier for China to make a few concessions as far as its Mekong hydro-politics was concerned. This was especially because the concessions made did not go as far as to negatively affect any of China's major foreign policy objectives, quite unlike a Chinese yielding in the South China Sea. In fact, more Chinese cooperation on water-related issues in the Mekong could also be seen as advantageous to Chinese interests at another front, namely, as a cushion against the newly US-launched LMI whose cooperation agenda comprised the areas of environment (including water), health, education, infrastructure development, and food and energy security (LMI 2017). As Chinese experts have confessed, China has to some extent been worried about LMI intentions and a potential hidden US agenda to gain greater political influence in the Mekong sub-region (Interviews 12 July and 4 August 2016). Altogether, its foreign policy situation vis-à-vis Southeast Asia in early 2010 underlines that China's Mekong hydro-politics does not take place in a vacuum. The next, and final, chapter will also take up this issue again and elaborate a bit more on it.

Interviews cited

Activist I, 3 October 2012, Bangkok, Thailand.
Activist II, 9 October 2012, Bangkok, Thailand.
Chinese expert I, 15 August 2012, Beijing, China.
Chinese expert II, 19 August 2012 and 4 August 2016, Beijing, China.
Chinese expert III, 21 August 2012, Beijing, China.
Chinese expert IV, 22 August 2012, Kunming, China.
Chinese expert V, 27 August 2012, Kunming, China.
Chinese expert VI, 29 August 2012, Kunming, China.
Chinese expert VII, 12 July 2016, Beijing, China.
CWPF representative, 17 October 2012, Vientiane, Laos.
MDRC-based water expert, 25 October 2012, Vientiane. Laos.
M-POWER representative, 23 October 2012, Vientiane, Laos.
MRC donor representative, 16 October 2012, Vientiane, Laos.
MRC official I, 24 October 2012, Vientiane, Laos.
MRC official II, 12 November 2012, Hanoi, Vietnam.
NMC Thailand official, 10 October 2012, Bangkok, Thailand.
WWF China representative, 14 November 2012, Hanoi, Vietnam.

Notes

1 Today, M-POWER is no longer really active. CPWF been transformed into the CGIAR Research Program on Water, Land and Ecosystems.
2 Officially, the US has consistently taken a neutral stance on the South China Sea disputes.
3 As already mentioned before, such a case actually happened in July 2012 when ASEAN failed to reach an agreement on the South China Sea issue mainly because Cambodia stepped in on China's behalf (BBC 2012).

References

Aradau, C. (2004) "Security and the Democratic Scene: Desecuritization and Emancipation," *Journal of International Relations and Development*, 7(4), 388–413.
Asia Times Online (2010) "When the Mekong Runs Dry," 13 March, www.atimes.com/atimes/Southeast_Asia/LC13Ae01.html.

Bangkok Post (2010a) "China's Dams Killing Mekong," Editorial, 25 February, www.savethemekong.org/news_detail.php?nid=93.

Bangkok Post (2010b) "China Asks Mekong States to Visit Dam, Wants to Counter Claims That It's Causing Drought," 10 March, www.savethemekong.org/news_detail.php?nid=101.

Bangkok Post (2010c) "China Denies Hogging Mekong River Water. Drought, Not Dams, to Blame, Says Counsellor," 12 March, www.savethemekong.org/news_detail.php?nid=103.

Bangkok Post (2010d) "China to Provide Water Data on Dams," 25 March, www.savethemekong.org/news_detail.php?nid=113.

BBC (2012) "ASEAN Nations Fail to Reach Agreement on South China Sea," 13 July, www.bbc.com/news/world-asia-18825148.

Bouphavanh, B. (2010) "Statement at the First MRC Summit," 5 April, Thailand, Hua Hin, www.mrcmekong.org/news-and-events/speeches/first-mrc-summit-3/.

Challenge Program on Water and Food in the Mekong (CPWF Mekong) (2013) "CPWF in the Mekong," http://mekong.waterandfood.org/archives/644.

China Daily (2010a) "Yunnan, Guangxi Reel from Severe Drought," 4 February, www.chinadaily.com.cn/cndy/2010-02/04/content_9424549.htm.

China Daily (2010b) "Drought Inflicts a Heavy Toll," 9 February, www.chinadaily.com.cn/cndy/2010-02/09/content_9447589.htm.

China Daily (2010c) "No End in Sight to Prolonged Drought in South," 15 March, www.chinadaily.com.cn/cndy/2010-03/15/content_9588270.htm.

China Daily (2010d) "Waiting for a Miracle Called Rain," 18 March, www.chinadaily.com.cn/cndy/2010-03/18/content_9606455.htm.

China Daily (2010e) "Drought Paralyzes Power Supply," 24 March, www.chinadaily.com.cn/cndy/2010-03/24/content_9631854.htm.

China Daily (2010f) "Drought in China Caused by Climate Change: Experts," 28 March, www.chinadaily.com.cn/china/2010drought/2010-03/28/content_9653182.htm.

China Daily (2010g) "China Taps Upper Mekong Water Resources Reasonably," 30 March, www.chinadaily.com.cn/china/2010-03/30/content_9664522.htm.

China Daily (2010h) "China Denies Dams Worsen Drought in Mekong Basin," 31 March, www.chinadaily.com.cn/china/2010-03/31/content_9664697.htm.

China Daily (2010i) "Reservoirs Not Cause of Drought," 1 April, www.chinadaily.com.cn/cndy/2010-04/01/content_9671835.htm.

China Daily (2010j) "Climate Change to Blame for Mekong Drought," 3 April, www.chinadaily.com.cn/world/2010-04/03/content_9684768.htm.

China Daily (2010k) "China to Boost Co-op with Downstream Mekong Countries," 4 April, www.chinadaily.com.cn/china/2010-04/04/content_9685698.htm.

China Daily (2010l) "United against Disaster," 6 April, www.chinadaily.com.cn/cndy/2010-04/06/content_9687682.htm.

Chinese Embassy in Bangkok, Thailand (CEB) (2010) "Information about the Severe Drought in Southwest China and the Hydropower Development in Lancang River," 1 April, www.savethemekong.org/admin_controls/js/tiny_mce/plugins/imagemanager/files/ChinaStatEng.pdf.

International Hydropower Association (IHA) (2013) "Hydropower Sustainability Assessment Protocol," www.hydrosustainability.org/Protocol.aspx.

Inter Press Service (2010a) "Chinese Dams Blamed As Mekong Level Falls," 17 March, http://proquest.umi.com.ezproxy.lib.nccu.edu.tw:8090/pqdweb?did=1985250511&sid=2&Fmt=3&clientId=23855&RQT=309&VName=PQD.

Inter Press Service (2010b) "China Flexes Hydropower Muscle," 27 August, www.ipsnews.net/2010/08/south-east-asia-china-flexes-hydropower-muscle/.

Lower Mekong Initiative (LMI) (2017) "LMI Plan of Action," http://lowermekong.org/about/lmi-plan-action.

Mekong Program on Water, Environment and Resilience (M-POWER) (2011) "Sustainable Hydropower Development in the Mekong," Roundtable, 27 September, www.mpowernetwork.org/Knowledge_Bank/Key_Reports/PDF/Dialogue_Reports/27Sept_Roundtable_China_Mekong_final.pdf.

Mekong Program on Water, Environment and Resilience (M-POWER) (2012a) "Hydropower Sustainability Assessment Protocol Stakeholder Training Workshop Takes Place in Laos," 22 February, www.mpowernetwork.org/Knowledge_Bank/Key_Reports/Media_Releases/PRESS_RELEASE_IHA_2012_02_22_Laos_training.pdf?tabid=34059.

Mekong Program on Water, Environment and Resilience (M-POWER) (2012b) "Second Visit by a Delegation of Energy Planners and Hydropower Developers from China," Summary Notes, 26–30 August, www.mpowernetwork.org/Knowledge_Bank/Key_Reports/PDF/Dialogue_Reports/China_exchange_visit_to_Cambodia_Summary_Report.pdf.

Mekong Program on Water, Environment and Resilience (M-POWER) (2013) "Advancing Hydropower Sustainability," www.mpowernetwork.org/Major_Projects/Hydropower_Sustainability/index.html.

Mekong Program on Water, Environment and Resilience (M-POWER) (2017) "About Us," www.mpowernetwork.org/About_Us/Overview/index.html.

Mekong River Commission (MRC) (2010a) "China Ready to Share Data on Mekong Water Levels Ahead of Regional River Summit," News Release, 26 March, www.mrcmekong.org/news-and-events/news/china-ready-to-share-data-on-mekong-water-levels-ahead-of-regional-river-summit/.

Mekong River Commission (MRC) (2010b) "MRC Hua Hin Declaration," 5 April, www.mrcmekong.org/news-and-events/speeches/mrc-hua-hin-declaration/.

Mekong River Commission (MRC) (2010c) "Mekong Prime Ministers Agree to Prioritise Climate Change as Summit Ends," News Release, 5 April, www.mrcmekong.org/news-and-events/news/mekong-prime-ministers-agree-to-prioritise-climate-change-as-summit-ends/.

Mekong River Commission (MRC) (2010d) "Mekong Commission Visits China Dams and Will Discuss Future Cooperation," News Release, 7 June, www.mrcmekong.org/news-and-events/news/mekong-commission-visits-china-dams-and-will-discuss-future-cooperation/.

Mekong River Commission (MRC) (2010e) "Report of the 15th Dialogue Meeting Between the Mekong River Commission and the People's Republic of China and the Union of Myanmar," 27 August, Cambodia, Phnom Penh, www.mrcmekong.org/assets/Publications/governance/15th-DialogueMeeting-report-full.pdf.

Mekong River Commission (MRC) (2011) "Report of the 16th Dialogue Meeting Between the Mekong River Commission and the People's Republic of China and the Union of Myanmar," 29 August, Laos, Vientiane, www.mrcmekong.org/assets/Publications/governance/16th-DialogueMeeting-Report-full.pdf.

Mekong River Commission (MRC) (2013) "Mekong River Commission and China Boost Water Data Exchange," News Release, 30 August, www.mrcmekong.org/news-and-events/news/mekong-river-commission-and-china-boost-water-data-exchange/.

Mekong River Commission (MRC) (2017) "About the MRC: Upstream Partners," www.mrcmekong.org/about-the-mrc/upstream-partners.

Nation (2010) "China's Dams Make No Impact to Upstream," 8 March, www.nationmultimedia.com/national/China-s-dams-make-no-impact-to-upstream-30124199.html.

New York Times (2010) "Countries Blame China, Not Nature, for Water Shortage," 1 April, www.nytimes.com/2010/04/02/world/asia/02drought.html?_r=0.

Nguyen, T. D. (2010) "Statement at the First MRC Summit," 5 April, Thailand, Hua Hin, www.mrcmekong.org/news-and-events/speeches/first-mrc-summit-4/.

Song, T. (2010) "Remarks at the First MRC Summit," 5 April, Thailand, Hua Hin, www.mrcmekong.org/news-and-events/speeches/first-mrc-summit-5/.

Storey, I. (2010) "China's 'Charm Offensive' Loses Momentum in Southeast Asia [Part II]," *China Brief*, 10(10), 7–10.

Talk Vietnam (2010) "Mekong River Commission Called onto the Carpet," 6 July, www.talkvietnam.com/2010/07/mekong-river-commission-called-onto-the-carpet/.

Vejjajiva, A. (2010) "Opening Statement at the First MRC Summit," 5 April, Thailand, Hua Hin, www.mrcmekong.org/news-and-events/speeches/first-mrc-summit/.

Wong, E. (2010) "Chinese Military Seeks to Expand Its Naval Power," *New York Times*, 23 April, www.nytimes.com/2010/04/24/world/asia/24navy.html?_r=0.

7 Conclusion
Making sense of China's (Mekong) hydro-politics

Lessons from the spring 2010 Mekong crisis for China's Mekong hydro-politics

A Chinese scholar at Yunnan University who has been following China's dam-building activities in the Mekong very closely has argued that large-scale dam building was a "very emotional issue," with "psychological factors" deeply involved. Therefore, during the 2010 Mekong crisis, "bad guys" were "simply needed" and China was an "easy target" (Interview 22 August 2012). In contrast, a Western scholar based at Chiang Mai University has contended that the crisis actually represented a good chance for China to appear like a "big benevolent brother" saying, "we are there, we can help" (Interview 11 October 2012). Apart from these two exemplary and very different personal statements, however, what did China's reaction to the criticism of its dams during the spring 2010 Mekong crisis tell us about the characteristics of and reasons for China's hydro-political approach to the Mekong in general as well as the cooperation–conflict balance existent in this approach in particular? Moreover, in how far did China's behavior during and following the crisis reveal old limits and new facets of its hydro-politics?

As shown throughout this book, China's Mekong hydro-politics had long exhibited a co-existence of both conflict and cooperation. The 2010 Mekong crisis only re-emphasized, and in fact further strengthened, this overall picture. Moreover, as likewise carved out before, the cooperative side of China's Mekong hydro-politics had usually remained mostly passive, that is, reactive to criticism deemed detrimental to Chinese foreign policy interests such as a positive image and a stable neighborhood. This, too, was largely reconfirmed by the events surrounding the spring 2010 Mekong crisis. Apart from these two broad continuities, however, there also were subtle novelties involved in China's reaction. Generally speaking, the degree of Chinese cooperation with the Mekong downstream riparian countries (MDRCs, i.e., Laos, Thailand, Cambodia, and Vietnam) on water-related issues in the Mekong has been relatively moderate. This can be explained by China's favorable geographical position as the Mekong's most upstream riparian country. It can further be understood through the fact that China also is the materially most powerful

Mekong riparian country. According to realist International Relations (IR) theory, the combination of these two features even tends to make for a totally uncooperative upstream hegemon (Lowi 1993: 10; also see Chapter 1). In the events surrounding the spring 2010 crisis, however, the cooperation–conflict balance in China's behavior tilted towards the cooperative side to an extent unprecedented. In particular, with the short-time sharing of dry-season hydrological data and the granting to MDRC representatives of a dam-visiting tour, China increased the transparency about its dam building to an unparalleled degree. Similarly, the Chinese promise to enhance cooperation going forward indeed produced a few tangible and previously unequalled results, such as some personnel interflow with the Mekong River Commission (MRC) in the years 2011 and 2012 as well as Hydropower Sustainability Assessment Protocol (HSAP) trial assessments on the Chinese Jinghong and Nuozhadu Dams in the same years.

Interestingly, however, and with the benefit of hindsight, this relatively cooperative Chinese behavior led to rather ambiguous assessments in the MDRCs. For a Thai expert, China had undergone "big changes" in its response to MDRC concerns on water issues after 2010 (Interview 2 October 2012). Similarly, a Western expert heavily involved in the HSAP cooperation with China was of the opinion that this was a "very positive development" in which all sides were very willing to engage (Interview 23 October 2012). In contrast, an MDRC-based Western activist reached the conclusion that there was "no sea change" in China's overall behavior towards the Mekong (Interview 3 October 2012). Likewise, an MRC donor representative found that the 2010 crisis had not produced any "sustainable" China-MRC cooperation (Interview 22 October 2012), and a Vietnamese scholar maintained that while China had shown more flexibility in the 2010 crisis, ultimately there were "no substantial changes" in Beijing's attitude (Interview 15 November 2012).

In a sense, all these assessments, albeit very different, can be seen as correct. On the one hand, there was more Chinese cooperation, and this was positive. On the other hand, however, China's more cooperative behavior surrounding the spring 2010 Mekong crisis should certainly not lead to the false assumption that all the MDRCs needed to do going forward was to press China hard enough for concessions, and concessions would be what they would get from China. To some extent, this worked. At the same time, though, China retained certain red lines that it was unwilling to overstep and that marked clearly defined limits to China's cooperative behavior. When, for example, comparing the list of demands the Save the Mekong Coalition (SMC) delivered to the Chinese government in its letter of complaint from 3 April 2010 (see Chapter 5) with what was actually achieved, the overall picture looks rather grim. Among the SMC key demands were the following: to stop all dam building on the upper Mekong River's mainstream; to release data detailing the operation schemes of the dams and showing past records of the river conditions before the dams were built; to cooperate with the MDRCs to establish a joint committee, in which people affected by dams from each country are represented in an effort to study and seek ways to manage the river in a just and sustainable way; and to revise the management of the completed dams and pursue approaches to manage their reservoirs without causing impacts to the downstream communities (SMC 2010: 2). None of these demands were realized – certainly not to a full degree at least. In reality, China did not all of a sudden begin to discuss and negotiate its Mekong dam-building plans with the MDRCs. Also, it remains true to date that (1) China's sharing of dry season data has not been repeated after 2010; (2) China continues to reject becoming an MRC full member; and (3) since it has not accepted that its dams cause negative impacts downstream, China has not compensated MDRC communities for economic losses.

As a result, therefore, China's reaction to the blame its dams received in the spring 2010 Mekong crisis included enhanced water-related cooperation with the MDRCs, but it was not tantamount to shifting to a mode of full-blown cooperation on these issues. In theoretical terms, this behavior corresponds with descriptions made earlier in this book: China is not simply, as realists would have one believe, a (fully) uncooperative upstream hegemon, even though it certainly has the potential to be one. Neither is China, speaking in institutionalist terms, a friend of river basin organizations – especially not multilateral ones and those narrowly focused on water management issues – because they could constrain China's hydro-political activities. Instead, China is somewhere in between, as China has followed an approach of rather loose on-and-off cooperation. This is in line with what securitization theory has to offer to explain China's hydro-political behavior. China's general preference for non-securitization, that is, an ideally very low-key status, of its hydro-political actions basically means that water-related cooperation is to some extent possible, but certainly no natural given. In pursuing non-securitization, China moreover seeks to frame its hydro-politics as part of a benevolent common regional development strategy, not as a zero-sum competition for water, food, and energy resources. Meanwhile, when yet faced with attempts at securitizing its hydro-political actions – usually because of too little cooperation – China's then employed reactive strategy of causing securitization failure entails an enhancement of water-related cooperation efforts which, however, is not necessarily sustained nor crossing certain thresholds. In other words, China does not favor hydro-political cooperation beyond the extent needed in order to calm the immediate waves of criticism and reassure its riparian neighbors of Beijing's goodwill. For China, it is therefore ultimately a cost-benefit analysis – and one in which China may well include the broader foreign policy context as well. And while there were voices from the activist sectors that were not satisfied with the scope of China's cooperation offers in the spring 2010 Mekong crisis, official MDRC government statements certainly were quite positive of China's reaction.

Nonetheless – and this qualifies as another noteworthy novelty in addition to the shifting cooperation-conflict balance – China's reaction to the spring 2010 Mekong crisis, especially the final response phase which what was labeled earlier as endeavors to reshape securitization moves, also involved cautious steps towards an approach that was interested in more long-term forms of cooperation and therefore was more active, too. This was also reflected in the assessment of a senior riparian MRC staff member who found that it seemed after the spring 2010 events that China was serious about more cooperation that was not just short-term (Interview 24 October 2012). As Chinese experts later revealed (Interviews 12 July and 4 August 2016), the spring 2010 Mekong crisis, which was not only the second Mekong crisis in three years but also indicated a rapidly growing intensity of criticism of China, made China realize the two following and related things. First, Mekong crises including blame of China's dam building represent an increasing problem for China's friendly neighborhood diplomacy and the country's positive image abroad. Second, in order to avoid similar crises and blame in the future, China has to do more so as to better be able to follow its preferred hydro-political strategy of pre-empting securitization attempts directed at Chinese actions – instead of having to reject those securitization attempts. Put differently, it seemed that the cost-benefit analysis was shifting in favor of new forms of cooperation.

In this regard, however, two crucial questions remained somewhat unanswered in the early aftermath of the spring 2010 Mekong crisis. First, were the cooperative measures China had taken to respond to the spring 2010 situation actually sufficient to pre-empt similar future blame from the MDRCs? This point was particularly relevant in light of the fact that the initial enthusiasm about enhanced cooperation, supposedly existent on both sides (China and the MDRCs), seemed to be slowly petering out in the course of 2012 already. Second, given the apparent limits to China's cooperative behavior in the Mekong as previously defined, how far would China be willing to further modify its approach in order to further strengthen cooperation with the MDRCs and therefore make sure that Chinese hydro-politics would actually not again be in the focus of criticism going forward? For this second question, it is worthy to take a short detour at China's record in its other major shared basins. Doing so should be conducive of getting a more comprehensive understanding of the broader patterns prevalent in China's international hydro-politics as well as of the preferred instruments in China's hydro-political toolbox.

China's performance in its other shared major rivers as a "cooperation marker"

As outlined in the introductory chapter, China shares many large rivers with the neighboring countries all around its periphery. Apart from the Mekong, which is certainly the most important international river in what I previously termed the southeast sub-region, China also shares major rivers in its northeast, northwest, and southwest (also see Chapter 1). What does the hydrological situation in these other major rivers look like? What have been the main water-related issues between China and its riparian neighbors? And what approach(es) to cooperation has China followed there?

China's major shared rivers in the northeast

Among China's shared rivers in its northeast, the Amur and, to a lesser extent, the Tumen are of particular interest in order to understand the hydrological characteristics as well as China's hydro-political approach in this sub-region. Importantly, both the Amur, which China shares with Russia and, to a small part, also with Mongolia, and the Tumen, where China's riparian neighbors are Russia and North Korea, are international rivers which do not cross, but rather mark the borders between their riparian states. As a result, these rivers are not faced with the typical upstream-downstream constellations in cross-border rivers, which often make cooperation extremely difficult.

The Amur is the longest boundary watercourse in the world and furthermore stands out as one of the few major river basins in the world whose mainstream has no dams or reservoirs. Around 54 percent of the Amur's catchment area is located within Russian territory, some 44 percent lie within China, and the remaining 2 percent belongs to Mongolia (Vinogradov and Wouters 2013: 5, 10). China and Russia are therefore the two key players when it comes to questions of joint water management in the Amur. This is even more the case as there is – due mainly to the reluctance of China (see Vinogradov and Wouters 2013: 17) – no trilateral treaty in place. Rather, the three riparian parties have signed bilateral agreements on the protection and utilization of their joint water resources (China and Russia in 1994 and 2008; China and Mongolia in 1994; and Russia and Mongolia in 1995). Despite the two bilateral water agreements and the existence of joint river commissions, however, water security challenges for the Sino-Russian dyad are mounting in the Amur. Critically in this regard, Russia finds itself in a much more vulnerable position than China – a fact that primarily emerges from the sharp contrast in population density (with Russia's Far East being sparsely and China's northeast densely populated) and resultant characteristics of land use in the basin (Simonov 2011: 95).

The first issue of concern for Russia relates to transboundary water pollution and, thus, water quality management. While pollution was a problem earlier, a turning point in attention was reached with the previously mentioned 2005 Songhua River incident, which temporarily cut off almost four million people, including those living in Russian cities along the Amur, of their water supply after a chemical plant explosion in the Chinese city of Jilin had polluted the river, which is the largest Chinese tributary to the Amur, with 100 tons of benzene (Gleick 2009: 83). In accordance with the economic and demographic disparities between Russia and China in the Amur, it is estimated that China contributes 87.5 percent to the total pollution of the upper Amur (Argun River), 75 percent in the middle section of the Amur, and 97.6 percent to pollution of the lower Amur (Ussuri River) (Vinogradov and Wouters

2013: 12). As a result, and following the 2005 incident, pollution control has become a crucial area of cooperation between China and Russia. At the same time, though, it has been reported that not only has the water quality in the Amur remained poor, but also the quality of joint monitoring efforts has remained low (Karakin 2011: 93).

Apart from water pollution matters, a second area of concern for Russia has been China's increasing water consumption in the Amur basin. While pollution has tended to overshadow consumption problems so far – in fact, it has been argued that there was a danger that China might not only limit its cooperation to the pollution issue, but would also deal with it only from the point of view of the local communal services and fisheries' interests in the Chinese section of the river basin (Karakin 2011: 93) – water quantity shortages will most likely become much more acute in the future. This is because China withdraws huge volumes of water from the entire basin, mainly for agricultural use in order to increase food production, but also for urban and industrial development – and this in an increasingly arid region. In the Songhua basin, for example, China's water demand is supposed to steadily approach the total runoff volume estimated at 75 percent of the needed supply. To alleviate the pressure on its soaring water demand, China has already implemented ten, and is planning to implement up to 20 more, large-scale water transfer projects between different tributaries of the Amur (Karakin 2011: 88, 90). Russian scholars have even speculated that China might have a complex long-term goal of hydro-engineering on the Amur mainstream, in which actual energy generation would not figure as prominently as the creation of strategic reserves of fresh water for several purposes, ranging from irrigation to more water diversion (Simonov 2011: 96).

Be that as it may, the present level of Sino-Russian water cooperation is insufficient in view of the severity of the problems. One key difficulty in overcoming the existing problems is that "China is rather reluctant to make concessions with respect to what it perceives as its sovereign right to use transboundary waters within its territory" (Vinogradov and Wouters 2013: 16). Meanwhile, maintaining favorable conditions for navigation in the Amur seems to be one of the few issues linked to joint water resources management, on which Russia's and China's national interests have concurred (Karakin 2011: 92).

The Tumen, which is a rather small border river compared to the Amur, is an interesting case to briefly look at for very different reasons. In this river, China has been a member, and, in fact, the driver, of a multilateral initiative – namely, the Tumen River Area Development Coordination Committee set up in 1996 and comprising all three riparian countries (i.e., China, Russia, and North Korea). However, the focus of the Tumen committee has never been on water management issues, but rather on supporting the Tumen River Development Program, and thus on trade, investment, and infrastructure development. This fact is further underlined by the program's later transformation in 2005 into the Greater Tumen Initiative (GTI), which incorporates a much-enlarged regional area, also bringing in non-riparian actors such as Mongolia's eastern provinces as well as South Korea's eastern port cities (Freeman 2010). The GTI, therefore, much more resembles the Greater Mekong Subregion (GMS; see Chapter 3) than an actual river basin organization dealing with water-related issues.

China's major shared rivers in the northwest

In China's northwest, the major international rivers of interest so as to get an understanding of the situation in and China's hydro-politics towards this subregion are the Irtysh and the Ili. Apart from the significant difference that both the Irtysh and the Ili are cross-border rivers (and not border rivers like the Amur and the Tumen) with China being the upstream country, the overall setting in China's northwest is very similar to the one in its northeast. This starts with the fact that, as with the Amur, China has again followed a strictly bilateral approach to river management. While the Irtysh not only flows from China into Kazakhstan, it also constitutes the main tributary to Russia's Ob River, one of the longest in the world. Similarly, the drainage area of the Ili not only comprises China and Kazakhstan, but to a lesser extent also Kyrgyzstan. On the one hand, China in 2001 signed the "Cooperation Agreement on the Utilization and Protection of Transboundary Rivers" with Kazakhstan, which also led to the setting up of a joint river commission. Furthermore, in 2011 both sides inked the "Agreement on Protection of Water Quality of Transboundary Rivers." Cautious steps have been taken even into the direction of regulating the allocation of shared water resources (Biba 2014a and Ho 2017: 150). The bilateral treaties comprise all of the two countries' 20-ish shared rivers. Cooperation in the past has gone so far that China provided Kazakhstan with emergency water supply to help mitigate a drought in summer 2014 (*Xinhua* 2014). On the other hand, despite hopes in Kazakhstan and Kyrgyzstan, China has rejected the idea of inclusive (i.e., trilateral) water management of the Ili basin. Likewise, and in spite of China's existing bilateral agreements with Russia and Kazakhstan (Russia and Kazakhstan also have a bilateral treaty covering the Irtysh), Beijing has again been reluctant to the notion of trilateral cooperation (UNECE 2009: 15, 47).

This constellation not only leaves Kazakhstan as China's key riparian neighbor in its northwestern region, China's water-related agreements with Kazakhstan also indicate that Beijing has been quite accommodating vis-à-vis Astana. Elsewhere, I have explained China's forthcoming attitude, noting that Kazakhstan is a vital partner for China in its fight against the so-called "Three Evils" of separatism, extremism, and terrorism, which are seen by Beijing as key sources of social unrest in its strategically important vast Autonomous Region Xinjiang Uighur bordering Kazakhstan. Also, Kazakhstan is a major exporter of oil to China as well as a transit country for natural gas from Turkmenistan – both critical assets for China's energy security and sustained economic growth. As a result, China has been willing to ease some of

Kazakhstan's concerns on water-related issues in return (Biba 2014a and 2014b; also Ho 2017). This, again, is an illustrative example of how issue-linkages between hydro-politics and other issue-areas exist in China's foreign policy.

Nevertheless, grave problems remain, with the key issue being Chinese water extractions in both the Irtysh and Ili basins, which are part of the largest arid zone on the Eurasian continent. In October 2004, then Chinese ambassador to Kazakhstan, Pei Shouxiao, affirmed that his country was counting on using as much as 40 percent of the Irtysh's effluence, although the river flows on Kazakh soil for most of its length (Allouche 2007: 52). Regarding the Ili, estimates say China consumes up to 70 percent (Asanov 2009). The reasons for China's huge water withdrawals need to be understood in light of China's 2003 White Paper on Xinjiang, which made a case for the expansion of cotton and energy industries as part of the "Develop the West" (*xibu da kaifa*) campaign. This has resulted in an unsustainable growth in water use. Cotton is a highly water-intensive crop, yet now takes up about half of Xinjiang's arable land, as Beijing regards textile exports to be of strategic interest. At the same time, Xinjiang is also China's leading domestic oil producer. To guarantee the future development of oil fields, water diversion schemes for the Irtysh and the Ili have long been considered inevitable (Biba 2014a). Back in the 1990s, China had already started using some of the Irtysh waters to provide water to the Karamai oil fields, as Beijing announced the construction of the Kara Irtysh-Karamai Canal to divert water from the Irtysh to Lake Ulungur (Allouche 2007: 52). Besides, China has built reservoirs for hydroelectric power plants and stuck to plans to transfer water from major tributaries of the mainstream rivers (such as the Kash, Kunes, and Koksu) into neighboring basins where agricultural and economic activities are also being intensively developed (Asanov 2009). On top of all this, continuing large-scale population migration into Xinjiang from other provinces will further intensify the demand for water (Biba 2014a).

Unlike the Amur for Russia's sparsely populated Far East, the Irtysh and the Ili represent critical sources of fresh water for millions of Kazakh people, particularly for their agricultural, industrial, and energy bases. Yet, China's huge water withdrawals are likely to precipitate several adverse effects, some of which can already be felt today. More precisely, rice production, for example, has already decreased, while hydropower generation and navigability could be affected in the future. The Irtysh is also the main source of fresh water for around 15 million people, mostly living in Kazakhstan's bigger northeastern cities, including the capital Astana. Water shortages could threaten urban and industrial development there. Environmentalists have even warned that Lake Balkhash whose major source of water is the Ili could become a desert, like the Aral Sea (Peyrouse 2007: 8–9).

Apart from these issues, it has been maintained that the scope of the joint river commission with China, with its focus primarily on monitoring and joint research, has been limited and that in particular the ultimate question of water allocation between the two countries has not been answered yet (UNECE 2009: 47). So far, therefore, despite the two agreements mentioned earlier, Kazakhstan has no tools available to veto Chinese actions on the Irtysh and Ili rivers (Interview 15 August 2012).

China's major shared rivers in the southwest

Turning to China's shared rivers in its southwestern region, the general situation changes in at least two significant regards: first, the levels of water quantity are all in all much higher; and, second, due to geographical constellations, that is, steep declines in the riverbeds flowing down from the Tibetan Plateau, hydropower generation gains center stage. The general situation therefore resembles the one prevalent in the Mekong. However, compared to its international rivers in the north, China has been less forthcoming on water issues when it comes to its shared rivers in the southwest. The primary, and also most contentious, example of this has been the Brahmaputra River, which China shares as the upstream country with India and Bangladesh downstream. The most noteworthy kind of cooperation China has agreed to is the sharing of some hydrological data. With India, China signed a first memorandum of understanding on the provision of flood season data from June to October every year in 2002. This memorandum was then renewed in 2008 and 2013, respectively, with the last one also extending the time frame for data provision from May to October (Liu 2015: 360 and Walker 2013b). In 2006, moreover, a bilateral expert-level mechanism was set up in order to facilitate dialogue on the flood season data sharing as well as related questions of emergency management. This development has to some extent paid tribute to Indian fears in the early 2000s of deadly flash floods coming from Chinese stretches of the river due to ineffective water management and deforestation (Biba 2014b: 37). More recently, in September 2015, China also agreed to provide Bangladesh with the same hydrological data it seems to actually sell to India (Siddique 2015).

Over the years, the fear of flash floods in India has given way to increasing concerns about Chinese dam building in the Brahmaputra. In 2010, China for the first time admitted that it was building a large-scale hydropower plant on the river's mainstream at Zangmu (*Asia News* 2010). At the end of 2015, all power-generating units of the dam became fully operational, while three more mainstream dams were approved by China's 12th Five Year Plan of Energy Development on 1 January 2013 and yet more are likely to follow (Liu 2015: 355–356 and Walker 2013a). Watts (2010) has argued that in 2010 already, there were at least 28 dams on the Brahmaputra that were either completed, planned, or under discussion by China. However, as China has been very secretive on its dam-building activities and has in general not followed an approach of prior notification vis-à-vis its neighbors, it remains sometimes difficult to know exactly how many dams are being planned, built, or completed in any given basin.

While large-scale dam building can have disastrous environmental consequences (see Chapter 4), Indian concerns have revolved more around the aspect of potential Chinese "water theft" (*Asia News* 2010). In particular, this concern has been linked to widespread speculations about possible Chinese plans to use the so-called "Western Route" of the South-to-North Water Transfer Project (see Chapter 1) to divert water towards China's arid north through the building of a mega dam at the Brahmaputra's Great Bend. So far, China has always pledged that all its dam-building activities in the Brahmaputra have only involved run-of-the-river projects, which do not store, let alone divert, water (see Biba 2014b: 38). Besides, debates about the actual feasibility of such diversion schemes have been highly controversial. Sinha (2012: 41) has summarized the Indian debate on this issue as follows:

> While it can be argued that many of the diversion projects on the Yarlung [i.e., the Chinese stretch of the Brahmaputra] are economically unfeasible and hence anxieties over them are excessive and alarmist, it can equally be argued that the proposed series of dams on the Yarlung, some of which may not be run-of-the-river, could potentially give China significant capacity to pressurise its neighbours and shape outcomes.

The problem for downstream India – a country with a similar record on water-related problems, population pressure, and food and energy security concerns like China – certainly is that the Brahmaputra is of critical importance. The river accounts for 29 percent of the total runoff of India's rivers and therefore represents a rare potential source of available water. In addition, of India's total hydropower potential, roughly 44 percent lies in the Brahmaputra basin. This potential could be greatly reduced, depending on Chinese upstream activities. However, hydropower plays an enormous role in the Indian government's objective to ensure electricity for the country's huge and growing population (Rahaman and Varis 2009: 67). In fact, India has been planning hydropower development schemes on a large scale itself. For the Brahmaputra and its tributaries alone, public and private companies have proposed – albeit implementation remains unclear – 168 massive dams in the upper reaches of the basin in Arunachal Pradesh and Assam (Hilton 2014).

All in all, it can be said that China's hydro-politics vis-à-vis India has been the most strained, and remains the most explosive, among all of China's riparian neighborhood relations. This must certainly be attributed to the fact that overall bilateral relations in this dyad have often been tense as well (see Biba 2016b). In particular, Chinese experts continue to emphasize that there can be no joint water treaty while there are still unresolved territorial disputes between the two countries (Interview 13 August 2016). This is especially the case as the Brahmaputra runs through a part of the disputed area, that is, Arunachal Pradesh. Besides, the Chinese side sometimes perceives of Indian accusations of Chinese behavior as hypocritical (Interview 15 August 2012). This is because India, itself an upstream country to Bangladesh, has had a similar record in terms of treaty practice and information sharing like China vis-à-vis India. Unlike in the Irtysh, for example, there has therefore been no common interest of downstream countries to establish forms of basin-wide inclusive water management in the Brahmaputra.

China's overall hydro-political record and inferences for the Mekong

The concise review of the situations and China's respective behavior in its major shared rivers around its entire periphery first of all reveals that, similar to the Mekong, cooperation and conflict coexist everywhere. At the same time, each sub-region certainly has its own set of hydrological and contextual peculiarities that differentiate one sub-region from the other. As a result, the details of China's approaches to each sub-region, or even each river basin, have also differed to some degree. Nonetheless, it is likewise possible to distill from the review a few overarching preferences in China's international hydro-politics. These comprise the following aspects in particular:

- *Treaty practice.* China has not been particularly keen on signing comprehensive water treaties with its many riparian neighbors. In fact, China has concluded water-specific treaties with only three riparian neighbors. These are Mongolia, Russia, and Kazakhstan (also see Chen et al. 2013: 219). Notably, Kazakhstan therefore is the only country with which China has inked treaties covering major cross-border rivers (in contrast to boundary rivers). As the question of water distribution is not included in these Chinese-Kazakh treaties, it is a fact that China has not yet signed a single agreement regulating the issue of water quantity in cross-border river basins.
- *River commissions.* In correspondence with its disinclination to sign water treaties, China has been reluctant to set up joint river commissions with riparian neighbors. This is coherent in that river commissions are usually the tangible expression of a previously inked water agreement. Consequently, river commissions with (full) Chinese membership only exist where China has also signed a treaty. Another aspect is the limited scope of existing commissions that largely focus on monitoring and research only and therefore lack a set of other important governance instruments such as full-blown disputes settlement mechanisms or stakeholder involvement.
- *Multilateralism.* Another very conspicuous fact is that China has clearly preferred bilateralism to multilateralism when it comes to joint water management. All treaties China has signed, just like all river commissions China has co-established, have been bilateral in nature. Meanwhile, China has been circumspect to join multilateral river management institutions and has been similarly cautious to empower multilateral organizations of which it has actually been a member to play a bigger role in questions of joint water governance. The latter is certainly true for organizations such as the Shanghai Cooperation Organization in Central Asia or the

previously mentioned Greater Mekong Subregion. Also, while the GTI is a multilateral forum, it does not discuss water issues.
- *Information sharing.* China has an ambiguous record on information sharing, and thus on transparency, with its riparian neighbors. On the one hand, China has – and this applies in particular to its cross-border shared rivers – rejected to negotiate its dam-building activities and river diversion plans with its downstream neighbors. Likewise, China has declined a full disclosure of those plans *ex ante*. On the other hand, China has been more forthcoming in terms of providing hydrological data. China has in particular shared flood season data with various riparian neighbors. At the same time, China has seen no incentive to also share dry season data, at least not on a regular basis. Other data potentially relevant for China's downstream neighbors, such as sediment load, have not been provided by China, either.

Summarizing these aspects, it becomes obvious that despite the different conditions across sub-regions and river basins, China's hydro-political preferences in its other major shared rivers, by and large, reflect those prevalent in the Mekong. First, the extent and scope of China's hydro-political cooperation with its many riparian neighbors have, generally speaking, remained rather low. As underlined several times throughout this book, this is mainly related to China's usually superior position vis-à-vis its riparian neighbors, both in geographical and in material terms. In addition, however, how the Chinese conceive of their international rivers and their actions in these basins has also hampered cooperation. For one thing, many Chinese tend to treat their international rivers in essence as domestic rivers, which therefore do not require international cooperation (Interview 21 August 2012). For another thing, many Chinese believe that dam building entails no negative impacts (downstream) and in particular does not reduce the amount of water flowing downstream, thus, again, limiting the need for international cooperation (Interview 15 August 2012).

Nevertheless, second, China has also engaged in certain forms of cooperation. In doing so, however, China has clearly not been interested in forms of institutionalized joint river management with its riparian neighbors. Treaties and concomitant institutions, especially multilateral ones, have above all been considered a possible constraint on China's freedom of unlimited future action and its discriminatory use of a river's resources. Hence, China has again and again preferred rather loose on-and-off cooperation models that provide much more flexibility. In sum, therefore, the look beyond the Mekong also reconfirms the theoretical tenets of this book. On the one hand, this look reveals that both realist and institutionalist IR theories are flawed when it comes to explaining China's international hydro-politics. In simplified terms, realism is too pessimistic about cooperation, while institutionalism is too optimistic; moreover, both are too static. This picture not only applies to the Mekong but also to China's other major shared rivers. Meanwhile, on the other hand, securitization theory, in combination with China's overarching hydro-political objective of non-securitization of Chinese behavior, is able to reflect rather well the dynamic character of co-existing cooperation and conflict in China's approach(es) to its shared rivers (also see Biba 2014b).

Returning to the Mekong now and comparing China's overall hydro-political record with its reaction to the spring 2010 Mekong crisis, a few more noteworthy inferences can be drawn. For one thing, it becomes obvious that the extent of China's *enhanced* cooperation in the spring 2010 Mekong crisis was still well *within* of what can be described as the usual bounds of the cooperative side of China's international hydro-politics. That is to say, the forms of increased cooperation China engaged in mainly occurred in the areas of information sharing and transparency enhancement. To be sure, China's increased cooperation at the time remains positive. However, the areas in which China was willing to cooperate more likewise represented those of rather low-hanging fruit. In other words, it was relatively easy for China to share more of the already existing hydrological data and enhance transparency through voluntary and often one-time measures. Meanwhile, these forms of enhanced cooperation did not entail any obligations for China – especially not those that could not be easily revoked again. For another thing, and following the first inference, it also becomes clear that China, despite its unprecedented cooperation measures in the spring 2010 Mekong crisis, still had a lot of room for potentially offering more to the MDRCs. This "more" particularly applied to forms of generally more institutionalized cooperation and thus would have been rather *outside* the usual bounds of China's hydro-political cooperation, especially in a multilateral setting such as the Mekong. To better understand if, and how far, China would go down this road in the years following the spring 2010 Mekong crisis, however, it is once again useful to expand a little on developments in terms of contextual factors, especially China's overarching foreign policy objectives and its broader international relations in Southeast Asia.

Stable contextual factors and the need for hydro-political change in the Mekong

In general terms, China's overall foreign policy goals have been relatively stable and durable since the beginning of the reform era in the late 1970s. That is to say, sovereignty and territorial integrity, economic development, and international status were China's key foreign policy goals in order to support the domestic legitimacy of the ruling Chinese Communist Party (CCP) before the spring 2010 Mekong crisis – and they have clearly remained in place after the crisis. It is correct that an increasing number of arguments have been made more recently along the lines, for example, that China's foreign policy is portraying a "new assertiveness" (Yahuda 2013), that China has abandoned Deng Xiaoping's long paramount foreign policy dogma of "keeping a low profile" (*taoguang yanghui*) only to present the new strategy of "striving for achievement" (*fenfa youwei*) (Yan 2014) and that China has even turned into a "post-responsible power" (Deng 2015). Meanwhile, Chinese official rhetoric is still full of the country's long-held peaceful rise/development doctrine, which itself continues to require a stable and friendly environment, both at the global and regional levels (see, for example, China State Council 2017). In addition, the Chinese government still upholds its good-neighborly policy, meant to promote win-win situations for itself and its neighborhood, including the Mekong sub-region and Southeast Asia more broadly (ibid.). Put differently, for China, a stable Southeast Asian backyard continues to be vital for promoting China's sustained economic development and for fostering China's image of a benevolent and responsibly rising great power, while unresolved territorial disputes also remain indicative of continuous discord.

If anything since the spring 2010 Mekong crisis has changed about China's foreign policy and the foreign relations context as relevant, in some way or another, for China's Mekong hydro-politics, then it is not so much the general issues, but more some of the specifics. A few aspects have stood out in particular. First, the South China Sea disputes have, all in all, become even more intense since 2010. China has certainly had its fair share in this development. Examples include China's unannounced moving of an oil rig into what Vietnam claims to be its own exclusive economic zone in May 2014, and China's very contentious large-scale land reclamation activities in the Spratly Islands, which have gained center stage ever since the second half of 2015 (Biba 2016c: 460).

Second, and to some extent a corollary of the intensified South China Sea disputes, China's relationship with the United States (US), both in general and in Southeast Asia in particular, has (further) deteriorated since 2010 (see, for example, Steinberg and O'Hanlon 2014). In the Mekong itself, the Lower Mekong Initiative launched by the US in 2009 has remained a thorn in China's side (Interviews 12 July and 4 August 2016). In the South China Sea, the US Navy in October 2015 carried out its first freedom of navigation operation (FONOP) near China's man-made islands. The FONOP aimed at making clear that China's artificial islands have no right to a 12-nautical-mile territorial sea under UNCLOS and that the US would not accept such a claim (Panda 2015). In a sense, this FONOP, just like the ones that followed, as well as the LMI can be seen as part of the US pivot/rebalance to Asia, announced by the Obama administration in late 2011 already. The original strategy was based on (1) increased US engagement with regional multilateral organizations such as the East Asia Summit; (2) enhanced US attention to regional economics and trade through the Trans-Pacific Partnership (TPP); (3) strengthened US security agreements with regional allies and partners; and (4) continued promotion of democracy and human rights in East Asia (Lieberthal 2011). The announcement of the pivot, however, raised concerns in Beijing and was widely perceived as a thinly veiled US endeavor to contain China's influence in East Asia (ibid.). Since assuming power in January 2017, new US President Donald Trump has abandoned TPP and left the future of the US rebalance somewhat unclear to date. Above all, however, he has maneuvered US–China relations into a tricky state of unpredictability, particularly for the Chinese side.

Besides, and finally, the Mekong itself was turned into the arena for a rather new contextual development. On 5 October 2011, two Chinese cargo ships were attacked on a stretch of the Mekong in the Golden Triangle (i.e., the border region between Myanmar, Laos, and Thailand), and all 13 Chinese crewmembers were killed and dumped in the river by suspected Myanmar-based drug traffickers. As a response, China temporarily suspended shipping on the Mekong. Moreover, China was quick to summon senior officials from Myanmar, Laos, and Thailand to Beijing and then "pressured the countries to participate in Chinese-led river patrols, intended to ensure security for the river trade" (Perlez and Feng 2013). In the meantime, China has sent advisors to Myanmar and Laos, whose police forces it helps train and equip, and has set up a joint police command office close to the Mekong in its Yunnan Province. As at July 2016, 48 joint river patrols of the four countries have been conducted since December 2011. The objective has been to enhance law enforcement on the river in order to counter drug smuggling, people trafficking and related crimes (*China Daily USA* 2016). This episode has certainly displayed how quickly and forcefully China can respond and bring countries in the Mekong into line if Beijing's vital interests are threatened.

In sum, the post-2010 crisis trajectory of contextual factors relevant for China's Mekong hydro-politics, that is, China's foreign policy goals in Southeast Asia, together with its on-the-ground foreign relations in this neighboring sub-region, convey the following unequivocal message: while China's broader foreign policy objectives have remained quite stable, some more specific developments in regional affairs since the spring 2010 Mekong crisis have at times made it somewhat more challenging, but not less important, for China to achieve these very objectives. This also means that the contextual factors continue to generally support a Chinese Mekong hydro-politics that is aimed at further stabilizing and strengthening China–MDRC relations and at helping promote a positive Chinese image in the MDRCs. If the spring 2010 Mekong crisis showed Beijing that these goals were put at risk, then the trajectory of contextual factors in the aftermath of the crisis further suggested that China might be well advised to explore new avenues in its Mekong hydro-politics.

From a reactive to a proactive Chinese Mekong hydro-politics?

More than two years after the spring 2010 Mekong crisis, a Chinese scholar would describe the events as a tipping point for China to re-evaluate its cooperation with the MDRCs on water-related issues. As a result, he said, there was an active reaction on the part of China to invest more in its hydro-political relations with the other Mekong riparian countries (Interview 19 August 2012). However, as previously indicated, in the course of 2012, it seemed that the enthusiasm for enhanced China-MDRC cooperation on water-related issues was already waning. To be fair, though, that this impression emerged was not only due to the limits of China's cooperation. With the benefit of hindsight, it rather becomes obvious that various relevant downstream actors also played a crucial role in this situation.

While the behavior of the MDRC governments and the MRC was previously described as "diplomatically smart" when it came to requesting Chinese support in the spring 2010 Mekong crisis (see Chapter 5), it also turned out very soon that the same actors did not actually have a clear or common understanding of how to proceed from the 2010 situation and what exactly to ask from China. As illustrated earlier, the MRC was the critical counterpart for China's official cooperation track following the spring 2010 Mekong crisis (see Chapter 6). Remarkably, however, when interviewing an MRC donor representative in fall 2012, he recalled a moment during the 2011 MRC dialogue meeting with China when China basically asked the MRC, "what do you want us to do?" and the MRC had no clear and straightforward response ready (Interview 22 October 2012). In a similar vein, a senior riparian MRC staff member has conceded that the organization had to become much more specific about what it actually wanted from China (Interview 24 October 2012). An expert outside the MRC has seconded this view, stating that the MRC in general neither paid much attention to nor had much knowledge about China. Rather, it was "common thinking" that engagement with China would be "difficult," so no one was particularly anxious to give it a serious try in the first place (Interview 23 October 2012). A Chinese scholar also agreed that there was no clear-cut MRC strategy vis-à-vis China (Interview 19 August 2012).

What then further weakened a joint MDRC/MRC hydro-political approach towards China was that since September 2010, the dam debates in the lower Mekong have shifted away from Chinese activities to those in the MDRCs themselves. More precisely, since September 2010 the focus of concern in the MDRCs has shifted from China to Laos, as the latter has begun with the initial construction phases for its first mainstream dams in the lower Mekong, primarily the Xayaburi, but later also the Don Sahong and Pak Beng Dams (also see Chapter 4). The Xayaburi Dam, the first Mekong mainstream dam downstream of China, is situated in northern Laos and is currently being built by one of Thailand's largest construction companies and financed by six Thai commercial banks. Thailand has also agreed to purchase some 95 percent of the energy generated by the dam (International Rivers 2014). According to the 1995 Mekong Agreement, MRC members are required to seek accord before building any dams on the river's mainstream. However, such accord was never sought for the Xayaburi Dam. Despite MRC donors' concerns and requests from further downstream Cambodia and Vietnam, Laos and Thailand even declined to study the dam's transboundary impacts before beginning construction (ibid.). As a result, the controversy over the Xayaburi Dam has not only created tensions between the four MDRCs and put the MRC in a difficult situation close to its dissolution after many donors dropped their funding, it has also entailed that NGOs, activists, and the media previously at the forefront of criticizing China have gradually directed their focus away from the Chinese dams and have instead picked up on the issue of downstream dams. The subsequent launch of the Don Sahong and Pak Beng projects has only strengthened these trends.

For China, as we now know, the combination of MDRC discord, MRC indetermination, and activist neglect meant a valuable gain in time to ponder the overall situation and devise a more comprehensive approach to China's hydro-political behavior in the Mekong. The outcome of this thought process can be witnessed since November 2015 when China in its Yunnan Province launched, together with the four MDRCs and Myanmar, the Lancang-Mekong Cooperation (LMC), an initiative already pitched at the November 2014 Summit Meeting between China and the Association of Southeast Asian Nations (ASEAN) in Naypyidaw, Myanmar. The LMC follows a so-called "3+5 cooperation framework" based on the three pillars of the mechanism and its five key priority areas. The three pillars comprise political and security issues, economic and sustainable development, and social, cultural, and people-to-people exchanges, and thus resemble the ASEAN approach. The pillars are combined with practical cooperation carried out in five key priority areas, namely, connectivity, production capacity, cross-border economic cooperation, water resources, and agriculture and poverty reduction. In March 2016, the LMC held its first leaders' summit. Also, the LMC has started establishing joint working groups on the key priority areas and is currently preparing its first five-year action plan (LMC 2016b).

To be sure, it is far too early to seriously assess the qualities of LMC. Nonetheless, a few things, with regard to China's Mekong hydro-politics, have been quite noteworthy from the start. First, and most strikingly, with the LMC China is for first time driving a *multilateral* mechanism that explicitly *includes* water resources management within its remit. This is in stark contrast to China's attitude towards other previously established Mekong initiatives: the Greater Mekong Subregion (GMS) has the same membership as the LMC, but it has focused on infrastructure, trade, and investment only. China has reportedly even prevented water issues to play a role on the GMS agenda (Hensengerth 2009: 331; also see Chapter 3). Meanwhile, the MRC has a (sole) focus on water resources management, but China has steadfastly rejected to become more than a dialogue partner. Consequently, the LMC certainly represents a new step in China's Mekong hydro-politics.

Second, it is likewise notable, however, that water resources management is not the only issue on the LMC agenda. In fact, the LMC agenda is rather broad and it remains unknown to date where the priorities of the LMC will ultimately be. Some Chinese experts highlight that water resources management should be in the focus of the LMC (Interviews 11 July and 12 July 2016), whereas other Chinese experts are more cautious in this regard (Interviews 1 July and 4 August 2016) so that it remains to be seen what role water will actually play in the LMC. Also, it still seems to be unclear what exactly water resources management means for the LMC. Meanwhile, a Vietnamese expert underscored that he did not see the added value of the LMC if its focus was to be on water. For this purpose, he emphasized, the Mekong countries had long established the MRC and China was welcome to join (Interview 12 August 2016). In any case, though, it can already be concluded that the LMC agenda, and thus China's new approach, prominently reflects Beijing's continued understanding that its hydro-politics is connected to other areas of its foreign policy and moreover feeds into its overall foreign policy goals. Hence, it is China's intention to link potential cooperation on water resources to other aspects of sub-regional collaboration so as to share potential benefits more evenly, from the Chinese perspective, across LMC members and the various LMC priority areas. This is because the Chinese think that in terms of water resources management, the MDRCs have nothing really to offer to China in return for the latter's cooperation. Therefore, MDRCs should reciprocate in other areas and thus the relatively broad LMC agenda (Interview 5 July 2016).

Zhang Jiuhuan, vice chairman of the China Public Diplomacy Association and a former Chinese ambassador to Thailand, has said that under the LMC roof downstream countries "concerned about the implications of the dam construction upstream [...] could raise the issue for consultation with countries upstream" (cited in Biba 2016a). Moreover, the Sanya Declaration of the first LMC foreign ministers' meeting highlighted that the LMC was set to

> [e]nhance cooperation among LMC countries in sustainable water resources management and utilization through activities such as the establishment of a center in China for Lancang-Mekong water resources cooperation to serve as a platform for LMC countries to strengthen comprehensive cooperation in technical exchanges, capacity building, drought and flood management, data and information sharing, conducting joint research and analysis related to Lancang-Mekong river resources.
>
> (LMC 2016a)

Against this backdrop, it certainly did not come at an inconvenient moment that China, after the launch of the LMC in November 2015 but still shortly before the first LMC foreign ministers' meeting in March 2016, immediately had a chance to prove its new hydro-political Mekong leadership. Reportedly upon Vietnam's request, China agreed to discharge water from its Jinghong Dam in a period from 15 March to 10 April in order to help alleviate another drought period in the lower basin (Tiezzi 2016). While it is unlikely that water released from the Jinghong Dam actually led to a (noticeable) water increase all the way downstream in the Mekong Delta in Vietnam, it was nevertheless a highly symbolic gesture that was meant to indicate China's benevolence – but also exhibited its control over the Mekong's water resources. Consequently, a Chinese expert remarked rather bluntly on this episode that in the future China might not be as forthcoming without some sort of compensation. In his view, this could go as far as to include MDRC support/concessions on the South China Sea dispute (Interview 5 July 2016).

As China's Foreign Minister Wang Yi has made clear, the LMC should generally "discuss easy issues first" and evolve in a gradual and project-driven manner (Biba 2016a). This is indicative that major breakthroughs in delicate water issues should not be expected from the LMC, at least not any time soon. At the same time, the Beijing-driven set-up of LMC already proves that international hydro-politics has enormously gained in importance and urgency for China. China has realized that crises like in spring 2010 bear potential to undermine some of China's major foreign policy objectives (Interview 4 August 2016). As a result, China now seems intent on playing a much more active role in water resources management and cooperation in the Mekong so as to prevent similar further crises. For this purpose, China has sought to establish its own institution, thereby hoping to shape the rules of cooperation and making sure that external actors such as the US and Japan are excluded (Biba 2016a). But it also seems that China's willingness to substantially increase joint water resources management going forward will not be for free for the MDRCs. Only time will therefore tell if the LMC really means a marked and sustained shift from a reactive to a proactive Chinese Mekong hydro-politics, including further enhanced and particularly more institutionalized water cooperation. For now, the LMC is clearly no rules-based river basin organization such as the MRC.

Policy recommendations for China's international hydro-politics

Transboundary water issues were for a long time not a priority area of China's foreign policy. This is shifting rapidly now. He (2015: 312), for example, has argued that the upstream-downstream situation prevalent in many of China's shared rivers

> has resulted in diplomatic tensions between China and its riparian neighbours – including as some examples increased uses on the Lancang River (Mekong), the Yarlung Zangbo River (Brahmaputra), the Ili River and the Irtysh River. These developments are linked with many interests: China's energy security, the livelihoods of its citizens in border areas, as well as regional security and stability, and thus have become one of the primary concerns in Chinese foreign affairs.

In a similar vein, Feng et al. (2015: 329) have maintained that "China's transboundary waters resources management continues to evolve as one of the most important emerging geopolitical issues for the nation and the region." Decision-makers in Beijing and scholars across the country alike therefore increasingly realize the potential of China's shared rivers to derail the country's good-neighborly policy and ultimately even its peaceful rise strategy. Conversely, these people also start to understand that a more cooperative management of international rivers could make a positive contribution to China's foreign policy goals and help stabilize and strengthen China's relations with its neighbors. Nevertheless, the challenges ahead are tremendous for China. The ultimate question for China will be how to meet domestic water demand for continued but sustainable socio-economic development while at the same time being a good neighbor and taking the water needs of its riparian neighbors into consideration. The following, finally, are a few policy recommendations for China that move gradually from relatively low-hanging fruit to more demanding aspects of water cooperation:

- First, increasing transparency is key, and not particularly costly, for China's international hydro-politics. More transparency, especially if it occurs on a regular and not crisis-driven basis, is likely to entail more trust, and more trust will be crucial. China should therefore revise its data sharing policy. For instance, it remains hard to understand why dry season hydrological data and sediment load are regarded as state secrets linked to China's national security. In fact, sharing all-year-round hydrological data would be very beneficial for downstream countries in various ways, including improving adaptability to short-term changes in water flow volumes.
- Second, a very similar point must be made in terms of dam building. As China's dam building will most likely continue in the Mekong (upstream the present cascade) and other major shared basins, China should embark upon a strategy of prior notification, have impartial impact assessments conducted, and follow up on their findings. Moreover, as more and more of its dams are completed now and have begun operating, it becomes increasingly significant that China also be more open about coordinating the operation schemes of these dams with its downstream neighbors, aiming, for instance, at a balance between maximizing power production and looking after downstream countries' environmental security.
- Third, and in the long run, China should become ready to negotiating with its riparian neighbors common and equitable rules of joint water resources management – rules that reflect the respective geographical positions (but not necessarily the respective power capabilities) and can one day lead to the inking of comprehensive and binding water treaties.

It is possible that the LMC represents a first cautious step in these directions and that the body will one day grow into fully representing such important functions. Much more, however, still needs to be done – both in the Mekong and in other rivers China shares with its neighbors. At the end of the day, only increased and institutionalized water cooperation can make sure that China and its neighbors will actually live in peace and harmony with each other.

Interviews cited

Activist, 3 October 2012, Bangkok, Thailand.
Chinese expert I, 15 August 2012, Beijing, China.
Chinese expert II, 19 August 2012 and 4 August 2016, Beijing, China.
Chinese expert III, 21 August 2012, Beijing, and 13 August 2016, Shanghai, China.
Chinese expert IV, 22 August 2012 and 1 July 2016, Kunming, China.
Chinese expert V, 5 July 2016, Kunming, China.
Chinese expert VI, 11 July 2016, Beijing, China.
Chinese expert VII, 12 July 2016, Beijing, China.
M-POWER representative, 23 October 2012, Vientiane, Laos.
MRC donor representative, 22 October 2012, Vientiane, Laos.
MRC official, 24 October 2012, Vientiane, Laos.
Western expert, 11 October 2012, Chiang Mai, Thailand.
Thai expert, 2 October 2012, Bangkok, Thailand.
Vietnamese expert, 15 November 2012, Hanoi, Vietnam.
Vietnamese expert, 12 August 2016, Shanghai, China.

References

Allouche, J. (2007) "The Governance of Central Asian Waters: National Interests versus Regional Cooperation," *Disarmament Forum*, 4, 45–56.
Asanov, M. (2009) "Kazakhstan Attributes River Depletion to China," *Central Asia Online*, 17 August, http://centralasiaonline.com/cocoon/caii/xhtml/en_GB/features/caii/features/2009/08/17/feature/03.
Asia News (2010) "China Builds World's Highest Dam, India Fears Water Theft," 24 April, www.asianews.it/news-en/China-builds-world's-highest-dam,-India-fears-water-theft-18230.html.
Biba, S. (2014a) "China Cooperates with Central Asia over Shared Rivers," *China Dialogue*, 24 February, www.chinadialogue.net/article/show/single/en/6741-China-cooperates-with-Central-Asia-over-shared-rivers.
Biba, S. (2014b) "Desecuritization in China's Behavior towards its Transboundary Rivers: The Mekong River, the Brahmaputra River, and the Irtysh and Ili Rivers," *Journal of Contemporary China*, 23(85), 21–43.
Biba, S. (2016a) "China Drives Water Cooperation with Mekong Countries," *China Dialogue*, 1 February, www.chinadialogue.net/article/show/single/en/8577-China-drives-water-cooperation-with-Mekong-countries.
Biba, S. (2016b) "New Concerns, More Cooperation? How Non-traditional Security Issues Affect Sino-Indian Relations," *Journal of Current Chinese Affairs*, 45(3), 3–30.
Biba, S. (2016c) "It's Status, Stupid: Explaining the Underlying Core Problem in US-China Relations," *Global Affairs*, 2(5), 455–464.
Chen, H., A. Rieu-Clarke, and P. Wouters (2013) "Exploring China's Transboundary Water Treaty Practice through the Prism of the UN Watercourses Convention," *Water International*, 38(2), 217–230.
China Daily USA (2016) "China, Laos, Myanmar, Thailand Complete Joint Patrol on Mekong River," 24 July, http://usa.chinadaily.com.cn/world/2016-07/24/content_26201702.htm.

China State Council (2017) "China's Policies on Asia-Pacific Security Cooperation," *The State Council Information Office of the People's Republic of China*, January 2017, http://news.xinhuanet.com/english/china/2017-01/11/c_135973695.htm.

Deng, Y. (2015) "China: The Post-Responsible Power," *The Washington Quarterly*, 37(4), 117–132.

Feng, Y., D. He, and W. Wang (2015) "Identifying China's Transboundary Water Risks and Vulnerabilities – A Multidisciplinary Analysis Using Hydrological Data and Legal/Institutional Settings," *Water International*, 40(2), 328–341.

Freeman, C. (2010) "Neighborly Relations: The Tumen Development Project and China's Security Strategy," *Journal of Contemporary China*, 19(63), 137–157.

Gleick, P. (2009) "China and Water," in P. Gleick (ed.) *The World's Water 2008–2009. The Biennial Report on Freshwater Resources*, Washington, DC: Island Press, 79–100.

He, Y. (2015) "China's Practice on the Non-navigational Uses of Transboundary Waters: Transforming Diplomacy through Rules of International Law," *Water International*, 40(2), 312–327.

Hensengerth, O. (2009) "Transboundary River Cooperation and the Regional Public Good: The Case of the Mekong River," *Contemporary Southeast Asia*, 31(2), 326–349.

Hilton, I. (2014) "It's Time for a New Era of Cooperation on the Yarlung Tsangpo," *China Dialogue*, 5 March, www.chinadialogue.net/blog/6756-It-s-time-for-a-new-era-of-cooperation-on-the-yarlung-Tsangpo-/en.

Ho, S. (2017) "China's Transboundary River Policies towards Kazakhstan: Issue-linkages and Incentives for Cooperation," *Water International*, 42(2), 142–162.

International Rivers (2014) "Xayaburi Dam," www.internationalrivers.org/campaigns/xayaburi-dam.

Karakin, V. (2011) "Transboundary Water Resources Management on the Amur River," in E. Shvarts, E. Simonov, and L. Progunova (eds.), *Environmental Risks to Sino-Russian Transboundary Cooperation: From Brown Plans to a Green Strategy. WWF Trade and Investment Program Report*, Moscow, Vladivostok, Harbin: WWF, 86–94.

Lancang-Mekong Cooperation (LMC) (2016a) "Sanya Declaration of the First Lancang-Mekong Cooperation (LMC) Leaders' Meeting – For a Community of Shared Future of Peace and Prosperity among Lancang-Mekong Countries," 23 March, www.fmprc.gov.cn/mfa_eng/zxxx_662805/t1350039.shtml.

Lancang-Mekong Cooperation (LMC) (2016b) "Joint Press Communiqué of the Second Lancang-Mekong Cooperation (LMC) Foreign Ministers' Meeting," 23 December, www.fmprc.gov.cn/mfa_eng/zxxx_662805/t1426601.shtml.

Lieberthal, K. (2011) "The American Pivot to Asia," *Foreign Policy*, 21 December, http://foreignpolicy.com/2011/12/21/the-american-pivot-to-asia/.

Liu, Y. (2015) "Transboundary Water Cooperation on Yarlung Zangbo/Brahmaputra – A Legal Analysis of Riparian State Practice," *Water International*, 40(2), 354–374.

Lowi, M. (1993) *Water and Power: The Politics of a Scarce Resource in the Jordan River Basin*, Cambridge: Cambridge University Press.

Panda, A. (2015) "Lassen Faire in the South China Sea: Takeaways from the First US FONOP," *The Diplomat*, 28 October, http://thediplomat.com/2015/10/lassen-faire-in-the-south-china-sea-takeaways-from-the-first-us-fonop/.

Perlez, J., and B. Feng (2013) "Beijing Flaunts Cross-border Clout in Search for Drug Lord," *New York Times*, 4 April, www.nytimes.com/2013/04/05/world/asia/chinas-manhunt-shows-sway-in-southeast-asia.html?_r=0.

Peyrouse, S. (2007) "Flowing Downstream: The Sino-Kazakh Water Dispute," *China Brief*, 7(10), 7–10.

Rahaman, M., and O. Varis (2009) "Integrated Water Management of the Brahmaputra Basin: Perspectives and hope for Regional development," *National Resources Forum* 33(1), 60–75.

Save the Mekong Coalition (SMC) (2010) "Stop Mekong Mainstream Dams: Let the Mekong River Flow Freely," *Third Complaint to the Chinese Government*, 3 April, www.savethemekong.org/admin_controls/js/tiny_mce/plugins/imagemanager/files/StattoChina3.4.10.pdf.

Siddique, A. (2015) "China to Give Brahmaputra Flow Data to Bangladesh," *The Third Pole*, 29 September, www.thethirdpole.net/2015/09/29/china-to-give-brahmaputra-flow-data-to-bangladesh-2/.

Simonov, E. (2011) "Hydropower and Water Resource Management in the Amur River Basin," in E. Shvarts, E. Simonov, and L. Progunova (eds.), *Environmental Risks to Sino-Russian Transboundary Cooperation: From Brown Plans to a Green Strategy. WWF Trade and Investment Program Report*, Moscow, Vladivostok, Harbin: WWF, 95–105.

Sinha, U. (2012) "Examining China's Hydro-behaviour: Peaceful or Assertive?," *Strategic Analysis*, 36(1), 41–56.

Steinberg, J., and O'Hanlon, M. (2014) "Keep Hope Alive," *Foreign Affairs*, 16 June, www.foreignaffairs.com/articles/asia/2014-06-16/keep-hope-alive.

Tiezzi, S. (2016) "Facing Mekong Drought, China to Release Water From Yunnan Dam," *The Diplomat*, 16 March, http://thediplomat.com/2016/03/facing-mekong-drought-china-to-release-water-from-yunnan-dam/.

United Nations Economic Commission for Europe (UNECE) (2009) "Capacity for Water Cooperation in Eastern Europe, Caucasus, and Central Asia: River Basin Commissions and Other Institutions for Transboundary Water Cooperation," www.unece.org/env/water/documents/CWC%20publication%20joint%20bodies.pdf.

Vinogradov, S., and P. Wouters (2013) "Sino-Russian Transboundary Waters: A Legal Perspective on Cooperation," *Stockholm Paper, Institute for Security and Development Policy*, http://isdp.eu/content/uploads/images/stories/isdp-main-pdf/2013-vinogradov-wouters-sino-russian-transboundary-waters-legal-perspective.pdf.

Walker, B. (2013a) "China Gives Green-light to New Era of Mega-dams," *China Dialogue*, 1 February, www.chinadialogue.net/blog/5678-China-gives-green-light-to-new-era-of-mega-dams/en.

Walker, B. (2013b) "China-India Deal on Water: Why We Should Be Sceptical," *China Dialogue*, 29 October, www.chinadialogue.net/blog/6451-China-India-deal-on-water-why-we-should-be-sceptical/en.

Watts, J. (2010) "Chinese Engineers Propose World's Biggest Hydro-electric Project in Tibet," *Guardian*, 24 May, www.guardian.co.uk/environment/2010/may/24/chinese-hydroengineers-propose-tibet-dam.

Xinhua (2014) "China, Kazakhstan to Enhance Cooperation by Implementing Silk Road Initiative," 13 September, http://news.xinhuanet.com/english/china/2014-09/13/c_126981612.htm.

Yahuda, M. (2013) "China's New Assertiveness in the South China Sea," *Journal of Contemporary China*, 22(81), 446–459.

Yan, X. (2014) "From Keeping a Low Profile to Striving for Achievement," *The Chinese Journal of International Politics*, 7(2), 153–184.

Index

Abrahamsen, R. 28, 125–6n1
Adamson, P. and Bird, J. 72
Afghanistan: renewable water resources in 6; water dependency ratio (2014) 12
Africa, water availability in 6
Agreement on Protection of Water Quality of Transboundary Rivers 168
Agriculture, Chinese Ministry of 13
Allouche, J. 169
America (North and South), water availability in 6
Amur River 10, 166–7, 168, 169
Anti-Secession Law (China, 2005) 49
Aradau, C. 32, 155
Arase, D. 56
Arends, B. 1
Asanov, M. 169
Asia, water availability in 6
Asia News 170, 171
Asia-Pacific Economic Cooperation 2
Asia Times Online: China and the Mekong 75, 84, 85–6, 87; Mekong crisis (2010) 98, 106, 135, 138
Asian Development Bank (ADB) 80; Mekong, China and the 73; Southeast Asia, China and 52, 53
Asian Infrastructure Investment Bank (AIIB) 2, 3
Association of Southeast Asian Nations (ASEAN) 2, 14, 61–2, 64n2; China-ASEAN free trade agreement (CAFTA) 55–6, 58, 63, 64, 156–7; China-ASEAN Investment Cooperation Fund 57–8; China's relations with 42, 47, 54–7, 57–60; Chinese interactions in response to criticism on 2010 Mekong crisis 140–41; membership of 55; primary importance of 74; Regional Forum 60, 62; Treaty of Amity and Cooperation (2003) 57
Atkins, R. 1
Atland, K. 37
Austin, John L. 26, 29

Ba, A. 58, 60
Babel, M. and Wahid, S. 82
Backer, E. 70, 73, 74, 75
Balzacq, T. 29, 30, 37
Bangkok Post: China and the Mekong 84–5, 86, 87; Mekong crisis (2010), criticism of China on 104, 105, 110, 112, 114–15, 117–20; Mekong crisis (2010), response of China to criticism on 132, 136, 138, 139
Bangladesh: renewable water resources in 6; water dependency ratio (2014) 12
Barnett, J. 29
Beilun/Ka Long River 10
Belt and Road Initiative (BRI) in China 2
Bhutan: renewable water resources in 6; water dependency ratio (2014) 12
Biba, S. 3, 4, 7, 17, 47, 49; China and the Mekong 70, 77–8, 79; China's Mekong hydro-politics, making sense of 168, 169, 170, 171, 174, 175, 179, 180; securitization theory, China's international hydro-politics and 31, 34, 35, 36, 39n3, 39n6–7
Bird, Jeremy 118–20, 139, 146, 149
Biswas, A. 78
blocking strategy 36
Booth, Ken 39n5
Bouphavanh, Bouasone 145, 146
Brahmaputra River 4, 10, 170–72, 180
BRICS (Brazil, Russia, India, China, and South Africa) 2, 3

British Broadcasting Corporation (BBC) 64n5, 158n3
British Petroleum (BP) 9
Brooks, S. 16
Brown, P. and Xu, K. 90n4
Brunei, China bilateral relations with 47
Bush, George W. (and administration of) 60
Buzan, B., Wæver, O. and de Wilde, J. 26–7, 28, 29–30, 32, 35, 38n1, 111
Buzan, Barry 26, 38n1

Caballero-Anthony, M. and Emmers, R. 36
Cambodia: China bilateral relations with 48; China outbound FDI flows to (2004–9) 51; echoes of blame in 108–9; flooding problems in 85; Mekong basin, characteristics of 70; Mekong water levels in (April 2010) 98; renewable water resources in 6; trade with China (1990–2009) 50; water dependency ratio (2014) 12; world trade with China (2009) 51
Carlson, A. 44
Central Intelligence Agency (CIA) 16
"century of humiliation" *(bainian guochi)* 44, 46
Challenge Program on Water and Food (CPWF) 149–50, 158n1
Chang, F. 62
Chang, G. 3
Chellaney, B. 5, 6, 7, 9, 10, 15
Chen, H., Rieu-Clarke, A. and Wouters, P. 12, 172
Chen Dehai 136
Chen Mingzhong 135, 140
Chheang, V. 52
Chiang Mai University: criticism of China on 2010 Mekong crisis 99; Mekong hydro-politics of China 162
China: Agriculture, Ministry of 13; Anti-Secession Law (2005) 49; Asia-Pacific Economic Cooperation 2; Asian Infrastructure Investment Bank (AIIB) 2, 3; Association of Southeast Asian Nations (ASEAN) 2, 14; Beilun/Ka Long River 10; Belt and Road Initiative (BRI) 2; BRICS (Brazil, Russia, India, China, and South Africa) 2, 3; "century of humiliation" *(bainian guochi)* 44, 46; China-ASEAN relations, spring 2010 Mekong crisis and 57–60; "community of common destiny" *(mingyun gongtongti)*, aim for 43; Confucius Institutes 2; "cooperation and coordination" *(hezuo yu xietiao)* 46–7; dam building, hydroelectricity and 7; development, generic "China model" of 1; Development and Reform Committee 13; distribution of water 8–9; domestic problems 3; domestic water situation 8–10; drought in, effects of 130–32; East Asia Summit 2, 55, 61, 175; energy generation 7, 9; Environmental Protection, Ministry of 13; "export champion" 1; Foreign Affairs, Ministry of 13, 47, 149; foreign policy goals 43–7; Forest, State Bureau of 13; fresh water, links to 3–8; G-20 1–2; Ganges River 10; "good-neighborly policy" *(mulin zhengce)* 4–5, 46, 140, 175, 180–81; gross domestic product (GDP) growth 1, 16; Health, Ministry of 13; Heilong/Amur River 10, 166–7, 168, 169; Housing and Urban-Rural Development, Ministry of 13; Ili River-Lake Balkhash 10; institutionalist perspective on international hydro-politics 2–3, 16–17; international hydro-politics of 3, 4, 12–13, 14–15, 17–18, 37–8; international hydro-politics of, theoretical lenses on 15–17; International Monetary Fund (IMF) 1–2; International Relations (IR) theory and rise of 2–3; international rivers 10–13; international rivers, foreign policy and 4–5; international status, concern about 45–6; Irrawaddy River 10; Irtysh-Ob River 10; Lancang/Mekong River 10, 13–15; mainstream dams 77; Mekong and 13–15, 18, 69–91; Mekong basin, characteristics of 70; Mekong dam building, blame as securitization attempts 111–14; Mekong downstream riparian countries (MDRCs) 14, 16; Mekong hydro-politics and, extreme challenge of spring 2010 for 129–30; Mekong hydro-politics of 19–20, 162–81; Mekong River Commission (MRC) 14; military expenditure 1; Mischief Reef Incident (1995) 57; "national rejuvenation" 2; natural resources, diversification of access to 47; neighborhood diplomacy 14;

Index   187

New Development Bank 2; New Maritime Silk Road 2; Nu/Salween River 10; outbound FDI flows to MDRCs (2004–9) 51; Pearl/North River 10; "periphery policy" *(zhoubian zhengce)* 46; political influence, extension of 1–2; Power Group 13; Qinghai-Tibet Plateau, freshwater reserves from 10; realist perspective on international hydro-politics 2, 15–16; reform and opening up policy (1978) 1; "rejuvenation" *(zhenxing or fuxing)* 46; renewable water resources in 6; rise of 1–3; securitization theory and international hydro-politics 17; Senge Zangbo-Indus River 10; Shanghai Cooperation Organization 2; shared river basins 11; shared water resources 4, 7; Silk Road Economic Belt 2; Songhua River incident (2005) 10; South China Sea 14; Suifen/Razdolnaya River 10; "superpower" status 2; Tarim River 10; Tourism, State Bureau of 13; Transport, Ministry of 13; Tumen/Tumannaya River 10; United Nations Security Council 1–2; United Nations Watercourse Convention (UNWC) and 12, 16; upstream hegemon, potential as 88–90; water availability, water-energy nexus and 5–7; water challenges, costs of 9; water conflict, potential for 5; water dependency ratio (2014) 12; water issues, national security and 7–8; Water Resources, Ministry of 13; World Bank 2; World Trade Organization (WTO) 1–2; world trade with MDRCs (2009) 51; Yalu/Amrok River 10; Yarlung Zangbo/Brahmaputra River 4, 10, 170–72, 180; Yuan/Red River 10; *see also* criticism of China on 2010 Mekong crisis; response of China to criticism on 2010 Mekong crisis
China-ASEAN free trade agreement (CAFTA) 142, 156–7
China-ASEAN Free Trade Area 55–6, 125, 156–7
China Daily 130–32, 134, 135, 136, 137, 142
China Daily USA 83, 176
China State Council 13, 175
Chinese Communist Party (CCP): Mekong hydro-politics of China 174–5;

Southeast Asia, China and 43, 44, 45, 57, 174
Chinese Embassy in Bangkok, Thailand (CEB) 136, 140
Ciuta, F. 31
Clinton, Hillary 61, 62
CNN 61
Commerce, Ministry of (China, MOFCOM), 51
Confucius Institutes 2
Consultative Group on International Agricultural Research (CGIAR) 149–50
Cooperation Agreement on the Utilization and Protection of Transboundary Rivers with Kazakhstan 168
cooperation-conflict balance, shifts in 37–8, 90, 164–5
cooperative water management, positivity in 180–81
Copenhagen School of Security Studies (CS) 17, 25–6, 27, 28, 29, 30, 31–2, 35, 38n1, 39n6, 125–6n1
criticism of China on 2010 Mekong crisis 19, 96–126; Cambodia, echoes of blame in 108–9; Cambodia, Mekong water levels in (April 2010) 98; Chiang Mai University 99; China as passive recipient of 132–3; China's Mekong dam building, blame as securitization attempts 111–14; criticism blocking 136–8; dam-building, rejection of attempts at securitization of 120–23; dams built by Chinese, blame on 99–111; Jinghong dam 101, 103; Laos, Mekong water levels in (April 2010) 98; MDRC activist groups and NGOs, blame directly from 100–103; MDRC attitudes to record-low water levels in lower Mekong 99–100; MDRC governments' reactions to China's Mekong dam building 114–17, 120–23; MDRC media, echoes of blame in 103–9; MRC attitudes to record-low water levels in lower Mekong 99–100, 113–14; MRC reactions to China's Mekong dam building 114–15, 117–23; re-shaping of criticism by China 142–5, 152–4; record-low water levels in lower Mekong, impacts of 97–8; record-low water levels in lower Mekong, speech acts referring to 111–12; Save the Mekong Coalition (SMC) 101–3, 112–13, 114, 125–6n1; spring 2010

Mekong crisis 96–7; Thailand, echoes of blame in 104–6; Thailand, Mekong water levels in (April 2010) 97–8; UN Watercourse Convention (UNWC) 112; US media, echoes of blame in 109–11; Vietnam, echoes of blame in 107–8; Vietnam, Mekong water levels in (April 2010) 98; Xiaowan dam 99, 101, 103, 104; Yunnan Academy of Social Sciences 99

Dachaoshan dam 78
Dalai Lama 44
dam-building: blame for downstream problems placed on 99–111; domestic drivers of 77–8; downstream attitudes to 79–83; flood and drought control capacity 79; flow regulation and 79; hydroelectricity and 7; impacts of 78–9; on lower Mekong 81; on lower Mekong, Strategic Environmental Assessment (SEA) of plans for 81–2; prior notification strategy 181; rejection of blame attached to 133–6; securitization of, rejection of attempts at 120–23; soil fertility and 79
dam cascade 78
damage control 138–42
De Stefano, L., Edwards, P., de Silva, L. and Wolf, A. 7
De Wilde, Jaap 26
Deng Xiaoping 1, 43, 174–5
depoliticization 36–7
Derrida, Jacques 26, 31
desecuritization 17, 25–6, 32, 35, 36–7, 39n6; modes of 33–4
Development and Reform Committee in China 13
Dinar, S. 16
diplomacy: diplomatic relations in wider context 156–8; early 2010 situation 63–4; regional diplomacy, China's foreign policy and 42–3
Don Shong dam 77, 81
Donor Consultative Group of MRC 73
Dore, J. and Lazarus, K. 76
Dosch, J. 52
Dosch, J. and Hensengerth, O. 52
Dupont, A. 5

EarthRights International 82
East Asia Summit: China 2, 55, 61, 175; Mekong hydro-politics of China 175; Southeast Asia, China and 2, 55, 61, 175
East China Sea, territorial claims in 44–5
economic development 15, 43, 45, 47, 52, 54, 63, 78, 81–2, 83, 121, 140–41, 143, 156, 174–5
Economy, E. 4, 8, 9
Elhance, A. 3, 69
Emmers, R. 32, 57, 59, 64n3
Energy Administration, Chinese National 149
energy generation 7, 9, 69, 167, 177; water availability, water-energy nexus and 5–7
Energy Information Administration (EIA) 9, 47
energy requirements 80
environmental issues 3, 7, 13–14, 27, 38n1, 43, 53, 108–9, 111, 117, 135, 149, 151, 171, 181; Mekong, China and 69, 80, 81, 83, 84, 89
Environmental Protection, Chinese Ministry of 13
Europe, water availability in 6
existential threat 19, 26, 27–9
Eyler, B. 80

Fan, H., He, D. and Wang, H. 4, 90–91n5
Feng, Y., He, D. and Wang, W. 10, 13, 180–81
flooding 29, 38–9n2, 58, 62, 86–8, 101–2; flood and dry seasons 71–2; flood hydrology 84, 86; flood season water levels 75; of Mekong (2008) 18, 84–8, 113, 125, 130, 132–3; natural floodplains 79; wet season flood control 78–9
Floyd, R. 26, 27, 29, 30, 32, 35, 39n3
Food and Agriculture Organization (FAO) 5, 6, 12
Ford, E. 8
Foreign Affairs, Chinese National Ministry of (MOFA) 13, 47, 149
foreign direct investment (FDI) 45, 49, 51, 58
Forest, State Bureau of 13
Fox, C. and Sneddon, C. 73
Fravel, T. 44
Freedom of Navigation Operation (FONOP) 175
Freeman, C. 168
Freeman, J. 79

G-20 1–2
Ganges River 10, 24
Ganlanba dam 78
Gleick, P. 7, 8, 9, 10, 166
Goh, E. 29, 55, 59, 60; China and the Mekong 70, 71, 79
Golden Triangle (Myanmar, Laos, and Thailand) 176
Gongguoqiao dam 77, 78
"good-neighborly policy" *(mulin zhengce)* 4–5, 46, 140, 175, 180–81
Greater Mekong Subregion (GMS) 52–4, 178; development of, China's interest in 53–4; intra-GMS trade 53; transport infrastructure, GMS and 52–3; Vientiane Summit (2008) 53
Greater Tumen Initiative (GTI) 167–8
Grey, D. and Sadoff, C. 28
gross domestic product (GDP) 1, 8, 9, 16, 46, 53, 56, 79
Grumbine, E., J. Dore, and J. Xu 81
Gurria, A. 28
Gurtov, M. 3

Ha, M. 74
Habich, S. 77
Han, H. 16
Hansen, L. 33–4, 35, 36–7, 39n4
He, D., Wu, R., Feng, Y., Li. Y., Ding, C., Wang, W. and, D.u 5, 10
He, Y. 10, 11, 180
Health, Chinese Ministry of 13
Heilong/Amur River 10, 166–7, 168, 169
Hensengerth, O. 53, 54, 178
Hidayat, M.S. 58
Hilton, I. 171
Hirsch, P. 81
Hirsch, P. and Jensen, K. 73–4, 91n7
Ho, S. 4, 168, 169
Hofstedt, T. 4, 8, 9
Holslag, J. 4
Hong, N. and Jiang, W. 59
Housing and Urban-Rural Development, Chinese Ministry of 13
Hu Zhengyue 115–16, 132, 136
Hua Hin Summit and Declaration (MRC, 2010) 135–6, 145–6
Hughes, C. 3
Hun Sen 48
Hunt, L. 76, 90n2
hydro-political change, need for stable contextual factors and 174–6
hydro-political record, inferences for Mekong in 172–4

hydrology of Mekong, China and 71–2
Hydropower Sustainability Assessment Protocol (HSAP): Mekong hydro-politics of China 163; response of China to criticism on 2010 Mekong crisis 150–51, 153

Ikenberry, G. John 2–3, 54
Ili River 168–9
Ili River-Lake Balkhash 10
India: renewable water resources in 6; shared rivers with 170–72; water dependency ratio (2014) 12
Indonesia-US military-to-military relations 60
Industrial Info Resources 90–91n5
information sharing, need for transparency and 173
institutionalist perspective on international hydro-politics 2–3, 16–17; Mekong hydro-politics of China 173–4
Integrated Water Resources Management 74
Inter Press Service 85, 98, 105–6; Mekong crisis (2010), response of China to criticism on 137, 146–7
International Centre for Environment Management (ICEM) 81–2
International Commission of Large Dams 134–5
international hydro-politics: of China 3, 4, 12–13, 14–15, 17–18, 37–8; China influence on 69–71, 87–8, 89–90; power constellations behind 87–8; theoretical lenses on 15–17
International Hydropower Association (IHA) 150
International Monetary Fund (IMF) 1–2, 49, 50, 51
International Relations (IR): securitization theory and 25; theory of, rise of China and 2–3
International Rivers 9, 81, 101–2, 177
international rivers 10–13; benefits of cooperation on 89; Chinese foreign policy and 4–5
International Training Program on Management of Flood Control and Disaster Mitigation 148
Irrawaddy River 10
Irtysh-Ob River 10, 168–9

Jackson, N. 36
Jacobs, J. 69, 73

Jia Jinsheng 134
Jinghong dam: criticism of China on 2010 Mekong crisis 101, 103; Mekong, China and the 78, 84; Mekong hydro-politics of China 163, 179; response of China to criticism on 2010 Mekong crisis 138–9, 144, 148, 151
Johnson-Reiser, S. 91n6
joint water resources management, need for 181
Junior Riparian Professional (JRP) Project, Integrated Capacity Building through 148
Jutila, M. 28, 125–6n1

Kara Irtysh-Karamai Canal 169
Karakin, V. 167
Kasit Piromya 116
Kaysone Phomvihane 49
Kazakhstan: renewable water resources in 6; shared rivers with 168–70, 172; water dependency ratio (2014) 12
Keohane, R. 16
Keskinen, M., Mehtonen, K. and Varis, O. 73, 83
Kuenzer, C., Campbell, I., Roch, M., Leinenkugel, P., Tuan, V.Q. and Dech, S. 4, 74, 76, 80, 81
Kurlantzick, J. 55
Kyrgyzstan: renewable water resources in 6; shared rivers with 168; water dependency ratio (2014) 12

Lai, H. 43
Lancang Hydro 131, 134
Lancang-Mekong Cooperation (LMC) initiative 178–80
Lancang/Mekong River 10, 13–15
land disputes 44
Laos: China outbound FDI flows to (2004–9) 51; flooding problems in 85; Lao National Mekong Commission (LNMC) 86; Mekong basin, characteristics of 70; Mekong water levels in (April 2010) 98; renewable water resources in 6; Thai investment in 82–3; trade with China (1990–2009) 50; water dependency ratio (2014) 12; world trade with China (2009) 51
Larson, D., Paul, T.V. and Wohlforth, W. 45
Le Duc Trung 107
Lee, S. 16
Li, M. 3

Li, Z. and Wu, F. 8
Li, Z., He, D. and Feng, Y. 4, 78, 79
Lieberthal, K. 63, 175
Lieberthal, K. and Oksenberg, M. 13
Liebman, A. 4, 15
Lim, Y. 3
Lim Kean Hor 117
Lim Tin Seng 53
Lindemann, S. 15
Liu, Y. 170
Liu Ning 135
Living River Siam 86, 99
Lower Mekong Initiative (LMI) 62, 64n4, 157–8; Mekong hydro-politics of China 175; response of China to criticism on 2010 Mekong crisis 156, 157–8; Southeast Asia, China and 61–2, 64n4, 156–7, 158, 175
Lowi, M. 15, 163

Ma Chaode 135
McDonald, M. 26, 30, 31
Magee, D. 4, 78, 90–91n5
Malaysia, China bilateral relations with 47
Manwan dam 78
maritime disputes 44; see also South China Sea
Matthews, N. 80, 83
Mearsheimer, J. 2
Medeiros, E. 43, 46, 47
Mehtonen, K. 80
Mekong, China and the 18, 69–91; Asian Development Bank (ADB) 73; Association of Southeast Asian Nations (ASEAN), primary importance of 74; basin population 82; Cambodia, flooding problems in 85; conflicts alongside cooperation, China's Mekong hydro-politics and 90; Dachaoshan dam 78; dam building on Mekong, domestic drivers of 77–8; dam building on Mekong, downstream attitudes to 79–83; dam building on Mekong, flood and drought control capacity 79; dam building on Mekong, flow regulation and 79; dam building on Mekong, soil fertility and 79; dam cascade 78; Don Shong dam 77, 81; Donor Consultative Group of MRC 73; "drought-prone" conditions 72; Electricity Generating Authority of Thailand (EGAT) 82–3; energy requirements 80; flood and dry seasons 71–2; flooding of Mekong (2008) 84–8;

Index

Ganlanba dam 78; Gongguoqiao dam 77, 78; governance of Mekong, China and 72–6; hydrology of Mekong, China and 71–2; impacts of dam building on Mekong 78–9; Integrated Water Resources Management 74; international hydro-politics, China and 69–71, 87–8, 89–90; international hydro-politics, power constellations behind 87–8; international rivers, benefits of cooperation on 89; Jinghong dam 78, 84; Laos, flooding problems in 85; Laos, Thai investment in 82–3; lower Mekong dam building, China and 81; lower Mekong dam building, Strategic Environmental Assessment (SEA) of plans for 81–2; mainstream dams 77; Manwan dam 78; MDRCs 69–70, 88–9; MDRCs, attitudes to upstream dam building 80; MDRCs, hydropower development 80–81; MDRCs, local communities attitudes to dam building 82–3; MDRCs, negative impacts of dam building for 78–9; Mekong Agreement (1995) 73, 75–6; Mekong Agreement (1995), national interests and 74; Mekong Agreement (1995), weakness of 74; Mekong characteristics 69–70; Mekong hydro-politics, China and 69–71; Mengsong dam 77, 78; MRC, China and 75, 88–9; MRC, criticisms of 73–4, 86–7; MRC, flood situation reports from 86–7; MRC, institutional functions 72–3; MRC, lack of inclusiveness 74–5; MRC, membership 72; MRC, relevance problem for 76; National Mekong Committees (NMCs) 73, 86, 98, 99, 107, 120, 122, 135, 152; Nuozhadu dam 77, 78; Pak Benk dam 77, 81; rock blasting on Mekong, China and 83; sustained development, importance for 71; Three Gorges Dam 76–7; Towards Ecological Recovery and Regional Alliance (TERRA) 84–5; upstream hegemon, China's potential as 88–90; Vietnam, flooding problems in 85; World Bank 73; Xayaburi dam 77, 81; Xiaowan dam 78

Mekong Agreement (1995) 73, 75–6; national interests and 74; weakness of 74

Mekong characteristics 69–70

Mekong crisis (spring 2010) 18–19; *see also* criticism of China on 2010 Mekong crisis; response of China to criticism on 2010 Mekong crisis

Mekong downstream riparian countries (MDRCs) 14, 16, 69–70, 88–9; activist groups and NGOs, blame directly from 100–103; attitudes to record-low water levels in lower Mekong 99–100; attitudes to upstream dam building 80; China's relations with 42, 48–54, 59–60, 63–4; Chinese outbound FDI with 50–51; governments' reactions to China's Mekong dam building 114–17, 120–23; hydropower development 80–81; local communities attitudes to dam building 82–3; media, echoes of blame in 103–9; Mekong hydro-politics of China and 162, 163–5, 174, 176–8, 179, 180; negative impacts of dam building for 78–9; responses of China to criticism on 2010 Mekong crisis 129, 132–4, 137–41, 143–7, 149, 151–7; world trade with (2009) 51

Mekong Flood Forum (MRC) 148

Mekong hydro-politics of China 19–20, 162–81; Agreement on Protection of Water Quality of Transboundary Rivers 168; Amur River 166–7, 168, 169; Brahmaputra River 170–72, 180; Chiang Mai University 162; Chinese Communist Party (CCP) 174–5; Cooperation Agreement on the Utilization and Protection of Transboundary Rivers with Kazakhstan 168; cooperation-conflict balance, shifts in 164–5; cooperative management, positivity in 180–81; dam-building prior notification strategy 181; East Asia Summit 175; Freedom of Navigation Operation (FONOP) 175; Golden Triangle (Myanmar, Laos, and Thailand) 176; Greater Mekong Subregion (GMS) 178; Greater Tumen Initiative (GTI) 167–8; hydro-political record, inferences for Mekong in 172–4; Hydropower Sustainability Assessment Protocol (HSAP) 163; Ili River 168–9; India, shared rivers with 170–72; information sharing, need for transparency and 173; institutionalist perspective on international hydro-politics 173–4; Irtysh River 168–9; Jinghong dam 163, 179; joint water resources management, need for 181; Kara Irtysh-Karamai Canal 169;

Kazakhstan, shared rivers with 168–70, 172; Kyrgyzstan, shared rivers with 168; Lancang-Mekong Cooperation (LMC) initiative 178–80; lessons from spring 2010 crisis for 162–5; Lower Mekong Initiative (LMI) 175; MDRCs and 162, 163–5, 174, 176–8, 179, 180; MRC and 163–5, 177–9, 180; multilateralism, need for move towards 172–3; Naypyidaw ASEAN-China Summit (2014) 178; northeast, shared rivers in 166–8; northwest, shared rivers in 168–70; performance on other shared rivers, "cooperation marker" of 165–6; policy recommendations for China's international hydro-politics 180–81; reactive to proactive Mekong hydro-politics, potential for movement 176–80; realist perspective on international hydro-politics 164, 173–4; river commissions, need for 172; Save the Mekong Coalition (SMC) 163–4; securitization theory and 174; Shanghai Cooperation Organization 172–3; Sino-Russian water cooperation 167; South China Sea disputes 175; South-to-North Water Transfer Project 171; southwest, shared rivers in 170–72; stable contextual factors, need for hydro-political change in Mekong and 174–6; Trans-Pacific Partnership (TPP) 175; transboundary water issues 180–81; transboundary water pollution 166–7; transparency, key of increasing 181; treaty practice, need for change in 172; Tumen River Development Program 167–8; UNCLOS 175; water consumption problem 167; water cooperation, demanding aspects of 181; Xayaburi dam 177

Mekong Program on Water, Environment and Resilience (M-POWER) 149, 150–51, 158n1

Mekong River Commission (MRC) 14, 75, 88–9; attitudes to record-low water levels in lower Mekong 99–100, 113–14; China and the Mekong 69, 70, 71, 72–6, 82, 84, 86–7, 90n2; criticisms of 73–4, 86–7; flood situation reports from 86–7; institutional functions 72–3; lack of inclusiveness 74–5; Mekong crisis (2010), criticism of China on 97, 100; Mekong crisis (2010), response of China to criticism on 138–40, 145–6, 148–9, 151–2; Mekong hydro-politics of China and 163–5, 177–9, 180; membership 72; reactions to China's Mekong dam building 114–15, 117–23; reactions to spring 2010 Mekong crisis from 117–20; relevance problem for 76; response of China to criticism on 2010 Mekong crisis and 129, 135–49, 151–5

Men, J. 56
Mengsong dam 77, 78
Menniken, T. 4, 15, 53, 80
Middleton, C. 97
Mirumachi, N. 17
Mischief Reef Incident (1995) 57
Mongolia: renewable water resources in 6; water dependency ratio (2014) 12
multilateralism, need for move towards 172–3
Myanmar: Mekong basin, characteristics of 70; renewable water resources in 6; water dependency ratio (2014) 12

Narine, S. 55
Nation 84, 86; Mekong crisis (2010), criticism of China on 98, 104–5, 106, 115, 116; Mekong crisis (2010), response of China to criticism on 132, 136
National Mekong Committees (NMCs) 73, 86, 98, 99, 107, 120, 122, 135, 152
natural resources, diversification of access to 47
Naypyidaw ASEAN-China Summit (2014) 178
negative desecuritization 32
neighborhood diplomacy 14; *see also* "good-neighborly policy" *(mulin zhengce)*
Nepal: renewable water resources in 6; water dependency ratio (2014) 12
New Development Bank of China 2
New Maritime Silk Road 2
New York Times 98, 109, 110–11, 116, 137
Nguyen Tan Dung 116, 145
Nickum, J. 11, 15
Noble, J. 1
non-securitization, China's preference for 33–4
North Korea: renewable water resources in 6; water dependency ratio (2014) 12
"North-South Corridor" 53

northeast, shared rivers in 166–8
northwest, shared rivers in 168–70
Nu/Salween River 10
Nuozhadu dam 77, 78

Obama, Barack (and administration of) 61, 62–3
Oceania, water availability in 6
Onishi, K. 16
Organization for Economic Co-operation and Development (OECD) 9

Pak Benk dam 77, 81
Pakistan: renewable water resources in 6; water dependency ratio (2014) 12
Panda, A. 175
passive recipient strategy 36
"peaceful development" *(heping fazhan)*, Chinese goal of 43
Pearl/North River 10
Pearse-Smith, S. 4
Pei Shouxiao 169
performance on other shared rivers, "cooperation marker" of 165–6
"periphery policy" *(zhoubian zhengce)* 46
Perlez, J. 83
Perlez, J. and Feng, B. 176
Petersen-Perlman, J., Veilleux, J. and Wolf, A. 29
Peyrouse, S. 169
Philippines: China bilateral relations with 47; Congress Archipelagic Baselines Act (2009) 58–9; US military-to-military relations 60
Phnom Penh Post 108–9, 116–17, 120
Pich Dun 120, 135
politicization, securitization and 32
Power Group in China 13

Qinghai-Tibet Plateau, freshwater reserves from 10

Radio Free Asia (RFA) 83, 86
Rahaman, M. and Varis, O. 90n3–4, 123, 171
Räsänen, T., Korponen, J., Lauri, H. and Kummu, M. 4
Ravenhill, J. 58
reactive to proactive Mekong hydro-politics, potential for movement 176–80
realist perspective on international hydro-politics 2, 15–16; Mekong hydro-politics of China 164, 173–4

record-low water levels in lower Mekong: impacts of 97–8; speech acts referring to 111–12
referent objects 27–9
Reilly, J. 51–2, 57, 64n1
"rejuvenation" *(zhenxing or fuxing)* 46
Ren, X. 3
response of China to criticism on 2010 Mekong crisis 19, 123–5, 129–58; preliminary scene-setting 123–5; Association of Southeast Asian Nations (ASEAN), Chinese interactions with 140–41; behavior of China *in toto*, synopsis of 154–6; Challenge Program on Water and Food (CPWF) 149–51; China and Mekong hydro-politics, extreme challenge of spring 2010 for 129–30; China-ASEAN free trade agreement (CAFTA) 142, 156–7; Consultative Group on International Agricultural Research (CGIAR) 149–50; criticism, China as cautious re-shaper of 142–5; criticism, China as passive recipient of 132–3; criticism, China as re-shaper of 152–4; criticism blocking 136–8; dam-building, China's rejection of blame attached to 133–6; damage control 138–42; diplomatic relations in wider context 156–8; downstream reactions, ambiguity in 145–7; drought in China, effects of 130–32; Energy Administration, Chinese National 149; Foreign Affairs, Chinese National Ministry of 149; future blame, China and prevention of 147–52; Hua Hin Summit and Declaration (MRC, 2010) 135–6, 145–6; Hydropower Sustainability Assessment Protocol (HSAP) 150–51, 153; International Commission of Large Dams 134–5; International Training Program on Management of Flood Control and Disaster Mitigation 148; Jinghong dam 138–9, 144, 148, 151; Junior Riparian Professional (JRP) Project, Integrated Capacity Building through 148; Lancang Hydro 131, 134; Lower Mekong Initiative (LMI) 156, 157–8; MDRCs and 129, 132–4, 137–41, 143–7, 149, 151–7; Mekong Flood Forum (MRC) 148; Mekong Program on Water, Environment and Resilience (M-POWER) 149, 150–51, 158n1; MRC and 129, 135–49, 151–5; phase

one, analysis of 132–3; phase one, China and severe drought 130–33; phase two, analysis of 136–8; phase two, China rejects blame on dams 133–8; phase three, analysis 142–5; phase three, China turns to damage control 138–47; phase three, downstream reactions to, ambiguity in 145–7; phase four, analysis 152–4; phase four, China works to prevent future blame 147–54; Water Resources, Chinese National Ministry of 149; World Wide Fund for Nature (WWF) 135, 149, 151; Xayaburi dam 151–2; Xiaowan dam 134, 138, 146–7; Yunnan Hydrology and Water Resources Bureau 148–9

Rice, Condoleezza 60

river commissions, need for 172

rock blasting on Mekong, China and 83

Roe, P. 30, 32, 33

Russia: renewable water resources in 6; water dependency ratio (2014) 12

Sadoff, C. and Grey, D. 89

Salter, M. 30–31, 35, 37, 39n7

Save the Mekong Coalition (SMC) 84, 163–4; criticism of China on 2010 Mekong crisis 101–3, 112–13, 114, 125–6n1; Mekong crisis (2010), criticism of China on 101–3, 112–13, 114, 125–6n1; Mekong hydro-politics of China 163–4

Schmeier, S. 80, 83

Schmitt, Carl 26

securitization failure 30, 34–5; audience role in determination of outcomes of 35–7; causes of 35; repoliticization and 36–7

securitization theory, China's international hydro-politics and 17, 25–39, 174; actors of securitization, states and beyond 26–7; blocking strategy 36; context 30–31; depoliticization 36–7; desecuritization 17, 25–6, 32, 35, 36–7, 39n6; desecuritization, modes of 33–4; dramaturgical analysis 30; environmental issues 27; existential threats 27–9; International Relations (IR) and 25; issues, existential threats and referent objects 27–9; negative desecuritization 32; non-securitization, China's preference for 33–4; outcomes of securitization 31–2; passive recipient strategy 36; politicization, securitization and 32; referent objects 27–9; securitization failure 30; securitization failure, audience role in determination of outcomes of 35–7; securitization failure, causes of 35; securitization failure, China and 34–5; securitization failure, repoliticization and 36–7; securitization processes, context-dependency of 30–31; securitization theory, conflict and cooperation in hydro-politics, co-existence of 37–8; securitization theory, key concepts of 25–31; sovereignty, threats to 29; speech acts and audiences 29–30; transformation strategy 33, 35, 37

Security: A New Framework for Analysis (Buzan, B. et al.) 26–7

Senge Zangbo-Indus River 10

Shambaugh, D. 63

Shanghai Cooperation Organization 2; Mekong hydro-politics of China 172–3

shared river basins 11

shared water resources 4, 7

Siddique, A. 170

Silk Road Economic Belt 2

Simonov, E. 166, 167

Sinha, U. 4, 15, 171

Sino-Russian water cooperation 167

Smil, V. 9

socio-economic development 75, 181

Song Tao 77, 140–42, 143–4, 152

Songhua River incident (2005) 10

South China Sea 14; "Chinese assertiveness" in 58–9; disputes in 175; tensions in 49; territorial claims in 44–5

"South-South cooperation," UN concept of 46–7

South-to-North Water Transfer Project 171

Southeast Asia, China and 17–18, 42–64; ASEAN, China's relations with 42, 47, 54–7, 57–60; Asian Development Bank (ADB) 52, 53; Brunei, China bilateral relations with 47; Cambodia, China bilateral relations with 48; China-ASEAN relations, spring 2010 Mekong crisis and 57–60; China's foreign policy goals 43–7; Chinese Communist Party (CCP) 43, 44, 45, 57, 174; "community of common destiny" *(mingyun gongtongti)*, Chinese aim for 43; "cooperation and coordination" *(hezuo yu xietiao)* 46–7; development of GMS, China's interest

in 53–4; diplomacy, early 2010 situation 63–4; East Asia Summit 2, 55, 61, 175; East China Sea, territorial claims in 44–5; economic development 45; foreign direct investment (FDI) 45; Greater Mekong Subregion (GMS), China and 52–4; Indonesia-US military-to-military relations 60; international status 45–6; intra-GMS trade 53; land disputes 44; Lower Mekong Initiative (LMI) 61–2, 64n4, 156–7, 158, 175; Malaysia, China bilateral relations with 47; maritime disputes 44; MDRCs, China's relations with 42, 48–54, 59–60, 63–4; MDRC's, Chinese outbound FDI with 50–51; "North-South Corridor" 53; "peaceful development" *(heping fazhan)*, Chinese goal of 43; Philippines, China bilateral relations with 47; Philippines Congress Archipelagic Baselines Act (2009) 58–9; Philippines-US military-to-military relations 60; regional diplomacy, China's foreign policy and 42–3; role of Southeast Asia for China's foreign policy goals 46–7; South China Sea, "Chinese assertiveness" in 58–9; South China Sea, tensions in 49; South China Sea, territorial claims in 44–5; "South-South cooperation," UN concept of 46–7; Southeast Asia, importance for China of 47; sovereignty, protection of 44; Soviet Union, collapse of 44–5; Spratly Islands dispute 58–9, 64n3, 175; Taiwan, relationship with 44, 48; territorial integrity, protection of 44; Thailand, China bilateral relations with 48; Trans-Pacific Partnership (TPP) 61, 175; transport infrastructure, GMS and 52–3; United States as factor in relationships 42, 60–63; US and Southeast Asia preceding spring 2010 Mekong crisis 61–3; Vientiane Summit (GMS, 2008) 53; Vietnam, China bilateral relations with 47, 48–9; Vietnam, Chinese activities in (2009 and 2010) 59
southwest, shared rivers in 170–72
sovereignty: protection of 44; threats to 29
Soviet Union, collapse of 44–5
Spratly Islands dispute 58–9, 64n3, 175
Starr, J. 7
Statistics Times 46
Steinberg, J. and O'Hanlon, M. 175

Stockholm Environment Institute (SEI) 7
Stockholm International Peace Research Institute (SIPRI) 1, 46
Storey, I. 49, 57, 58, 59, 138
Stritzel, H. 30
Suhardiman, D., Giordano, M. and Molle, F. 73, 74
Suifen/Razdolnaya River 10
Sundaravej, Samak 86
Sutter, R. 45, 55, 60
Suwit Khunkitti 116, 139
Swaine, M. 2

Taiwan, Chinese relationship with 44, 48
Talk Vietnam 146
Tarim River 10
Terra Daily 115
territorial integrity, protection of 44
Thai National Mekong Commission (LNMC) 152
Thai News Agency (TNA) 87
Thai People's Network on Mekong (TPNM) 86–7
Thailand: China bilateral relations with 48; China outbound FDI flows to (2004–9) 51; echoes of blame in 104–6; Electricity Generating Authority of Thailand (EGAT) 82–3; Mekong basin, characteristics of 70; Mekong water levels in (April 2010) 97–8; renewable water resources in 6; trade with China (1990–2009) 50; water dependency ratio (2014) 12; world trade with China (2009) 51
Thanh Nien News 98, 107–8, 112, 116
Thayer, C. 59
Three Gorges Dam 76–7
Tiezzi, S. 179
Tourism, Chinese State Bureau of 13
Towards Ecological Recovery and Regional Alliance (TERRA) 84–5
Trans-Pacific Partnership (TPP): Mekong hydro-politics of China 175; Southeast Asia, China and 61, 175
transboundary relations, controversial issues in 7–8
transboundary river basins 7
transboundary waters 10, 13, 29; conflict and cooperation over 37; interactions 38; pollution of 166–7; resource management for 180–81; sovereign rights to 167
transformation strategy 33, 35, 37
transparency, key of increasing 181

Transport, Chinese Ministry of 13
treaty practice, need for change in 172
Trump, Donald 175
Tumen River Development Program 167–8
Tumen/Tumannaya River 10

United Nations (UN) 38–9n2; Convention on the Law of the Sea (UNCLOS) 175; Economic Commission for Europe (UNECE) 168, 170; General Assembly (UNGA) 12; Security Council 1–2; Watercourse Convention (UNWC) 12, 16, 112
United States: Department of Defense (DoD) 62; Department of State (DoS) 61, 62; as factor in relationships 42, 60–63; media in, echoes of blame in 109–11; Southeast Asia preceding spring 2010 Mekong crisis and 61–3; Trade Representative (USTR) 61

Vejjajiva, Abhisit 115, 132, 136, 145
Vientiane Summit (GMS, 2008) 53
Vientiane Times 98
Vietnam: China bilateral relations with 47, 48–9; China outbound FDI flows to (2004–9) 51; Chinese activities in (2009 and 2010) 59; echoes of blame in 107–8; flooding problems in 85; Mekong basin, characteristics of 70; Mekong water levels in (April 2010) 98; renewable water resources in 6; trade with China (1990–2009) 50; water dependency ratio (2014) 12; world trade with China (2009) 51
Vinogradov, S. and Wouters, P. 166–7
Voice of America 97, 98, 109, 110, 111, 112, 116

Walker, B. 170
Wall Street Journal 109–10
Waltz, Kenneth 26
Wang, D. and Yin, C. 63
Wang, F. 43, 45
Wang, H. 45, 46
Wang Yi 180
water availability, water-energy nexus and 5–7
water cooperation, demanding aspects of 181
water dependency ratio (2014) 12

water issues, national security and 7–8
Water Resources, Chinese National Ministry of 13, 149
Water Technology 9
Watts, J. 170
Wæver, Ole 25–6, 29, 30, 32, 33–4, 35, 36–7
Wen Jiabao 53
Wilkinson, C. 39n4
Will, G. 52, 53
Williams, M. 26, 32
Wolf, A., Natharius, J., Danielson, J., Ward, B. and Pender, J. 11
Womack, B. 52
Wong, E. 157
World Bank 2, 9; Mekong, China and the 73, 80
World Trade Organization (WTO) 1–2
World Wide Fund for Nature (WWF) 135, 149, 151
Wouters, P. 12
Wouters, P. and Chen, H. 12

Xayaburi dam: Mekong, China and the 77, 81; Mekong hydro-politics of China 177; response of China to criticism on 2010 Mekong crisis 151–2
Xi Jinping 43
Xiaowan dam: criticism of China on 2010 Mekong crisis 99, 101, 103, 104; Mekong, China and the 78; response of China to criticism on 2010 Mekong crisis 134, 138, 146–7
Xinhua 84, 168

Yahuda, M. 2, 59, 174
Yalu/Amrok River 10
Yan, X. 2, 46, 174
Yarlung Zangbo/Brahmaputra River 4, 10, 170–72, 180
Yeophantong, P. 4
Yoffe, S., Wolf, A. and Giordano, M. 69
Yuan/Red River 10
Yunnan Academy of Social Sciences 99
Yunnan Hydrology and Water Resources Bureau 148–9

Zawahri, N. and Hensengerth, O. 16
Zeitoun, M. and Mirumachi, N. 17, 37–8
Zhang, H. 4
Zhao, S. 1, 3, 5, 46, 55
Zhou Xuewen 135